Table of Contents

Foreword

Steve Case
Chairman and CEO, America Online®

To the editors of the *Empire County* [California] *Argus* newspaper in May 1854, the accidental discovery of gold at Sutter's Mill and the resulting gold rush ". . . was the commencement of a new era in the affairs of the world—the opening of a wide and extended field of enterprise which has infused new life into every department of society."

In fact, the California Gold Rush, the first of modern times, did hold out the promise of closing a gap between haves and have-nots that at the time was as wide as the distance that divided the nation from East to West. For the men and women who pioneered that divide, the gold they sought offered endless possibilities to anyone with a dream and sufficient determination. Yet, because supplies of gold are finite and the process of finding it capricious, many participants were left disappointed and destitute even as others were enriched.

Nearly 150 years later, the Internet Rush extends the same promise of equalization as its metallurgic predecessor—without its limits on time, space, and physical resources. By sparking a revolution, not just in this country but around the globe, that is fundamentally changing the way we communicate, get our news, and conduct commerce, the interactive medium has once again "opened a wide and extended field of enterprise"—one that this time truly can involve "every department of society."

Unlike the gold rushes of past times, the interactive medium offers more than enough "gold" to go around, if we can recognize its direction and realize its full potential.

I became a "forty-niner" of sorts myself when I entered the online world in the mid-1980s. The small team that was then America Online® was fascinated with technology's power to connect people in new ways and to create new communities among people who live on opposite ends of the country—and opposite ends of the world.

It's almost hard to remember or believe, but in 1985, an online service was a couple of hundred people chatting after work. Personal computers were very much a novelty in those days.

Still, what we saw then, and still see today, is a medium that would one day be as central to people's lives as the telephone or the television . . . and even more valuable.

While about a quarter of American households are online today, in the coming century, as people access the Internet not just from personal computers but from televisions and telephones and other devices, the online medium will reach a mass-market audience worldwide equal to or greater than those two devices.

But more important than the reach of the new medium will be its impact. The gold of the Internet is the medium's power to offer a singularly unique interactive experience to each individual. Each person is empowered to create and shape his or her own online experience. The Internet allows friendships to blossom across continents, students to visit the world's greatest museums without leaving their classrooms, and patients to have their cases reviewed by doctors hundreds of miles away.

And of course, the medium is also beginning to have a significant impact on how we conduct commerce—sparking innovation and creating jobs along the way. For the time being, business-to-business commerce is developing fastest. That's because businesses have the resources to build powerful, secure networks that are able to move data quickly, and because companies are learning that the medium allows them to manage inventories more efficiently and to benefit from the real-time order and delivery of services. In fact, by the year 2000, more than $300 billion of business-to-business commerce will be conducted online.

But even in the commercial sphere, the true riches of the medium relate to its empowerment of the individual consumer. Through the Internet, consumers now have more information at their disposal than at any time in history. Powerful search engines allow consumers to locate products they need quickly and then to carry out that transaction with the click of a mouse. And instead of waiting for the store down the street to open, a consumer can make his purchase online at the time that fits his schedule best. It might by 4:00 P.M.; it could well be midnight. This added convenience and control—allowing people to buy what they want when they want it—is the single most important factor driving the growth of electronic commerce.

The result is the greatest power shift, from merchants to consumers, in the history of commerce. During the next few years, electronic commerce is projected to explode. Online consumer sales are projected to reach $20 billion by the year 2000. But more important, the interactive medium is changing the way consumers research and then buy goods and services and the way businesses and advertisers tailor and sell those services—in the process fundamentally uprooting entire industries and distribution systems.

For example, by the year 2000, half of all auto sales will involve the Internet. By 2001, online entertainment and travel tickets alone will exceed $10 billion. By 2002, mutual fund assets in online accounts will top $240 billion.

What does this mean for companies engaged in commerce today, or tomorrow? First, it means that the medium will offer unmatched potential to reach mass-market consumers conveniently, competitively, and creatively. But second, it means that realizing that potential will result in fundamental, wrenching adjustments as its impact spreads to other businesses.

Companies will have to recognize that every business process is affected by the Internet—production, marketing, advertising, sales, distribution, customer relations, inventory, finance, and billing. For example, the medium will redefine the marketing relationship. In the offline world, several steps across several media are required before actually concluding a transaction. Advertisers need to get the consumer's attention, which typically is done through a thirty-second television ad. Then they need to provide more information and answer questions, which is often accomplished through a print ad, a sales call, or direct mail. And finally, the transaction occurs in a store, through the mail or over the phone.

But online, all three steps can be accomplished in a matter of seconds—again enhancing the power of consumers to control the transaction even as it increases its efficiency and effectiveness for marketers.

To a certain extent, the industry's enhanced control on the consumer side will serve to underscore the characteristics or qualities that define the most successful offline businesses. More than ever, the consumer will be king, and the consumer, on- or offline, likes convenience. Our experience so far has shown that people don't care about the technology behind the new online opportunities and applications. In fact, most people want the technology to be invisible. Simplicity and ease of use are key. If it's complicated or confusing, programmers or merchants have lost their audience. A technological "breakthrough" only matters if it matters to consumers.

At the same time, those of us who have been working in and observing the online industry during the last two decades have learned enough to know only that we know very little. If there is a constant in our relatively brief experience with the Internet, it's change. To succeed as a company doing business on the Internet requires innovation, flexibility, and the ability to adapt. You have to be nimble.

That means that success in this new world will also require an openness and ability to undertake a broader and farther-ranging examination of the impact a more connected society will have on individual businesses, entire industries, and the overall economy. The truth is, this isn't about merely tweaking a marketing effort to fit a new medium. It's about re-engineering a business to reflect a significant change in society. Just as the car helped create suburbs that led to development of malls and new opportunities for retailers, so, too, will a more connected society lead to a new set of opportunities for those businesses able to identify new ways of doing business.

But we will only realize the benefits of the online medium for consumers and businesses alike if we take the steps that are necessary to integrate it into society in a way that stimulates trust rather than fear, confidence rather than uncertainty. And there are currently some very real concerns that require our attention. We need to find ways to make the online experience more consistently rewarding as well as safe and secure for children. There's been a lot of progress made with technological breakthroughs, parental controls, filtering technology, and better education efforts, but any company wanting to do business online needs to commit itself to serving the special needs of children.

Likewise, building public confidence that individual privacy can be protected in the new interactive world is essential to the growth of the medium. Without that confidence, people will shy away from electronic commerce and pull back from the promise of a more connected society. Consumers need to trust the medium and trust the businesses they are interacting with across the medium.

At the same time, we need to ensure a consistent and pre-dictable policy environment as this new medium continues to mature. The Internet now reaches enough people in the United States and around the globe to compel governments, businesses, consumers, and others to wrestle with how traditional legal and regulatory issues play out in this new environment. From intellec-tual property to international trade, and from protecting speech to prosecuting criminals, all the rules are changing.

Finally, to realize the full mass-market potential of the Internet, we need to expand its reach. The Internet is having a major impact on certain parts of society. For the 25 percent of American house-holds now online, the new medium has provided new ways to shop, learn, and communicate with friends and family members. Still, 75 percent of American households—and many more around the world—haven't ventured online. We need to find ways to ensure affordable access to all parts of society.

As we achieve this last goal, we need to remember that we are working to shape and define a medium that will continue to evolve as more and more people come online. When they do, how will they change the medium? How will their needs and expectations differ from those of the first to venture into cyberspace? The short answer is no one knows exactly how the medium will evolve or what its ultimate economic or social impact will be.

The journey is only beginning. The technology is still developing, and the audience, while growing fast, is nowhere near its peak. Even our ways of comprehending this new medium and its potential uses haven't fully developed. How companies doing business online conduct themselves and interact with consumers in these formative years for the medium—and the extent to which we demonstrate leadership in achieving its full potential to benefit society—will have a great deal to do with the ultimate shape and impact of the Internet.

As was the case with the original "forty-niners," dreams, determination, and a sprinkle of luck have a lot to do with success in today's gold rush. Of course, a solid business model doesn't hurt. But unlike our mining predecessors, we have the benefit of working with a resource of nearly unlimited reach, potential, and adaptability—and the time and opportunity to reflect and adjust our approaches.

Indeed, we are at an exciting crossroads—when the medium is big enough to be relevant, but still small enough to be shaped.

Acknowledgments

First and foremost, we wish to thank the more than two dozen contributors who devoted their time and effort to sharing their knowledge of the online and Internet business with our readers. They committed to this project with no guarantees and spent many solitary hours at their word processors at a time when their businesses needed them most. For that dedication, we are most appreciative.

We'd especially like to thank Steve Case for his contribution to this book and for his many efforts on behalf of the industry. Thanks also to his staff at AOL; Dave Eisner and Jim Whitney were always responsive and a pleasure to work with.

We would like to thank the Internet Alliance (formerly the Interactive Services Association), the trade group whose early support helped launch this project, and the place where we came to know so many of the experts who contributed to this book.

The following people allowed us to interview them at length: Mark Benerofe, Lee DeBoer, Josh Grotstein, Danny Krifcher, Mario Marino, Michael Mazza, Claudia Mengel, Bob Myers, Martin Nisenholtz, Tom Ponosuk, Gene Quinn, Iana Schmitzer, Lisa Simpson, Juan Viega, and Audrey Weil. Their insights, experiences, and advice helped to shape and improve our thinking and editing.

Many more people gave us their support and counsel, reviewed proposals, referred us to additional sources, steered us through the publishing process, and contributed to the overall development of the book: Richard Adler, Gary Arlen, Bill Burrington, Judi Galst, Mark Johnson, Jack Radziewkowski, Lee Rosenbluth, Evan Rudowski, Michele Rutkowski, Sam Simon, and Ruth Stanit. We thank them all.

We would also like to thank Ron Schultz, who helped us shape our initial inspiration into a book proposal and then stuck with us until the last galley had been proofed. Finally, we want to thank Ed Walters, Editor-in-Chief of Adams Media, who believed in this book and whose steady and supportive hand has made it a reality.

—Christina Ford Haylock & Len Muscarella

I wish to thank Len Muscarella for his faith, patience, and good humor during the two-year process of writing this book. I could not have done it without him. I would like to acknowledge colleagues to whom I am especially grateful: Alan Daley at Bell Atlantic who helped get me started in this business; Al Lau, who opened doors for me at Citibank and taught me many valuable lessons along the way; Sam Simon for his long time support and counsel; and Catherine Allen, who first gave me the idea and encouragement for doing this book and shared so generously from her own publishing experience. I also wish to thank those people in my personal life, my family and friends, whose love and support sustains me. I especially wish to thank my best friend and husband, John, whose presence in my life has made all the difference.

—CFH

I would like to thank Christina Ford Haylock for coming to me with the idea for this book two years ago, inviting me to co-edit it with her. Thanks to my wife, Sally, for teaching me through example that perspiration is the catalyst that turns inspiration into success. I want to thank my daughters, Anne and Nicole, for understanding that Daddy has another, sometimes demanding life and for loving me unconditionally. I want to thank Eric Thoroman and Kathy Walsh of Interactive Media Associates, Inc., whose support was a constant throughout the project. And I want to thank CBS managers who introduced me to the online business in the early 1980s, and who instilled in me the understanding that talented, hardworking individuals make the difference.

—LM

Introduction

Commerce on the Internet, which was almost nonexistent in 1996, is projected to be a $200 billion industry by the year 2000 (IDC). No matter where we turn these days, we are confronted with another amazing statistic, another success story, another anecdote of how the Internet is going to change the way we work, play, communicate, and shop. Yet, there is a dangerous paradox emerging.

The hype surrounding each Internet "hit," be it Yahoo! or Amazon.com or GeoCities, has resulted in hundreds and thousands of other companies rushing to the Internet like moths to fire. And too many have found themselves singed by financial losses, disillusionment, and regret. We saw unrealistic expectations, followed by disappointment and frustration. And we felt, in particular, that the information available about the Internet contained too much "get rich quick" hype and not enough real understanding about building and managing effective Internet-based business strategies.

This is the situation that prompted us to write and compile this book. Its many contributors agree with the pundits that the Internet is changing our world. But we believe this will come about more as an evolution than a revolution, more as the result of thoughtful restructuring than the lightning-flash discovery of a new technology. Businesses and people will adapt, and products and services will be built in incremental steps, providing a transition from what exists today to where we will be tomorrow. This transition requires leadership, skillful management, and flexibility. We believe that with the right approach, planning, and proper utilization of resources, any company can use the Internet to effectively communicate its ideas; reach its customers, clients, constituents, or partners; sell products; or operate more efficiently.

History supplies the basis for our conviction. Back in the early to mid-1980s—years before the World Wide Web was established and a decade before Netscape was founded—there was a small cadre of business leaders who believed in a marketplace whose foundation would be networked computers. They were pioneer evangelists, spreading their gospel to skeptics both inside and outside of their companies. They shared a belief that online interactive services had the potential to significantly change our lives, both personally and professionally. They convened under the auspices of a trade association called the Videotex Industry Association, now the Internet Alliance, and they represented industries including telecommunications, computer hardware and software, manufacturing, banking, travel, retailing, and publishing, among others.

They collaborated to move the industry forward, defining standards and establishing privacy and security requirements. They even issued a report, called Gateway 2000, in 1987, predicting that by the end of the twentieth century, virtually everyone in North America would have access to a wide range of easy-to-use, electronic interactive services available in their offices, homes, and in public places. And they were not far off.

To paraphrase Ted Turner, these people "were interactive before interactive was cool." And they had compiled a significant body of learning in their years of research, development, and experimentation.

Yet when the Internet exploded into the public and business consciousness in 1994, it seemed to obliterate all of the history, and the learning, that went before it. In the height of the Internet frenzy and hype, no one seemed to remember that CompuServe had been offering online shopping since 1975; or that Prodigy based its business case, in 1984, on the conviction that advertising must be a key revenue source; or that "community" features had been championed by America Online® since its name was Quantum Computer Services (1985). The open standards and ubiquity of the Internet understandably had wiped the technology slate clean of those Byzantine early years of proprietary software. But the valuable business lessons learned in these early years were often discarded as well.

Net Success brings these lessons back to the forefront while addressing the challenges facing today's business executive in a Web-Centric world. This book has been written by many of the most successful and enduring executives in the industry today, including Steve Case, Chairman and CEO of America Online®; Eric Hippeau, President of Ziff-Davis Publishing; Blake Darcy, President of DLJ Direct; and Bill Randle, Executive Vice President and Managing Director of Huntington Bancshares. Many of the writers are veterans of those early days, including Richard Adler, Hilary Thomas, Elaine Rubin, Sam Simon, Leslie Laredo, Paul Lewis, Reggie Brady, and Harley Manning. They were the early prospectors, who know where the gold has been found in the past and, perhaps more importantly, where it hasn't. They also know where it might be in the future. These executives are people with views based on the jobs they've held and the business propositions they have implemented; executives like Tony Christopher of Fujitsu, Jim Pisz of Toyota, and Link Hoewing of Bell Atlantic. They are the developers of successful Internet strategies and carry with them the wisdom of those experiences. The advice is based on their experience. The lessons learned are enlightening. The recommended approaches are pragmatic and grounded in business principles.

This book is not about Internet predictions or forecasts for the future. It will not instruct the reader how to get rich quick, or how to be the next Yahoo!, nor will it provide simple answers. It will clearly lay out the challenges facing *established* companies and industries, rather than those who have come to exist purely as a result of the Internet. It is also about how to do business in a bimodal world and how to adapt and operate in a complex and changing environment.

This is not a book about technology. Although Internet technology is constantly evolving, we do not believe that technology, or the inability to grasp the technology, is a major hurdle for companies to overcome. The challenge is harnessing the business opportunity presented by the Internet. *EXPENSE*

The pages of this book are filled with real stories about how many leading companies in their industries are creating Web-centric organizations. The chapter on Intranets and Extranets explains in detail how Toyota has addressed this challenge. These are stories about the hard issues facing companies and executives alike who are in the midst of this undertaking; issues like the elimination of inter- mediaries, discussed in the chapters on brokerage, health care, and travel; the blurring of industry lines and facing of new competition, described in the chapter on banking; the managing of the new with the old, outlined in the chapter on public policy; and leading change, illustrated throughout. But beyond stories, we will provide a resource for comprehensive and effective action—a sane voice in the whirlwind of exaggeration. The chapters on design, direct marketing, advertising, and electronic retailing dispel the myths and offer a clear course of action.

We have divided the book into three parts to help readers get to their area of interest more quickly. We encourage everyone to read Chapters 1 and 2, because they offer our view of the Internet marketplace and the elements that make it so difficult for many companies to manage. Part One offers insights and instruction on the many facets of conducting business on the Web. Part Two, *Business-to-Business Uses of Internet Technology*, addresses the use of Internet technologies within an organization and with its trading partners. And Part Three, *How the Internet Is Helping to Transform Industries*, demonstrates how some of the most mature segments of Internet business and commerce are adapting to, and being changed by, this network of all networks.

We encourage the reader to reach outside of his or her own functional area or industry while reading this book. As the Internet pioneers recognized early on, they often learned more about doing business on the Internet from people in other industries than from people in their core business. And the challenges and issues facing companies and whole industries are often more alike than one would assume.

While we have edited the book to read cohesively, we have left room for the individual authors' creativity and ways of expressing their own ideas. Each has drawn from his or her own experiences. Therefore, there may be several sides to an issue represented. We have not tried to simplify what is complex, or present a unified opinion where one does not exist. We believe this has added value to the work.

A high technology truism states that the consequences of change are often overestimated in the short run and underestimated in the long run. As you will read, *Net Success* is built over time. It is built by opening up the flow of information. It is built by collaborative thinking, overcoming cultural hurdles and putting the tools and know how in the hands of everyone in the workflow. We hope this book will spark your own creative thinking and serve to contribute to your Net Success.

—Christina Ford Haylock and Len Muscarella

#### ONE

Making Sense of the Internet

Christina Ford Haylock, President, Ford Communications, and
Len Muscarella, Managing Director, Interactive Media Associates, Inc.

The image has become commonplace. Call it geek chic. Staring back from the pages of our favorite news or business magazine is a thirty-something male sporting a broad smile. Unlike the other men in the magazine, he is dressed in a decidedly casual fashion, as if he just stepped out of the student union. The headline reads, "The Internet has made him a multi-millionaire."

This is the Internet story that has dominated the media during the latter part of this decade. Investors have stampeded to Internet stocks. Companies that were barely heard of a year before are suddenly worth hundreds of millions of dollars. And kids barely out of college are suddenly titans of what is arguably the most dynamic industry of the twentieth century.

But there is a flip side to this Internet gold rush. You have to read the fine print of "The Internet Economy" hype to understand that only a handful of Internet ventures are profitable. In fact, even the most successful Internet services companies, from an investment standpoint, by August 1998, still have yet to experience operating profits for even one quarter. That has been true for some of the biggest brand names on the Internet. Yahoo!, the Internet portal whose name is almost synonymous with consumer Internet services, had a market value of $6.9 billion in the summer of 1998, but lost $32 million on revenues of just $71 million during the first half of that year. In July of 1998, the stock of Amazon.com, the Internet bookseller, was trading at 35 times sales and 1,470 times cash flow. It, too, had yet to experience its first profitable operating quarter.

Admittedly, both Yahoo! and Amazon.com experienced explosive revenue growth that helped fuel their stock prices. In the case of Amazon.com, its sales of $87.4 million in the first quarter of 1998 represented a 446 percent increase over the previous year's. But the fact remains that even the hottest, best known, and best capitalized Internet businesses have yet to move into the black.

This ROI (return on investment) gap has been even more acute for the tens of thousands of large and small companies trying to make their own way in a Web-centric world. These companies usually operate far from the magazine cover stories and the Silicon Valley investor galas. Most are merely trying to grab hold of the Internet train before it leaves the station. We call them encumbered companies. They are encumbered operationally, saddled with legacy systems, potential marketing channel conflicts, and personnel and organizational structures that were not designed with the Internet as their focus. And they are encumbered financially, with stockholders (or private owners) and boards of directors that are accustomed to operating profits, and who don't like the income statements of the aforementioned Internet industry leaders. (One of the ironies of the Internet gold rush is that investors are so caught up in the hype, that Web-based start-ups can actually be described as *less encumbered* financially than many billion-dollar corporations.)

For encumbered companies in particular, which represent the vast mass of corporate America as we approach the year 2000, the Internet has been far from a gold mine. According to market researcher ActiveMedia Inc. (as reported in *Business Week*), although commercial Internet sites exploded from 2,000 in early 1995 to 414,000 in 1998, only one in three was profitable.

Many companies whose business models are not appropriate for consumer-focused commercial sites are trying to force the square peg into the round hole, leading to even more disastrous results. Too few are seriously examining how Internet technologies can increase productivity and save money through Intranets, which are intracompany information, transaction, and communications services, and Extranets, which are private networks of information, transaction, and communications services between a company and a defined universe of users (customers, partners, distributors, or sales offices).

Senior management of these companies are mostly aware that the Internet, in all of its forms, holds great promise for their firms. It doesn't take a visionary to see that the combination of Moore's Law—which holds that computer power doubles every year—and societal trends [See Chapter 2 by DYG, Inc. on 7 Consumer Trends That Will Fuel Internet Commerce] points to a quantum shift in the way business will be conducted.

But these same senior managers often get caught up in the hype, expecting quick results at low investment. Even those who understand may get impatient when the Internet, which they keep hearing is as simple as rolling out of bed, becomes an all-consuming business challenge.

The simple fact is: The Internet is not so simple.

Why Is the Internet So Vexing to Some Companies?

The term "The Internet" has become the catch phrase for a vast, complex set of business activities that really cannot be represented by two words. Yet too many people insist on doing so, oversimplifying this varied and complex set of functions and applications. The generalization contributes to the difficulty of integrating and managing an Internet initiative in an encumbered company.

The Internet is actually a multidimensional, multidisciplinary, and multipurpose medium (or channel). This complexity defies simple answers; there is no single formula for success. But there are principles that emerge for the successful implementation of Internet initiatives in a corporate setting. And many of them are contained in the writings assembled in the chapters of this book.

THE INTERNET IS MULTIDIMENSIONAL
Effective use of the Internet can be one-to-one, one-to-many, or many-to-many.

One-to-one communications via the Internet are the hallmark of its communicative power. There is no other medium through which so many can be served so individually. Using toll-free phone numbers and trained telephone operators is prohibitively expensive for any function other than order taking. But using the computer to make the same information available without human intervention creates a personalized experience at a reasonable cost. Custom responses, those that cannot be computerized, can be handled less expensively and more thoroughly via e-mail.

But one-to-one communications is just one dimension of the Internet's power. When the Internet is used for one-to-many communications, it resembles broadcast media. This application of the Internet, as a flexible, facile broadcast or mass medium, remains the business model that—with the exception of electronic commerce—was responsible for the most revenue on the Internet at the end of 1998. The much talked-about portal sites—including Yahoo!, Excite, and AOL.com—all derive the bulk of their revenues from advertisers who want to reach the audiences they assemble. Aggregating audiences, and selling them to advertisers, is a business as old as newspapers. But it is one of the most important dimensions of the Internet today.

And the Internet also operates in the dimension of many-to-many; that is, a place for users to congregate and share ideas among themselves. So crucial is this dimension of the Internet that we have devoted a chapter in this book to it: community. America Online® was the first online system operator to understand the importance of community, and it rode that understanding to become the dominant Internet ISP and online service provider in the world.

Given the many dimensions in which the Internet operates, it's no surprise that companies trying to use it effectively can find it difficult to derive and enunciate a strategy. If and when they do, their work has only begun, because one of the most difficult aspects of the Internet is that it requires cross-functional management expertise.

THE INTERNET IS MULTIPURPOSE

The fact that the Internet is multipurpose, and that it can serve the corporation in so many, varied ways, is both the promise and the problem in many business environments. It causes confusion, mis-understanding, and lack of focus.

Almost every business understands that the ultimate power of the Internet must be seen through ROI. But ROI is a goal, not a strategy. And the varied ways that the Internet can impact the bottom line can sometimes seem at odds. The most obvious potential of the Internet is to increase revenues—by reaching new, otherwise inaccessible markets with products and services. But focusing on increased revenue alone can cause missed opportunities for companies.

The long-term payback of increasing the quality of customer service or increasing customer loyalty and reliance by providing value-added services is more difficult to measure than increased sales. But those types of initiatives may be even more accessible, and no less important, than simple Internet sales.

Then there is the entire expense side of the ledger. The Internet's power to provide higher-quality customer service at lower expense than traditional means—such as toll-free phone calls answered by customer service reps—has been proven by industry leaders such as Federal Express and Cisco Systems. Millions of dollars of postage have already been saved by companies who have shifted a portion of their communications budget to the Internet, and away from print and mail. And handled properly, Internet transactions can be more streamlined and less costly than orders that require human intervention.

In addition, the Internet can facilitate productivity and creativity gains by promoting collaboration and information sharing between customers and the company, between vendors and the company, and among employees of the company, as will be made clear in the Business-to-Business section chapter on Intranets and Extranets.

Obviously, "The Internet" is a loaded phrase, which makes it incumbent on the managers and leaders within a company to be explicit about what goals they want to achieve with their Internet initiative.

THE INTERNET IS MULTIDISCIPLINARY

Just who controls a company's Internet initiative? It is exactly the multifaceted and multidimensional aspects of the Internet that makes this decision so difficult. Internet initiatives do not fall neatly into existing organizational structures. In many organizations, the Information Technology department was the first to know about and play with the Internet. This was particularly true in the early years, when a curious technical person might actually have created *your-company.com* without the knowledge or inclusion of anyone else in the company. Once the Internet came into broader awareness, it was common for turf battles to ensue among marketing, corporate communications, product management, and public affairs departments, among others. In many companies it actually became a race of sorts to gain the recognition of being the first department with a Web site. In large, complex organizations, it was even more chaotic, with separate business units competing for control. Portal and brand issues were hotly debated. And in smaller companies, the practice persists, even today, of leaving the technology organization in charge of the Internet because they can talk the language.

The initial results of such actions were usually disastrous. With no clear leadership and little or no coordination among key departments, the Web sites produced were entities unto themselves—with no clear purpose, no stated objectives, and no results. For companies who have come later to the Internet, this may still be true.

But even when an Internet initiative is properly organized with appropriate leadership, its multidisciplinary demands can test an organization. This is particularly true in encumbered companies, where bureaucracy can be thick and where departments are organized and staffed to address traditional business functions, not the demands of running an Internet program.

Internet initiatives require teams with strategic, marketing, technical, graphic design, communications, publishing, and operations capabilities. The organizational challenge of assembling, managing, and empowering such teams is immense, as is described throughout the book.

The Adaptive Organization

The Internet industry, with all of its promise, change, speed, and unpredictability, is a perfect metaphor for our times. It is both driver and passenger in this chariot of change. Markets are fragmenting, or morphing, with scary speed. Industries are converging, and new business models are forming. Competition is coming from nontraditional sources, and alliances between competitors are becoming more common. Career employees are being passed over for specialized knowledge and skill workers. A customer-driven culture is replacing a corporate-driven culture. The pace of business is speeding up—as demonstrated by rapid technological innovations, faster time to market, and shortened product life cycles. Although time has collapsed in other eras of business, there is no experience with this level of immediacy, whether it be customer feedback, the dissemination of information, or the streamlining of business processes.

In this environment we believe the winners will be the adaptive organizations; organizations that are designed and managed to exploit change. The adaptive organizations will find the right balance between business process and creativity, between quality mandates and a software-industry mentality that says "adjust as you go along." It will instill a core competency for managing risk in a world of radical change. It will make flexibility a best practice.

The adaptive organization will empower its people to run beyond the road blocks while taking the time to teach them ethics and business principles. It will use the natural tensions that exist between the rigors of business discipline and the rate of change in this environment to provide its checks and balances.

Success in this environment requires building bridges: establishing positive interactions and relationships throughout an organization. This means bringing together older workers, valued for their wisdom, business skills, loyalties, and ethics, with the younger, more technically skilled workers, who may be impatient with process and loyal only to themselves. It will require bringing together Internet executives and managers, with their specialized skills and knowledge, and core business executives and managers, with their understanding of the company and its industry, competition, customers, and products. It will require the forging of new partnerships that will align former competitors who now must ally themselves against the new competition. Internet success will reveal an increasing dependence between large mature companies and small start-up companies. It will also join marketing partners whose interests do not always coincide.

There are many obstacles to attaining this new order. Resistance to change is strong in human nature, even for those who buy into a new concept. There is fear of an uncertain future and concern of being displaced in the new order. Internet initiatives may seem marginal to the core business, and its imperatives too different to be readily supported by core management. Often, the person brought in to lead the Internet or e-commerce charge is from outside the corporation, even the industry. This leads to natural tensions, distrust, and lack of understanding, and can be seen as a threat.

Implementing Internet Strategies

Much is being written about the "fast company" and managing in the new world order. But are there unique aspects to effective management of Internet strategies? The answer is one of emphasis. It is also a matter of flexibility, education, perseverance, and constant communication.

MARRYING THE NEW WITH THE OLD

Interviews were conducted with more than a dozen of today's senior executives responsible for their corporations' Internet businesses, representing such companies as Citicorp, Sony, NBC, Bell Atlantic, Viacom, the *New York Times*, and Chase Manhattan Bank, among others. What emerged was a common attitude and priority when approaching their work. They made it clear that while no executive's job is easy, to effectively marry Internet strategies with business strategies requires remarkable skill on many levels. The Internet executive relies heavily on the support and cooperation of the core business units. The challenge lies in figuring out how to bring the core business to bear, take full advantage of core assets, and bring the fundamental attributes of the corporation into this new world.

Respect for the core business, its history and tradition, along with a keen understanding of its environment, is absolutely essential. This means attending core business meetings, keeping abreast of its initiatives, and making an emotional connection with the people. It means bringing people from the core business into the

Internet organization at all levels. It means treating the core business as a client. It means engaging in activities designed to strengthen, enhance, and support the core business.

Conversely, it is just as important to insinuate the Internet-based business into the core, to develop roots. People need to understand the Internet and its thesis. The job is to get the core business to see things from new points of view, to be willing to work in a different way and to develop champions for the cause.

SELLING THE BUSINESS CASE

Creating a business case for the Internet is often the difference between knowing when to be bold and when to be conservative. One has to start with an argument that is more qualitative and sometimes overstates the returns to get going, while developing three- or five-year plans that are really impossible to project. One has to be an evangelist, capturing not only the mind but the imagination and heart of the audience. Personal communication skills are magnified.

It is important to sell the concept before developing a viable business model and assumptions. Then it's a matter of defending the business, the choices, and the deals. The Internet executive has to show where value is created and answer hard questions about the underlying assumptions. This requires a lot of complex and dense presentations. He has to be prepared to continually reinvent the business plan, deal with change, and be comfortable when he is not standing on firm ground. The Internet executive has to have a great deal of self-confidence.

Once in the market, it is critical to use tools to measure market share, revenues, and other quantitative performance criteria. But once in the market and not meeting revenues, the positioning switches to staying alive. The Internet executive has to skillfully manage expectations and create an environment that supports the missteps that accompany the development of new business, while applying the lessons learned to new efforts. He has to convince an audience that he is building a strategic core asset for the business. And this is where the presence of real leadership, commitment from senior management, and support from the core business is critical.

MANAGING THE PROCESS

There are other difficulties. Timing in this environment is critical but often hard to predict. The speed of change is staggering. There are new competitors, new technologies, new events every day. It is a constant battle to stay informed and remain relevant. It is even harder to stay focused.

People with a certain mind-set and skill who feel comfortable with risk and accept radical change are needed. In this environment, one must build eclectic teams that marry the old with the new, marketing with operations, creativity with business discipline. A level of cooperation must be achieved that brings the best of everyone together to solve a problem. Constant communication and information exchange helps keep everyone relevant. It takes work to keep everyone focused every day. The workload must be paced so people don't burn out. Once the necessary skills have been taught, there must be a clear path so they can do their job.

Five Principles

As we said earlier, there is no single formula for success in this environment. Yet some guidelines emerge. From the writings of the authors in this work, and from interviews with many more leading Internet executives in preparation for this book, five principles surface that hold value for any company that is evaluating, or reassessing, an Internet initiative. These principles are particularly appropriate for managers of encumbered companies, who must deal with the added complexity and legacy operations of an ongoing business.

1. The Internet is not a strategy: It serves the business strategy. Successful Internet initiatives share one thing in common—they are integrated into the fabric of the company's business strategy, and do not stand alone. The companies using the Internet successfully understand this fact.

Whether the company's objective is market share, revenue growth, expense reduction, or repositioning, any Internet initiative should be integrated as an element of that plan. The interactive components of information, entertainment, and commerce may stand alone in certain respects, but they must always address an objective of the core business. This holds true for both Fortune 100 companies and small not-for-profit organizations.

Integration of the Internet into overall business thinking and strategy is also critical. At its best, the Internet is not the subject of a temporary task force. It is not a special project. It is a way of doing business that everyone in the organization has to understand, buy into, and participate in. This includes all phases of the business process, from the corporate to the department level. It includes marketing, advertising, corporate communications, public relations, legal and regulatory, and customer support. Each business discipline should be looking to incorporate the use of the Internet into its delivery mix to achieve its objectives.

2. Internet initiatives require commitment and leadership. Whether the top executives in a company are enthusiasts or skeptics, hard charging or cautious, it is crucial that they provide commitment and leadership while developing Internet business models, products, and processes. Many contributors in this book acknowledge the leadership that enabled their early initiatives to launch, and enabled them to endure the inevitable setbacks that occurred along the way. Leadership empowers and emboldens Internet managers to learn from their mistakes, make changes, adjust to new circumstances, and persevere.

Nowhere was this demonstrated more dramatically than in Bill Gates's decision in 1995 to embrace the Internet, turning Microsoft's direction on a dime, demanding that every employee, every project, and every process be Internet focused.

Both Bill Randle, Executive Vice President of Huntington Bancshares, Inc., and Blake Darcy, President of DLJDirect, the Internet brokerage arm of Donaldson, Lufkin and Jenrette, write about the importance of the support of their management during the early years. Darcy was among the first to launch online brokerage services, initially through Prodigy and then AOL, years before the World Wide Web exploded. Because of his investment in and focus on the online services, Darcy was late moving to the Internet. And he was frustrated by the media's attention to Internet brokerage services at the expense of more established, larger online-based services, such as his own.

But as he makes clear in his chapter on the brokerage industry, his management supported him and provided the resources necessary to launch his Internet product.

Many Internet "failures" come down to executives who only pay lip service to the Internet initiatives, stop funding at the first sign of trouble, allow internal forces to undermine them, and fail to empower those they choose to lead. Leadership provides clear direction and perseverance during difficult times.

3. The Internet requires the re-examination of intermediate relationships. Much has been made of disintermediation through the Internet, and examples abound in this book—particularly in the stock brokerage and travel industries. But the Internet has also created new intermediate relationships—for companies who aggregate and affiliate. In fact, a whole new set of middlemen is exploding on the Internet.

Priceline.com has turned airline ticketing on its head by enabling travelers to name their price for a flight. Auto-by-Tel.com and CarPoint have become new intermediaries in the new car business. And a plethora of digital auctioneers have emerged to bring buyers and sellers together in a number of merchandise categories.

Traditional business intermediaries—travel agents, stock brokers, bankers, book and music producers and sellers, and car dealers—who are most threatened by the Internet have an even greater urgency to understand the medium. Creative thinkers in these areas are already identifying ways that they can use the medium to solidify their positions.

One such creative program is being developed by Andrew McKee and is outlined in Chapter 16, "Travel." McKee and his investors are developing an Internet-based private network—an Extranet—that will provide small travel agents with tools that can help them combat the trend toward disintermediation.

From a manufacturer's perspective, it is essential to understand how the Internet can revolutionize the concept of channels. From a middleman's perspective, it is a matter of survival to understand the impact of the Internet.

4. Internet-technology advances are overrated: It's business-model advances that count. Internet-technology advances always grab the headlines. It happened with Java, Shockwave, QuickTime, and RealAudio. But there is a lag in the commercialization of these advances that is every bit as immutable as Moore's Law. The adoption lag is the two- to three-year period that occurs between a product announcement and its widespread acceptance in the marketplace, particularly the consumer marketplace. In the chapter on design, Harley Manning of Forrester Research details how this lag plays out in the development of Web sites.

Unless the desktop that services are being delivered to can be controlled, as in the case of some Intranet and Extranet programs, the adoption lag is a reality that has to be lived with.

Emerging Internet business models are much more important to track, evaluate, and adopt. Take, for instance, the emergence of auctions in 1997 with eBay, community offerings in 1998 by GeoCities, or the launch of travel sales through Priceline.com. These examples show that business-model advances can create competitive advantages or lost opportunities very quickly. And the gap that is created may not be easily overcome.

5. Partnering is the key to success in the Internet's multifunctional environment. Whether intraorganization or interorganization, partnering to bring all the necessary skill levels to the table is crucial. The Internet executive understands that his success is dependent on the development of the industry, its laws, its infrastructure, and its customer base. He also understands it is often necessary to go outside one's company to leverage the necessary talents, resources, and products to accomplish his objectives.

The history of online and Internet partnerships is a checkered one, littered with both spectacular hype and spectacular failures. No two deals are alike, but some attributes of a quality partnership endure.

First, the deal must be good for all parties.

Second, don't expect to anticipate or to accommodate every detail on the front end. Write a good contract, then put it away.

Third, the success of most partnerships is in the handoff from the negotiating team to the various operating units. Make sure they are ready to catch the ball.

Fourth, have a means in place to resolve disputes.

Fifth, set benchmarks. Measure, review, and adjust. Communicate results.

Sixth, do what the organization does well.

Seventh, pick partners who have a good reputation and can teach the company something about being in this business.

Eighth, be prepared to defend the partnership to the core business.

Asking the Right Questions

When planning, evaluating, and revising Internet initiatives, keep the following questions in mind:

How can the Internet help me reach my business objectives in a way that is better, delivers revenue, or reduces costs?

In what way does the Internet enhance what I am already doing? Have I looked at ways of improving business processes ?

Is anyone doing this with any success? What does it take? What does it cost? Does the investment justify the expense? Am I clear about what to expect?

What commitment am I (my company) prepared to make?

Do I have the right resources in house? Is everyone involved?

Have I caused people in the organization to understand the true value and purpose of what I am doing?

Am I spending enough time letting senior management know how things are going and solidifying their support?

Have I aligned myself with colleagues to ensure their cooperation and support?

Are my people focused on the right things, hampered by the corporate politics, working too hard?

Am I on track or do we need to readjust, given changes in direction, circumstance, or the environment?

Am I talking with everyone; getting out of the office; keeping up with people, developments, and events?

What issues on the policy, regulatory, and industry levels affect me, and what can I do to influence this?

Throughout this book, our authors will pose questions like these to the readers that challenge their thinking about managing and developing Internet initiatives. These are for the readers' practical use, to make sure that the right questions are being asked so that the right results are realized. There are plenty of opportunities on the Internet to be imaginative, innovative, and creative. But that doesn't mean that the wheel has to be reinvented with each new initiative. What follows is the experience, insight, and knowledge of those who have had net success.

#### TWO

Seven Societal Trends Driving Consumer Interest in the Internet and E-commerce

Madelyn Hochstein, President, DYG

DYG SCAN is a trend-identification program that since 1987 has tracked consumer social values and predicted shifts in the social and consumer agenda for the country. SCAN uses annual national surveys among a representative sample of Americans aged eighteen and older as well as focus groups and secondary-source research such as Census data to track social values and spot trends. SCAN is a service of DYG, Inc., a full-service marketing and social-research company with headquarters in Danbury, Conn.

It is essential for anyone who is considering an Internet-based initiative to understand the audience it is trying to address. Although millions are using the Internet, millions more are not. When considering doing business on the Web, one should be clear if the target is likely to be responsive to an Internet-based communication. At DYG, we use a trend-identification program called SCAN [1] to help our clients understand shifts in social values and behaviors and link these to the development of business and product strategies. What we clearly see is a confluence of events and attitudes that will result in an even greater role for the use of the Internet and e-commerce for businesses and consumers. The following trends are driving interest in the Internet and should prove useful in understanding your audience's desires, concerns, and motivations.

1. Long-term rise in educational attainment. Over the past four decades, an increasing number of Americans have completed high school and college. In 1998, 24 percent of adult Americans (25+) had four-year college degrees, compared to 11 percent in 1970. And the Census projects that these numbers will continue to rise among all ethnic and racial groups well into the next century. SCAN data on values related to the acceptance of technology suggest that the more educated our population, the better the outlook for use of the Internet in all ways—from information gathering to entertainment to commerce; currently, the people most attracted to the Internet are college educated.

It is vital for Internet marketers to recognize that educational status defines the receptive consumer. The values and attitudes of this segment are unique and must be factored into any marketing effort.

2. Increasing acceptance of technology as a problem solver. The key values trend that gives impetus to greater use of the Internet, including transactions and shopping, among better-educated Americans is the belief that "technology solves more problems than it creates." Indeed, educated consumers increasingly believe this, despite growing sophistication about both the up- and downsides of the new consumer technologies.

The 1980s' giddy fascination, especially among upscale men, with the gadgets of telecommunications technology has sobered with discussions of benefits blended with observations about "always being on call and at work" thanks to laptops and cellular phones. Awareness of privacy issues and the singular concern about exposure of children to pornography and predators on the Internet (given the massive trend in the country toward child-centeredness) are also evident.

However, educated consumers still see the benefits of technology outweighing the drawbacks. On the assumption that privacy and safety will be ensured, they embrace the Internet as a consumer problem solver. It is the direction of the future for better-educated consumers.

The success of e-commerce rests with keeping the underlying social value of "benefits outweighing the drawbacks" in place by addressing privacy and safety concerns and constant reinforcement of problem-solving capabilities.

3. Simplification. This will be one of the most potent long-term consumer trends of the next century, especially among the better-educated, upscale consumers so vital to the success of e-commerce.

Nearly forty years of the pursuit of "having and doing it all," from careers to material acquisition to quality-of-life experiences to family and children for both men and women, has left a generation exhausted, overloaded, time constrained, and feeling stressed and overwhelmed. The fundamental baby boomer goal for the next decade is downshifting—setting priorities, jettisoning the unnecessary or unpleasant, avoiding hassle, and freeing up time to concentrate on the important stuff: family, health, and well-being, and as discussed below, fun.

The Internet in all its functions, including e-commerce, is seen by better-educated baby boomers as a perfect conduit for simplification of information gathering and shopping. Much of the perceived problem solving attributed to technology derives from this view.

"Freeing up time" and "reducing hassle and stress" are at the top of the list of what marketers must deliver to find success on the Internet.

Consumers see traditional ways of doing transactions and shopping as highly stressful and hassled because they involve dealing with people who are rude, uninformed, and disrespectful.

The design of Internet marketing must communicate respect for the consumers' time and respect of them as intelligent people. Marketers must take every step to ensure that this new medium is as hassle free and stress reducing as possible in order to win with consumers.

4. Preference for a home-based lifestyle combined with only pleasant and safe outings. Several factors support a long-term, home-based approach to lifestyle. The simplification trend noted above is first among equals in creating a consumer view that quality of life is best achieved within the home. Next, the dramatic return of family and child orientation as a central baby boomer focus, and the widely accepted belief that home is where the family is. And finally, there is the extraordinary fear of societal threats—crime, germs, pollution—that one may encounter outside in such settings as supermarkets, department stores, and malls.

The Internet and e-commerce are central engines for facilitating a home-based lifestyle in which the only reasons to go outside are to have fun with the family and friends and to engage in healthful sports activities.

We can therefore add the facilitation of a home-based lifestyle to the list of benefits delivered by technology.

5. Passionate pursuit of leisure and entertainment. Just as better-educated consumers are increasingly shifting attention to family, they are also shifting their focus from work and career (which have proven to be less rewarding and not the source of satisfaction that they had hoped they would be) to leisure and pleasure.

Better-educated consumers are also expanding the definition of leisure. First, it must be productive either in the sense of physical fitness sports or in the sense of accomplishing something, such as learning or increasing one's cultivation. But it must also be fun and entertaining. Indeed, the overarching trend emerging as a result is that all activities in life must have a leisure component in the sense of being entertaining, enriching, or just plain fun. One of the long-term trends for the next century is the moving away from compartmentalization and achieving a blend of all aspects of life; the relevant blend here is shopping and transactions blended with fun, entertainment, and cultivation.

Internet marketers must take the need for these environmental factors into their designs—just delivering on the functionality of simplification and home-based, while critical, is not sufficient. E-commerce must also be an "experience."

6. Making connections. The thirty-year trend toward focus-on-self and defining individuality as a set of "my needs" is rapidly drawing to a close. It will be replaced with a new conception of individualism based on "my network"—the friends, family, and others that I share values and views with define who I am and what makes me unique. The new trend will be about reaching out to others with mutual interests and shared values. The Internet facilitates the creation of affinity groups worldwide and vastly expands the connections one can make.

Marketers have the opportunity to establish the sense of family with customers that leads to loyalty to and advocacy for products or services. In creating their sites, marketers must take into account the subtle benefit of belonging and connectedness that can be delivered to the consumer, and take steps to demonstrate and actively pursue this understanding.

7. Customer-in-charge. The final relevant trend builds from rising education levels but also reflects a revolution in social values when it comes to the marketplace. The past twenty years of American social history have seen a rise of distrust and cynicism about all of its institutions, including the marketplace—manufacturers, service providers, and most especially retailers. The traditional hierarchies are gone, and the consumer has taken over the relationship in the marketplace.

The social-values trends underlying this shift in who is in charge are the rising belief in self-reliance, the willingness to bypass traditional distribution channels to get value and better treatment, doing one's homework, confidence in one's self as an expert, and a desire to go straight to the "brand" one has confidence in, cutting out the middleman.

Clearly, these values support the future potential in e-commerce and use of the Internet for information gathering and shopping. They are critical for anyone who is doing business on the Internet to take into consideration.

Consumers will come to marketers on the Internet on their own terms, which include highest quality and greatest value; excellent treatment and respect, as defined by simplification in all aspects of the process; plentiful information to make informed choices; clear, differentiated, and strongly imaged branding; enough choices to create a sense of control, but not so many as to create a sense of work; and clear signals of understanding that the customer is charge.

Taken together, these seven trends suggest the following for marketers looking to the Internet for success:

Know your target—the audience is, and will be for a long time to come, the better-educated consumer.

Be vigilant—keep those educated consumers believing that the benefits outweigh the problems (and the benefits are home-based and hassle free) and make sure that privacy and safety don't become problems.

Make it simple—when e-commerce delivers stress reduction, it wins; if it winds up a hassle in its own right, the consumer will walk away.

Recognize that using the Internet, even for e-commerce, is about more than "getting something done"; the Internet offers educated consumers a medium for making connections and marketers should leverage the unique ability of the Internet to facilitate connectedness and affinity.

Functionality isn't enough—delivering hassle-free, home-based information gathering and transactions is the price of admission; the home run is, well, a home run; make it fun, entertaining, an experience.

Accept the notion that the Internet consumer is "the boss" and play by his or her rules—highest quality and great value; excellent treatment and respect; simplification in all aspects of the process; plentiful information to make informed choices; clear, differentiated and strongly imaged branding; enough choice to create a sense of control, but not so many choices as to create a sense of work.

Success on the Internet will come from never forgetting it's the consumer who is in charge and setting the terms for doing business with you; knowing their terms and respecting them is the key to winning.

## PART ONE

Internet
Applications

One way to look at the Internet is as a specialty practice within a business enterprise. The management of an Internet initiative requires skills in a number of disciplines and an understanding of the capabilities and assets of the medium.

The seven chapters in this section comprise some of the essential disciplines for a company that wants to do business using Internet technologies. In several cases, the chapters address disciplines that are well understood in the "traditional" business realm. Most large corporations are filled with practitioners in areas such as advertising, direct marketing, and public relations/corporate communications—or they have outside vendors that provide the expertise. But there are different strategies and tactics to be used in the Internet versions of those disciplines, and the following chapters provide keys to making them work for a company.

Two chapters in this section, Virtual Communities and E-commerce and Merchandising, address two of the most popular and promising applications of the Internet at the end of the 1990s. The Community chapter provides the reader with the essentials of understanding this powerful online tool and how it can be harnessed by companies who want to be successful on the Internet. The E-tailing chapter addresses the attributes that make consumer e-commerce such a powerful application, and provides direction for how companies can make the most of their online retailing initiatives.

The final chapter in the Applications Section is on Legal and Public Policy Issues on the Internet. It is designed to provide the reader with an understanding of how some of the most common, accepted business-law concepts—such as copyright, trademark, and sales tax—can be threatened by this new medium that seems to defy time and space.

#### THREE

The Action-Oriented
Design Imperative

Harley Manning, Senior Analyst, Interactive Technology Strategies,
Forrester Research

First generation Internet design was characterized by the simple repurposing of print material. But as services get more interactive, site design
must rise to a higher standard. Harley Manning provides perspective on
Internet design today, and predicts the design imperatives of the near future.

Within two years, your current Web site will be a
memory. You will have redesigned and rebuilt it at least once, possibly twice. This should not come as a surprise.

Design on the Web is in a constant state of change. Few, if any,
site designs stand the test of time. Think about how many of your
favorite sites look the same as they did two years ago. In fact, how
many of your favorite sites from two years ago are still among your
favorites today?

In a 1998 study conducted by Forrester Research, 74 percent of
respondents were either planning to redesign their sites within the
next six months or were engaged in a constant series of design iter-
ations. This is a ferocious rate of change compared to the frequency
of design changes for any other medium.

The frequent redesigning and rebuilding of Web sites is costly. Some of the cost components are easy to identify, others are hidden.

Forrester estimates that Fortune 1000 companies are paying $50,000 to $100,000 for "look and feel" designs of major sites. A site blueprint specifying navigation and function averages another $125,000. And the cost of creating a new design is just the tip of the iceberg. Once the design is complete, there are production costs that will typically exceed the cost of the design and could exceed the original cost of producing the site. Unless the existing site is shut down while the new site is being produced, these costs will be incurred on top of the site's current run rate.

Figure 3.1. Web Redesign Schedules

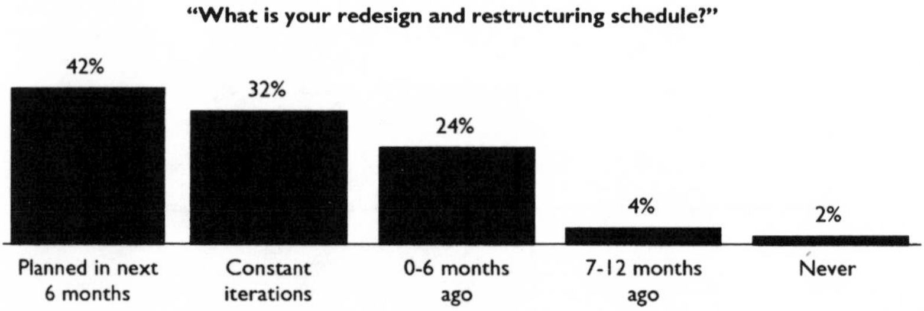

"**What is your redesign and restructuring schedule?**"

42%	32%	24%	4%	2%
Planned in next 6 months	Constant iterations	0-6 months ago	7-12 months ago	Never

Reproduced with permission of Forrester Research, Inc.

There's also the unmeasured cost of user dissatisfaction, as current users are forced to relearn site navigation. Even when a redesign improves a site, some new learning must take place. This will often elicit negative user feedback about the new design. But what users are really saying is, "Why are you making me learn this site all over again?"

Why are site designs changing so rapidly? Is such a rapid rate of change inevitable? As it turns out, the drivers behind the change are well understood and certain to continue for at least the next five years.

The most obvious driver for design change is the relentless pace of Web browser releases. This pace is not going to slow.

Major browser releases happen every one and a half to two years, and will continue to do so for at least the next five years.

Simultaneously, older browser releases overhang the market. This creates an ever-increasing tension between the desire to take advantage of new capabilities and the need to reach a broad audience.

Before year-end 1999, the state-of-the-art browsers in the marketplace will be 6.0 releases from Microsoft and Netscape. They will support features like font embedding, XML, and "smart browsing."

Figure 3.2. Web Browser Development Time Line

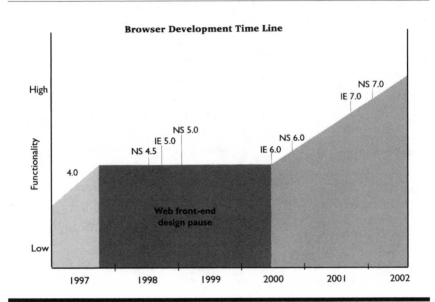

Reproduced with permission of Forrester Research, Inc.

But it doesn't stop there. By mid-2001, 7.0 releases will be widely available. They will support features like automatic update, HTML 4.0, and voice recognition. And while these features might sound like technobabble now, they will provide real benefits to users of sites that take advantage of them.

As of this writing, Web sites are designed for *at best* a 4.0 browser release from Microsoft or Netscape. It is far more likely for a site to have been designed—or even redesigned—to accommodate a lower level of browser such as Netscape Navigator 2.0. Web designers are facing increasing difficulties in trying to address the many combinations of browser versions and bandwidth in the marketplace.

Another recent study by Forrester found that many firms have pulled advanced capabilities like Java and frames off their sites, dumbing down to accommodate old browsers and slow connections.

Still another factor driving design change is the rise of Internet data marts. Data marts are databases or collections of databases designed to help managers make decisions about their customers. This development allows companies to leverage information about customers and users to deliver dynamic, personalized content that combines transactional capabilities with a high level of interactivity. At Forrester we call this "transactive content." Making the switch from static, one-size-fits-all content to transactive content requires design changes at all levels of site architecture.

Increasingly companies will connect their Web sites with customer databases, order-entry systems, and other legacy systems. Sophisticated personalization capabilities made possible by companies like Brightware and Net Perceptions will be integrated into the basic functions that all users experience. Static HTML pages will give way to templates populated by content drawn from Oracle and Informix databases.

But none of these developments will "just happen." They will require a major, focused design effort.

Furthermore, large companies will begin using the Internet not just as a marketing vehicle but as essential business infrastructure. This will focus increased attention on Web sites as part of a strategic mix of Internet-enabled applications, ranging from desktops to alternative devices like Palm Pilots and smart phones. As use of the Internet becomes more central to how business is conducted, the quality bar will rise for design, function, and performance of applications delivered through the Web.

As a direct result of these change drivers, Web projects will become less and less like publishing projects and will increasingly come to resemble traditional software development projects.

As functional complexity increases, costs for Web projects will rise. As companies become more dependent on the Web for day-to-day business, more will ride on success or failure of a site. Designing a usable interface for Web sites will therefore become even harder than it is today, as site designers wrestle with how to present more content and more function . . . and not overwhelm users.

Design As a Strategic Advantage

In this environment, the design of a Web site can become a strategic advantage. Effective use of design will allow a company to benefit in a number of ways.

An effective design will allow the provider to better predict and control costs. For example, a design should include flexible rules for how and where the site will add new content (as opposed to updating old content). Establishing these rules in the design phase of the project will greatly reduce the need for ongoing design changes, as well as pushing out the time until the next major redesign.

A layered site design can allow a company to react more quickly and effectively. Separating content from presentation and function in the design reduces the effort to change any of the three later. In addition, a strong conceptual model streamlines decisionmaking about whether or not to make changes in the first place.

Perhaps most importantly, an effective design can help satisfy and retain users. There are measurable human factors that can be used to objectively evaluate the impact a site design has on its users. An effective Web site design can improve the experience for users in several *measurable* ways. For example, using consistent language on buttons and prompts reduces the time it takes users to perform tasks by 25 percent. Users come to a site with goals. Effective design will help them to attain their goals more quickly and easily.

A design can be used to reduce the number of errors users make while performing common tasks on a site. If someone hasn't been exposed to how software designers deal with error, this idea may seem jarring. Users typically think of errors as mistakes they make that are somehow their fault. Software designers think of errors as a user's best approximation of the correct action. In other words, the user took what appeared to be the right action to achieve a goal. Software designers use well-known principles to improve the likelihood that a user will take the correct action in the first place. There are no bad users, but there are less-than-perfect designers and designs.

Subjective satisfaction is another human factor that software designers measure. This is typically done by having users assign a numerical value to how much they enjoyed using the software. So although the factor being measured is subjective, it is assigned an objective number—by users—that will serve as a benchmark that can be remeasured over time to gauge improvement. If an organization thinks that user satisfaction with its site isn't terribly important, it might want to keep in mind that it's an important predictor of whether or not the user will ever return.

We've seen some of the ways that better design can improve a site in measurable ways. But with rising costs, rapid technological change, and increased functional complexity, how will designers cope, let alone move beyond current levels of usability, to achieve a strategic advantage for their sites?

As Web projects become more like software projects, Web designers will have to look to the methodologies of the software industry. This will result in a move to a new design imperative that will combine best practices from media design and production with principles of computer-human interaction. This is called action-oriented design.

A good part of this new design movement will take place naturally. The Web may be the newest new medium but it certainly isn't the first new medium. There is a natural progression to the design of all new forms, media or otherwise. New forms start out by imitating older forms, then evolve into what the new form will eventually become. Early automobile designs copied carriage designs (hence, the name "horseless carriage"). Early television programs copied both radio and live theater. So, too, the Web is struggling from its early imitation of print and broadcast media and toward what it will ultimately become.

Four Phases of Web Design

The four progressive phases of Web design evolution mirror the phases that many Web designers pass through in their development. There are many examples of sites on the Web today that correspond to the first three phases. The fourth phase is one that is only now beginning to emerge. The four phases are:

1. Applying What We Already Knew. Here the designer applies lessons from established media. Consequently, the site tends to look like a printed page, a video still, or a CD-ROM. Interactivity often suffers and performance is usually poor due to heavy graphics.

2. *Imitating What We See.* As the designer becomes immersed in the realities of Web design, new design problems pop up that can't easily be solved by applying lessons from other media. At this point, the designer looks to how other sites solved these problems, and adapts those solutions. But although the designer is growing in knowledge, there is still no deep conceptual framework of understanding. A borrowed solution may not be appropriate and can even cause usability problems that are worse.

3. *Learning by Experience.* The feedback mechanisms of the Web are an incredibly valuable tool for learning. Study of server logs shows how users move through a site. Users voice their likes and dislikes through e-mail. But be warned: Although users know when they have a problem, they are not the right ones to design the solution. In addition, internal users are a constant source of data. As a Web designer enters the third phase, the design is typically simplified so that it will work better on a variety of browsers, the size of pages is reduced so that it will work better over low bandwidth, and it moves toward more consistency in page layouts. These are all positive developments, even though the designer may still lack an underlying framework of understanding.

4. *Software Design Awareness.* Some new media designers have begun to look beyond the current state of Web design and become aware of the principles and methods used by software designers. At the same time, the Computer-Human Interaction (CHI) community—largely academic and previously focused strictly on software—has begun to adapt and apply its work to the Web. What we are just beginning to see on the Web is a design approach that owes as much to science as to art. It is a more rigorous, principled approach to new media design. It is characterized by designers taking what they have learned from both past lives and recent experience, and applying it through structured methodology to produce designs that are measurably superior to past efforts. This is the beginning of action-oriented design.

Why is action-oriented design important? Users come to a site with goals. So, too, Web site owners have business goals that can be attained only by driving specific user actions, such as viewing pages (drives ad revenue) or making transactions (drives electronic commerce revenue).

Inevitably, sites add more content, more function, and more graphics. In a Forrester study of new media executives responsible for their companies' Web sites, the top responses to the question, "What will you add to your site in 1998?" were "more content" and "personalization." In the same study, site owners said that their top challenge was "making the site attractive." Ensuring ease of use came in fourth.

In the midst of this increased complexity, helping users attain their goals while leading them toward actions that support business goals is not easy. To achieve success, designers will need to clearly understand user goals, business goals, rapidly evolving site functionality, and software design methodologies. Talent and experience alone will not get the job done.

Figure 3.3. Web Developers' Approaches and Challenges
Reproduced with permission of Forrester Research, Inc.

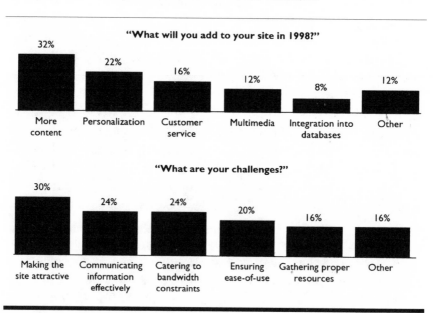

Crucial Steps Toward Action-Oriented Design

How can a site be taken from its current design to an action-oriented design? To get off the merry-go-round of trial-and-error design changes, there are specific steps that can be taken before the next redesign.

The first step is to determine specific user goals that you want your design to facilitate. These should be specific goals such as finding a particular document or completing an order for a product. This is the most critical task. If the process doesn't start with a good grasp of user goals, there should be little expectation that anything else done will improve the site's usability.

The next step is to benchmark the site's usability relative to the specific set of goals. Vendors can help identify and measure human factors like the time it takes to learn specific tasks, and the number of errors users make in performing those tasks.

The third step is to set measurable goals for improving a site's usability. For example, if the most frequent task users perform on a site takes five clicks, a goal should be set for cutting it down to three clicks. If users make an average of two navigation errors during a typical session on a site, a goal should be established for reducing that number to one or none.

Critical user tasks must be prototyped and user tested as part of the design process. A rough HTML prototype can be created quickly and cheaply with any of several popular tools. Prototyping and testing will add two to three weeks to the front end of a schedule and $12,000 to $25,000 to a typical budget for a large site, but it will all come back—and more—if a single major design flaw is corrected before a site is built.

For those sites where $25,000 sounds more like the total budget than the testing budget, there are low-cost alternatives. The two or three most critical tasks on a site can be quickly mocked up using a tool like Microsoft FrontPage or NetObjects Fusion. Then a handful of representative users can be brought in as they watch and try to perform the tasks. This won't provide the full benefit of a professional usability audit, but it will likely catch any egregious errors. For more insight on user testing on a budget, see Bruce Tognazinni's excellent book, *TOG on Interface*.

As the site is being designed and built, schedule checkpoints at critical steps along the way. For any proposed changes to the design, ask how usability will be affected. Will the changes add an extra step to a task? Are we adding clutter to a page, making it harder for users to pick out what they want?

Once a new site is live, it should become a habit to consider how changes and additions will impact the measurable site goals for usability. The ultimate goal is to make usability become part of the culture and not an afterthought. This can be accomplished by treating usability like any other measured business goal. Usability goals, like business goals such as gross sales and ROI, should be specific and measurable, with periodic progress reviews.

If a company already views design as a strategic component of its overall business plan, then evolving a Web site to action-oriented design will be a natural move. But for many organizations, it won't be so easy.

A company's current Web designer may not be versed in software-design principles. A company's current new media organization probably doesn't consider design a strategic priority that has equal weight with site goals like usage and completed orders. Then there are the pressures of keeping an existing site live and current. Nothing interrupts a good design session like having everyone leave to handle a server outage or put a late-breaking story on the home page.

Even more troublesome is that, many people have become used to making design decisions based solely on corporate identity guidelines. This is not to say that corporate identity is unimportant. An organization cares about its corporate logo and design guidelines, and it should. It probably paid plenty for them. But understand that color and text have a measurable impact on site usability. Graphics and multimedia do, too. It's possible to use colors in ways that will distract users from accomplishing their goals. It's not only possible but common for sites to slow performance to a crawl with elaborate graphics and animation. That flying, spinning, morphing logo that looked so great in the television ad just doesn't work when it is stuffed through a 28.8 modem. So, when striving to keep an identity on the Web in line with an identity in other media, it pays to always consider the impact on users.

At the extreme, some company Web sites show far more fascination with themselves than with their users. If the site is all about a company's logo, mission statement, and new ad campaign, it won't have to buy extra servers to handle all the traffic, because, just like a party guest who can only talk about himself, the site will be a bore . . . and attract about as much interest as a boring person. If generating site traffic or converting lookers into buyers is important, start by remembering the first rule of user experience: Provide something that users will find interesting or useful.

The best way to avoid these problems is to treat a Web site like the marketing channel it will become, not the stealth initiative it started out as. So, when planning communications, sales, and brand initiatives across channels, include a Web site in those plans. Otherwise the site will suffer and the company will, too—in lost customers, extra expense, and possible embarrassment.

To succeed in this transformation, user experience will need to be included in the site's measures of success. Changes will be required in the way design is planned for and evaluated. The same kind of measured accountability that is demanded from site traffic and ROI goals should be expected from design goals. If design is taken seriously, it can deliver serious results.

Virtual
Communities

Richard P. Adler, Principal, Digital Places, and Anthony J. Christopher, Principal, Digital Places

Community-of-interest formation is perhaps the single unique attribute of interactive media. Richard P. Adler and Anthony J. Christopher provide a scholarly analysis of the derivation and importance of virtual communities, and suggest ways that they can be employed to generate both fun and profit.

W e [are] convinced that cybercommunity members [are] the most focused and loyal of online users. Their emotional involvement in these communities suggests powerful opportunities for marketers to build brands.[1]

—*Myra Stark, Saatchi & Saatchi Advertising*

Anyone who is interested in doing business on the Internet needs to be aware of virtual communities. Perhaps no other technique is potentially more powerful for aggregating and communicating with specific target audiences. But, as we shall see, participating in a virtual community requires fundamental changes in how companies and organizations relate to their customers and the ways in which they conduct business.

What Are Virtual Communities?

Virtual communities allow people with common interests to meet, communicate, and share ideas and information with each other through an online network such as the World Wide Web. Through these activities, participants develop bonds with other members of the community and with the community as a whole. Over the past few years, the creation of virtual communities has emerged as one of the most distinctive—and potentially important—capabilities of the Internet.[2]

Virtual communities can be built around groups of individuals who belong to a particular demographic group (e.g., college students or working women or parents or African Americans or seniors) or who are part of a profession (e.g., farmers or doctors or computer programmers) or who share a particular personal interest (e.g., investing or drinking wine or playing backgammon or traveling). Because the participants in a virtual community share common interests, they have a good deal to talk about with each other. And once they are established, these communities provide a new way for companies to reach customers who are likely to have a special interest in their products.

As we shall see, the Internet has been playing a role in the development of virtual communities since its early days. However, it is only in the past few years that the concept has received widespread attention.

Initially, interest in online virtual communities was limited to those individuals who participated in them and a small band of journalists and sociologists who studied and described them. More recently, interest in virtual communities has grown as they have been seen as a powerful new tool that can create new business opportunities and can be a source of substantial revenues. Understanding the dynamics of virtual communities is emerging as a critical business skill in the new networked world.

Table 4.1: Types of Virtual Communities

TYPE OF AFFINITY	COMMUNITY	MEMBERS
Demographic	Tripod	College students
	iVillage	Women
	Babyplace.com	New parents
	NetNoir	African Americans
	SeniorNet	Older adults
Professional	Agriculture.com	Farmers
	Physicians Online	Doctors
	IDG Net	Computer professionals
Personal interest	Motley Fool	Individual investors
	Virtual Vineyard	Wine drinkers
	Expedia	Travelers
	Gamegrid	Backgammon players

A Brief History of Virtual Communities

The first virtual communities emerged about a decade after the establishment of the Internet. Starting in the early 1980s, a network called USENET was set up to link university computing centers that used the UNIX operating system. One function of USENET was to distribute "news" on various topics throughout the network. Participants were able to set up their own "newsgroups" on topics of shared interest. These were bulletin board–type discussions where participants could send messages to a newsgroup on a given topic and read the messages sent by others.

Initially, all of the newsgroups focused on technical or scholarly subjects, but so-called "alt" and "rec" groups that focused on non-technical topics such as food, drugs, and music began to appear. Before long, the number of newsgroups started to grow exponentially. From 158 newsgroups in 1984, the number grew to 1,732 groups in 1991 and to 10,696 groups in 1994.[3] By 1998, there were more than 25,000 different newsgroups in existence.

Newsgroups initially developed in the noncommercial environment of the Internet. But commercial services began to take note of and exploit the trend. CompuServe hosted a number of "forums" that allowed people to share professional and personal interests. The popularity of these forums played an important role in the growth of CompuServe throughout the 1980s. The Well, based in the San Francisco Bay area, flourished as a place where online pioneers could gather to meet and talk with one another.

In the early 1990s, America Online® (AOL) was establishing itself as an easy-to-use service for a mass audience. While it provided news and reference information and other kinds of services, AOL emphasized the value of person-to-person communication and the benefits of participating in virtual communities. In fact, AOL provided a home for many popular online communities such as the Motley Fool, which served individual investors (and which was one of AOL's biggest early successes); NetNoir, which focuses on Afrocentric culture; Blackberry Creek, which is designed to appeal to preteenagers; and SeniorNet, which is intended for older adults. In fact, AOL's emphasis on community building was one of the factors that helped it to reach its dominant position among online services.

The publication of *The Virtual Community* by Howard Rheingold in 1993 introduced the concept to a broader audience.[4] The book's author was not merely an observer of the phenomenon but an active participant. Rheingold was a member of The Well and much of the book was based on his experiences there. He was one of the first to assert that online networks were emerging as an important social force that could provide rich and authentic community experiences.

The concept of virtual communities received greater attention with the 1997 publication of the book *Net Gain* by John Hagel III and Arthur G. Armstrong.[5] The work gained credibility from the authors' affiliation with the well-known consulting firm of McKinsey & Company and the fact that the book's publisher was the Harvard Business School Press. Hagel and Armstrong acknowledged Rheingold's work, but extended it by arguing that virtual communities have economic as well as social significance. Like Rheingold, they recognize that virtual communities are based on the affinity among their participants that encourages them to participate in ongoing dialog with each other. Interchanges between participants helps to generate "Webs of personal communication" that reinforce the sense of identification with the community.

The authors then go on to explain how virtual communities can create value by creating linkages between community members and companies interested in reaching them. At the simplest level, virtual communities can attract vendors who have products or services to sell that are relevant to community members (e.g., airlines in a travel-oriented community, or diapers in a community of new parents). From this perspective, virtual communities are similar to special-interest magazines that attract advertisers who want to target a specific market segment.

But virtual communities do more: They can allow community members to *interact* with vendors to express their preferences or provide feedback on a particular product. And because they communicate with one another, community members can band together to share information and seek additional benefits, such as discounts, from vendors. Because of these aspects, virtual communities have the potential to transform and expand the relationship between vendors and their customers. In fact, companies have an opportunity to become *participants in virtual communities*, not merely sponsors of or vendors to them.

How "Authentic" Are Virtual Communities?

A lively debate has been going on for some time over how authentic virtual communities are. In describing what goes on in the virtual environment, Howard Rheingold has written that:

> People in virtual communities use words on screens to exchange pleasantries and argue, engage in intellectual discourse, conduct commerce, exchange knowledge, share emotional support, make plans, brainstorm, gossip, feud, fall in love, find friends and lose them, play games, flirt, create a little high art and a lot of idle talk. People in virtual communities do just about everything people do in real life, but we leave our bodies behind.[6]

Not everyone agrees with this perspective however. Skeptics argue that virtual communities lack some of the critical elements that define "real" communities, especially communities that are geographically based. For example, after visiting an online community,

Clifford Stoll in his book *Silicon Snake Oil*, asked: "What's missing from this ersatz neighborhood? A feeling of permanence and belonging, a sense of location, a warmth from the local history. Gone is the very essence of a neighborhood: friendly relations and a sense of being in it together."[7]

Who is right? One way that virtual communities differ from "real" communities is, precisely, that they are "virtual." They exist only in cyberspace. While it takes effort to move away from a physical place, it takes virtually no effort for an individual to leave a virtual community and move on to another. But that does not mean that participants don't really care about their communities. In fact, many participants care passionately and remain actively involved in virtual communities for years. And many virtual communities have discovered that participants develop friendships so strong that they will go to the trouble of meeting other participants in person. In the case of both SeniorNet and Fujitsu's WorldsAway (and in many other virtual communities as well), individuals who originally met online have arranged to meet in the "real world."[8] In some cases, these get-togethers have become regular events.

A number of social scientists have begun to investigate the extent to which virtual communities resemble or differ from "real" communities (see sidebar, "Elements of a Community"). For example, a recent study by Teresa Roberts of Sun Microsystems looked at whether participants in Internet newsgroups do, in fact, feel that they "belong" to a community. She interviewed participants in thirty Internet-based newsgroups and found that 61 percent of the respondents reported that they had formed friendships online and that two-thirds of them felt a sense of "belonging to their group." The study also found that the most important determinant of a feeling of belonging was the extent to which individuals participated in and contributed to the group.

Capitalizing on Virtual-Community Opportunities

The Web offers the opportunity for people worldwide to collaborate on any topic they desire; this is the essence of virtual communities. The best virtual communities foster collaboration and cooperation among participants to the benefit of all the members and the

ELEMENTS OF A COMMUNITY

Teresa Roberts of Sun Microsystems lists six dimensions of a community:

- *Cohesion:* the sense of there being a group identity and that an individual belongs to the group.
- *Effectiveness:* the impact that the group has on the members' lives and the outside world.
- *Help:* the perceived ability of members to ask for and receive various kinds of assistance.
- *Relationships:* the likelihood of group members interacting individually, including forming friendships.
- *Language:* the prevalence of specialized language.
- *Self-regulation:* the ability of the group to police itself.

A group of researchers at the Annenberg School of Communication at the University of Southern California have identified four major components that contribute to creating a "sense of community":

- *Need fulfillment* deals with how well a participant's needs are satisfied by a community.
- *Inclusion* is the extent to which participants are open and encouraged to participate in each other's plans and activities.

- *Mutual influence* is the extent to which participants openly discuss issues and affect one another.
- *Shared emotional experiences* include sharing events that specifically arouse feeling and are typically memorable—trips, birthdays, anniversaries, weddings, and so forth.

Finally, a group of anthropologists commissioned by the advertising agency Saatchi & Saatchi identified five different types of virtual communities, based on the primary interest that motivates participation:[9]

- *Just Friends* are people who want to meet others, and socialize.
- *Enthusiasts* share a specific interest. Socializing is less important to them than talking about the common interest.
- *Friends in Need* are support groups built around a specific problem such as living with cancer or substance abuse.
- *Players* come together to participate in games ranging from fantasy sports leagues to role-playing or board games.
- *Traders* seek communities where they can trade possessions with one another.

It is important to recognize that the same person may assume one of these roles at one moment, and another role at a later time, and therefore may well participate in multiple communities.

participating organizations. But how do an organization's commercial interests fit in here? How can a business market its product or service within this egalitarian framework?

The answer lies in the marketing strategy employed. Consider three types of strategies: mass marketing, direct marketing, and collaborative marketing. In mass marketing, product companies promote their image and generate awareness in order to sell more. In direct marketing, companies provide prospects more product information to create more knowledgeable buyers in order to sell more. In collaborative marketing, companies support prospective customers in understanding and evaluating alternatives, and in finding the right product or service to meet their needs—they help prospects to know more, earn their trust, and thereby sell more.

The Web in general, and virtual communities in particular, supports direct and collaborative marketing strategies.

Virtual-community opportunities can be incorporated into a business's marketing operations through three different approaches—these are hierarchical, with each subsequent approach requiring greater investment and commitment than the previous one. The first is about direct marketing, the second and third involve collaborative marketing. None are mass-marketing strategies: The Internet is not, and may never be, an effective mass-marketing vehicle.

1. *Sponsor*—advertise in a community or sponsor community content
2. *Participate*—provide content as an interactive participant in a virtual community
3. *Build*—create and maintain a virtual community of customers

Each of these approaches is discussed below.

Advertising and Sponsorships in Virtual Communities

Virtual communities are made up principally of Web pages that contain various types of content; advertisements can be placed on or integrated with the Web pages delivering this content.

Decisions to advertise or sponsor content in virtual communities are similar to making advertising-placement decisions in traditional media. The central considerations are the market focus and the theme of the community—that is, what are the demographic/psychographic characteristics of a community's participants? A search should be conducted for communities that are aggregating people in the business's target market and whose themes are in line with the image desired. Virtual-community services that are focused on one market—for example, Tripod's focus on the GenX market, NetNoir's focus on Afrocentric culture, Planet Out's focus on the gay and lesbian market—can provide rich sources of prospects for promoting appropriate products and services.

Advertising rates on community sites reflect their ability to aggregate people with common traits. The "run of the site" banner ads on community sites like Tripod (a Generation X community) and iVillage (parenting and women's communities) can cost as much as 100 percent more (on a cost-per-thousand-impressions basis) than "run of the site" banners on search or portal sites such as Yahoo! and Excite, which attract more diverse audiences. The more targeted the virtual community, the higher the ad rates will be—sites such as GeoCities and Globe.com, often hailed as virtual communities, garner rates only slightly higher than the search engines because their services are made up of diverse sets of "neighborhoods," which cannot deliver groups with specific attributes with as much precision as targeted community sites like Tripod and iVillage.

Sponsorships differ from advertising in that the sponsor is identified more closely with production of content—for example, an HMO might sponsor a stress-reduction forum and refer its patients to the site carrying that content. Sponsorships do not directly promote the sponsor's product or service—the promotion is for the community content/service being offered, and the sponsor's name is associated with that content/service. On SeniorNet, for example, MetLife's Mature Market Group sponsored a "Solutions Forum" that enabled older people to collaborate on addressing important issues and problems. MetLife benefited from publicity generated by the Forum and the "halo effect" of being associated with an innovative project and a good cause.

Sponsorships are familiar in the sports world; examples include cigarette and beer companies' sponsorship of auto racing, and bank and financial services' sponsorships of tennis and golf tournaments. Companies choose the sporting events that attract people who presumably would be good customers for their products and services. The same is true of virtual-community sponsorships. Examples include a car rental company sponsoring a forum on Driving Tours of Europe in a travel community like Expedia, or an online brokerage service sponsoring a guest-chat series in an investment community like Motley Fool. In most cases, the sponsor's payments for the sponsorship will be a function of the cost of producing the content and the Cost per Million (CPM) of the number of impressions created.

Here is how iVillage, a successful developer of women's communities on the Web, describes sponsorship opportunities on its site, ". . . our integrated sponsorship model allows marketers to take advantage of the unique attributes of the online medium and to build relationships with consumers in ways that are impossible in traditional media . . . sponsorships integrate marketers into our communities, making them valued contributors to the dialogues that are ongoing on all our sites."

As an advertiser works with sponsorship opportunities within a virtual community, its staff will become familiar with the content that is of most interest to that community. The organization's management can then determine whether or not to move on to the next level and become an active participant in a virtual community.

Participating in the Community

When an organization moves from sponsoring virtual-community content created by others to creating content within the community, it must be prepared for direct interaction with community members. In deciding to participate, management should be certain that they have staff resources with the expertise/information that will be of interest to the community, and that these staff members have the interactive skills to represent the organization effectively within the community.

The organization's staff that interacts with community members will be the organization's liaison to the community. So, in a very real sense, by participating, the organization joins the community. This interaction can be very valuable, but it can be fraught with risk. For example, an organization participating in a virtual community is potentially exposed to the commentary of critics and unhappy customers. How the organization responds to these critiques will be carefully watched by the members of the community. The organization could also receive a lot of responses and queries to issues arising out of its contributions. If the organization is not pre-pared to respond promptly to the queries, it could develop a reputa-tion as an organization that does not stand behind its information.

Given the risks, why would an organization want to incur this exposure? First, through effective participation, the organization can build a base of support among community members that yields loyalty and goodwill for the organization (and/or its products and services). Second, the critiques can occur whether or not the orga-nization is participating. The organization is better off being present as a member of the community where its staff (and, hopefully, other members) can respond to critiques with other information and per-spectives. Third, because users will spend more time on interactive-content pages (such as message boards or chat rooms) than on passive-content pages, there are greater brand-exposure opportuni-ties with interactive content.

Another consideration in deciding to participate in a commu-nity is that the organization must be prepared to represent the inter-ests of the community members above the interests of its products or services. In order for the organization to gain and maintain cred-ibility with community members, its staff must be prepared to forthrightly address the limitations of its products and services as the need arises. Members must be able to trust that their best interest is being served and that they are not being exploited.

Once an organization is comfortable with the ways in which it will participate in the community, there are myriad "deals" it can make that benefit itself, the community members, and the commu-nity developer. Here is an example that illustrates a typical interplay of organizations around a community business: A parenting com-munity learns from its members that they want to create a group focused on coping with stress. The speakers and discussion moder-ators for a new stress-reduction subcommunity could be con-tributed by an organization that offers stress-reduction products (anything from drugs to foot massagers) or by an HMO that has a lot of stressed-out parents. Let's say that the product organization has the expertise and the HMO wants to provide a resource for its stressed-out parents. The product organization offers expertise by providing information on the community Web pages and/or staffing the speaker and discussion-moderator positions. In this example, the HMO plays an advertiser/sponsor role, and the product organization fills a participant role.

Whenever possible, content should be planned to include and emphasize member-created content. This will facilitate the creation of content that is both attractive to the community members and cost-effective for the content providers. For example, a forum on caregiving for the elderly could be structured as a message board that allows members to share tips and experiences with other members; professional contributions from doctors and nurses could be limited to responses to questions about medical issues passed to them by the message-board moderator.

Organizations can often take advantage of the active members of a community for disseminating factual information about a topic. For example, a technology company might allow people who are qualified—as verified by online questionnaires or telephone interviews—to answer questions in forums and chat rooms about its products. For example, there are many avid Navigator or Internet Explorer browser users who could help new users in an Internet Users community if Netscape or Microsoft developed a program for certifying these people. These programs empower users and give them status within the community, and they lower the cost of providing information.

Organizations need to carefully consider the staffing required for participating in a community. A speaker making a one-time appearance in a chat room requires only a few hours of time. But moderated message boards, regularly scheduled chat sessions, and themed rooms in virtual worlds require that staff be available on an ongoing basis.

Finally, in planning all content, consider the topics that will and will not be covered; also consider how extensive, how deep, and how timely the information will be. Costs will be directly related to these decisions; for example, if information has to be very timely, then more staff time must be dedicated to maintaining it.

When an organization is prepared to focus on supporting the needs of one demographic, professional, or interest group, it can consider creating its own virtual community.

Building a Virtual Community

The decision to create a virtual community requires a lot of planning since it involves new ways of doing business. Business models in the new medium are different from brick-and-mortar business models, and these models are evolving. There will be lots of change over the next few years. Flexibility with regard to expectations, technology, and user needs is a necessity. Some of the fundamental considerations we believe will continue to be important even in the maelstrom of change that is the Internet are discussed below.

The first step is to choose the focus of the community. Be specific about the target audience; this is the group for whom the community developer will be an agent. Identify which group or category of people can be best served with the knowledge, relationships, services, and resources available to the organization that will create and operate this community.

The primary directive for any virtual community is that its operations be focused on serving the needs of its members. Many businesses that play an *agent* or *broker* role are well positioned to extend their current operations to the creation of virtual communities. Travel, real-estate, and financial-services agents base their businesses on meeting the needs of customers today and have an opportunity to extend their model into the new commerce medium: the Internet. Organizations that provide services to existing, real-world communities have the greatest opportunities to build virtual communities. Examples include professional, hobbyist, or alumni organizations; schools and training organizations; health-care organizations; and government agencies.

Companies in distribution and retail businesses also have significant opportunities to form virtual communities within their current market segments. These businesses are already serving their customers' needs in selecting the manufacturers and products that their customers want, and rejecting those that they do not want. There will certainly be start-up virtual-community businesses that will compete with existing sales channels. Some of the product categories that we believe offer significant virtual-community opportunities are: recorded music, home repair, auto purchase and maintenance, children's toys and educational products, clothing, sporting goods, food, and dining.

Product manufacturers and high fixed-cost service operations have more limited opportunities to build virtual communities. These production organizations have less flexibility in addressing the needs of community members while promoting sales of their products and services. They also face a greater risk of negative commentary becoming group-wide opinions that undermine sales. However, some producers will be successful in creating communities around customers' support, application, and service needs related to their products. Customers can help each other, and the manufacturers can reward the most helpful participants in such areas as advance availability of new products, discounts, and status in the community. In addition, producers can use the community to conduct customer research. Savvy manufacturers can, in a sense, create their own Nielsen or J.D. Power studies on an ongoing basis. With proper management, a manufacturer could conduct research that provides the information to dramatically increase efficiencies in product development and marketing.

Generating Revenue

There are three types of revenue that can be generated by a virtual community: (1) subscription fees paid by members, (2) advertising and sponsorship fees from organizations wishing to promote themselves to the community, and (3) margins or transaction fees from sales made to community members. There are trade-offs among these categories. For example, the amount of advertising and transaction fees that can be generated by a community will be directly related to the number of participants in the community. Subscription fees will significantly reduce the number of participants in the community and thereby reduce the amount of advertising and transaction revenue.

How will the community generate profits? Revenue growth can be difficult to forecast in the early stages of any business, let alone Internet businesses where value propositions, competition, technology infrastructure, and market size are all changing rapidly. Internet businesses generally are receiving large amounts of capital these days, and virtual communities are beginning to be recognized as warranting significant investments. We believe many businesses should be making investments in virtual-community opportunities.

We recommend that, when deciding how much to invest in creating a virtual community, the investment be allocated as a function of management's understanding of real revenue potential or other tangible measures of value to the organization. Following this dictate, "less sooner" will help keep costs in line with predictable values being returned. Launch a focused set of services, evaluate the numbers and the type of people who use those services, sell a few sponsorships to marketers interested in that segment, and learn step-by-step how to build value in the business. Over time, the profitable mix of investment in content, promotions, staffing, and infrastructure will come into focus. Plan to significantly increase investments in the venture after the architecture of revenue and value streams for the business are understood.

A common mistake in early virtual-community businesses has been to invest too heavily in the acquisition or creation of editorial content. If advertising and transactions will be the major revenue sources, then investment in growing the user base will yield more near- and long-term revenue than investing in passive content. The management of interactive (member-created) content is more challenging but fits the strategies of building the user base and mitigating investment requirements.

At SeniorNet, we used to say that members were initially attracted by the information provided by the organization, but they stayed for the community. The task of the community developer is to provide the means for the people who come for the information and services, to interact with one another and become a community.

Trust is a central issue in developing virtual communities. Successful community developers work hard to earn the trust of the members. If members feel exploited they will move on. Whatever roles marketers play—sponsor, participant, or developer—they must be respectful of the fact that the community in many regards belongs to the members. Serving the members is the first and foremost goal. Decisions that compromise this goal can undermine the trust relationships in the community and jeopardize the stability of the group.

A specific example of building trust is the issue of privacy. Privacy of personal information is fundamental for growth of virtual communities. Community developers must assure individuals that their personal information will not be used without their knowledge or permission. Marketers' need to know member demographic, psychographic, and purchase profiles, and even their need to deliver promotions to individuals with specific traits, can be met without compromising individual privacy.

Encouraging Member Participation

For individuals, becoming involved with and committed to the life of a virtual community is a process that takes time. Randy Farmer, an early pioneer in creating virtual communities, has identified four stages of user participation:[10]

> *Passives*—seek effortless entertainment or information
> *Actives*—participate enthusiastically in activities and topics created by others
> *Motivators*—create topics and plans activities of interest to other community members
> *Caretakers*—serve as intermediaries between community members and community staff members; are usually seasoned Motivators

Our estimate, based on usage data across several communities, is that the distribution of users across these categories breaks down as follows: approximately 85 percent are Passives, 12 percent are Actives, 2.5 percent play the role of Motivators, and 0.5 percent are Caretakers. Total time spent "within" the community is dominated by the Actives and Motivators. These are the people who create the majority of the content, which in turn attracts the 85 percent of passives who represent the bulk of the participants. The "care and feeding" of these leaders is critical to the success of the community.

An important goal of community development is to move people from passive readers to active contributors. The stronger the participation of the community members, the more lively and engaging the interactive member-created content will be.

Figure 4.1

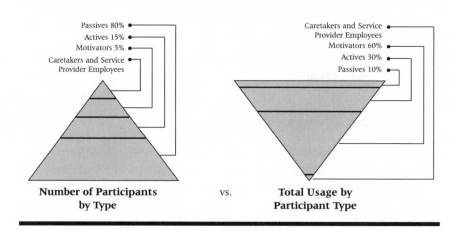

Passives 80%
Actives 15%
Motivators 5%
Caretakers and Service
Provider Employees

Caretakers and Service
Provider Employees
Motivators 60%
Actives 30%
Passives 10%

Number of Participants   vs.   **Total Usage by**
by Type   **Participant Type**

Staffing a Virtual Community

Creation of a virtual-community business requires many of the staff
skills required to build any successful Web business: technology
integrators, system administrators, Webmasters, marketing, and
sales people. In addition, a virtual community requires two other
key staff roles: executive producer and community manager. A successful virtual community will need a savvy executive producer—
someone familiar with online communications technologies, aware
of cost/return trade-offs in the business, and creative in the development of content, partners, and services that will be interesting to
the nascent community. The executive producer's job is to direct the
creation of attractive content services that generate revenue. The
performance measures of an executive producer are total membership and revenue.

Another person who is critically important to success is the
community manager, who is responsible for overseeing all member-
generated content. The community manager sets the standards for
the community interaction—what is acceptable and unsuitable—
and is responsible for recruiting, training, and motivating remote
staff. Performance measures for the community manager include
member retention and the ratio of community staffing costs to
total members.

Remote staff includes principally the Caretakers and to varying extents Motivators. Remote staff will typically be volunteers who host or moderate chats and message boards, respond to members being harassed in chat rooms, and archive community-created content. In our experience, the selection, training, and support of these volunteers is fundamental to growth of the community. Selecting mature, responsible caretakers will foster the creation of a strong, self-governing community.

The content and focus of a community may evolve in unpredictable directions. However, the creation of safe, inviting interactive environments for the large numbers of members required to make the virtual community successful is a function of the skill and effectiveness of the community caretakers. The virtual community organizations that create effective processes for recruiting, training, and motivating remote staff will have created an enduring asset.[11]

Virtual Worlds—Real Estate Where Virtual Communities Gather

Virtual worlds are a relatively new phenomenon that offers exciting new capabilities for building virtual communities. They are real-time, multimedia social meeting places—graphical spaces where people embodied as "Avatars" gather, interact in public and private spaces, own and share objects, and spend lots of time online. Our data indicate that virtual worlds generate user-session lengths and frequencies of visits that are two to eight times greater than other virtual communities. We believe that as virtual-world platforms become more widely available, the formation of virtual communities will be greatly accelerated. Through virtual worlds, community developers can offer richer and more engaging services to online users and more effective promotional vehicles to businesses and organizations.

Virtual worlds provide participants with significantly expanded expressiveness, and the result is a more immersive interactive experience. In a virtual world, members create distinctive graphical representations of themselves, called Avatars. Avatars provide participants with the ability to express emotions through happy, sad, angry, or puzzled faces, as well as the ability to make gestures such as waving, shrugging, jumping, or bowing. In some virtual worlds, Avatars can collect and exchange virtual objects that range from jewelry and other sartorial items to furniture and collectibles for their personal spaces. These objects offer a range of innovative opportunities for

VIRTUAL-COMMUNITY BUILDING BLOCKS

As we have seen, a virtual community can be formed around a single message board. However, robust virtual communities typically make use of a range of technologies that support person-to-person and person-to-group communications. The primary enabling technologies are described below.

Most virtual communities provide for both "synchronous" (real-time) communications, through text chat and instant messaging, and "asynchronous" (non-real-time) communications, through message boards, mail lists, member and community Web pages, and surveys. As a generalization, real-time communication is usually social in nature, while non-real-time communication tends to be more cognitive and topic focused.

In addition to these key building blocks, virtual communities also depend on a member database and may also include technologies to support registration; electronic commerce; directories of products, services, and suppliers; and searches for such things as member profiles, community documentation, reports, articles, transcripts, and archives.

Text Chat

Text chat is the exchange of written statements and responses among a group of people who are "present" together online, "in a chat room together." A chat room can be available twenty-four hours a day or may be available only at scheduled times when a moderator is present or when a guest is "speaking" on a specific topic. Chat rooms

can be public, open to everyone, or private, open only to invited guests.

Text chat was invented by CompuServe in the late 1970s and has been a critical element in the popularity of America Online®. Approximately one-fifth to one-third of online users enjoy the real-time social interaction offered by text chat.

Chat-room regulars contribute strongly to creating a sense of "community" on a site. Chatters often have a strong sense of belonging and occasional visitors to an active community know that they can almost always find a group of regular chatters online with whom to socialize.

Instant Messaging

Instant messaging allows a user who is online to find out if a friend or acquaintance is also logged on at the moment. "Buddy lists" automatically display the names of friends who are online at the same time a user is online. Friends can use instant messaging to engage in a private one-on-one text chat with one other. This exchange is displayed in a dedicated window and can take place at the same time that members are engaged with other aspects of the community, for example, reading Web pages, posting on message boards, participating in a chat room.

Community managers can use instant messaging to keep members informed of current events; for example, when a scheduled guest is about to begin a presentation, an instant message can be sent that says, "tonight's speaker will be on in five minutes . . . If you are interested in participating, click here."

advertising. Community sponsors can include facsimiles of their products within the virtual world environments; the product facsimiles become part of the users' in-world experiences and make much stronger impressions than advertisements about the product.

Message Boards

Message boards, also referred to as newsgroups or discussion forums, support ongoing discussions, generally on a single topic, over a period of months or years. An individual posts a message on a board that can be read at a later time by others who then post their responses. Unlike chat, participants in a board need not be online at the same time. Since past messages remain available, a transcript is created over time that provides a record of the discussion.

Some message boards are open to all; others require permission from a moderator to join. Messages on simple boards are organized sequentially; more sophisticated boards allow for "threads" in which messages on subtopics are linked to one another.

Mail Lists

Mail lists allow a user to send an e-mail to one e-mail address where the mail list server automatically forwards the message to everyone who has subscribed to the list. This type of communication supports the creation of subgroups within the community based on specific topics.

As with message boards, there are open lists to which anyone can subscribe and closed lists that require permission for subscription. A community manager can create and administer a mail list, or it can be administered by a member of the community, based on a topic of interest to him/her.

Member Web Pages

Many communities provide members with the opportunity to create and maintain their own Web pages. Sites such as GeoCities, Xoom, and AngelFire are primarily based on individually developed Web pages organized into "neighborhoods of people who presumably share common interests."

Member profiles will become an important feature of communities over time. Their precise format will vary, based on the theme of the community; for example, in a golf community, participants will be interested in such things as other members' handicaps or courses played. In an investment community, participants might be interested in other members' stock picks, asset diversification, or other investor characteristics. These profiles could be tied in to the developer's member database, which will also include the members' demographic information and possibly their responses to survey questions. Privacy terms will become critically important.

Surveys and Other Features

The ability to ask questions of a community's members and tabulate responses can be extremely helpful in delivering services desired by the community. Information about who members are, what they want, and what they like is also valuable for attracting advertisers and sponsors and for justifying a community's advertising rates.

Other emerging features that add additional capabilities to virtual communities include the ability to form and manage subgroups within the community; group calendars, which allow people to coordinate their schedules; and virtual worlds, which add a graphic dimension to textual, and soon voice, communication.

Objects in virtual-world environments can also contain links to Web pages. For example, a furniture object such as a chair or table could link to a furniture manufacturer sponsoring the community. Virtual objects can be provided to Avatars who participate in a demonstration of a manufacturer's product. The Web links to these objects can provide discount coupons that encourage purchases. The possibilities for rich new means to reach customers with promotional vehicles will evolve with virtual worlds.

Figure 4.2: The Palace

Virtual-world technologies are still in a very early stage of evolution. WorldsAway, from Fujitsu, and The Palace, from Electric Communities, are the two most significant current sources of virtual-world services and technologies (see screen shots). The Palace is the simplest form of an avatar virtual world, offering an integration of graphic images with text chat and a straightforward server installation. The richest interactive experiences today are available with WorldsAway, which provides more extensive user-controlled animations and interactive objects.

Virtual worlds could eventually attract a majority of virtual-community participants. On America Online® (AOL), 70 percent of all subscribers visit chat rooms at least once a month, and 15–20 percent of subscribers are heavy or regular users; that is, two or more chat sessions per week.[12] Fujitsu's research indicates that about half of text chatters strongly prefer WorldsAway to text chat, and about one-fifth of the people who do not like text chat do enjoy WorldsAway, indicating that penetration could extend well beyond the 20 percent of active text chatters and approach the 70 percent of occasional chatters.

Today there are significant hurdles for a user to overcome to use virtual worlds. Multiple megabytes of software must be downloaded and, as with any new application, individuals must learn how to use the software. As developers mitigate the hurdles, these environments will become increasingly popular and potentially could achieve penetrations equivalent to or greater than those of text chat. Until the downloads and user-interface issues are mitigated however, we believe that only about 10 percent of total community participants will use virtual-world services.

Figure 4.3: WorldsAway

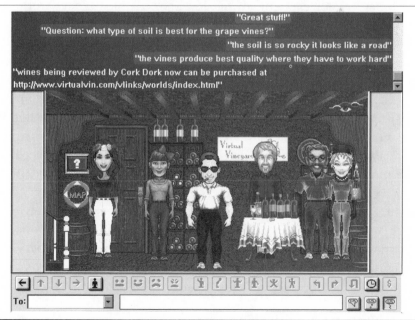

Despite low near-term numbers, there are still strong reasons for community developers to begin utilizing these environments today. First, virtual worlds generate usage rates that are multiples of any other virtual-community building block. WorldsAway users averaged eight one-hour sessions per month when fees were around $2 per hour; when fees dropped to flat monthly rates ($5–$20), usage expanded to twelve three-hour sessions per month. With longer-than-average online sessions, virtual-world users offer more advertising and sponsorship opportunities. Also, advertisers in virtual worlds can learn a great deal about developing effective interactive advertising techniques that will benefit them in the future.

Moving Toward Community

In the end, virtual communities, although they rely on a variety of technologies, are not about technology. They are about people. They represent a new kind of social institution that provides new ways for individuals with common interests to meet and interact with each other. They also represent an important new economic force that is opening up new avenues of interaction between companies and their customers. We believe that virtual communities will become a major element in the development of the new world of electronic commerce.

As we have seen, virtual communities can inspire a genuine, even a passionate, sense of belonging among their members. Strong bonds of friendship can be developed and sustained online. Successful virtual communities seem likely to endure for many years. However, loyalty to a community can be quickly dissipated if its members feel that they are being misled or exploited in some way. Participants can abandon a community with a single click of the mouse.

Perhaps no factor is more critical to the long-term success of virtual communities than trust—among members and between members and sponsors. Anyone wishing to capitalize on the opportunities offered by virtual communities must appreciate the vital importance of being a good community citizen. The reward for success is the prospect of building relationships with customers that may well be stronger and more valuable than those that can be created by any other marketing strategy.

■　■　■

1   Myra Stark, "A Fly on the Virtual Wall: Cybercommunities Observed," *Digitrends Quarterly*, Summer 1998, page 27.
2   There are also opportunities for the creation of virtual communities on intranets within organizations. Much of this chapter, especially in the section on "building virtual communities," applies to intranet environments, but the primary focus of this chapter is on public Internet-based communities.
3   Peter H. Salus, *Casting the Net*. Reading, Mass.: Addison-Wesley Publishing Company, 1995, pp. 146–148.
4   Howard Rheingold, *The Virtual Community*. Reading, Mass.: Addison-Wesley Publishing Company, 1993.
5   John Hagel III and Arthur G. Armstrong, *Net Gain—Expanding Markets Through Virtual Communities*. Boston: Harvard Business School Press, 1997.
6   Rheingold, *The Virtual Community*, page 3.
7   Clifford Stoll, *Silicon Snake Oil: Second Thoughts on the Information Highway*. New York: Anchor Books, 1996.
8   In both SeniorNet and WorldsAway, there have actually been multiple marriages of people who met online. To our knowledge, no studies have yet been done to determine if these marriages are more or less successful than those of couples who meet in more conventional ways.
9   Myra Stark, "A Fly on the Virtual Wall: Cybercommunities Observed," *Digitrends Quarterly*, Summer 1998, page 26.
10   F. Randall Farmer, "Social Dimensions of Habitat's Citizenry" in *Virtual Reality Case Book*. New York: Van Nostrand Reinhold, 1994, pp. 87–95.
11   There is a rapidly growing body of guides and resources, in both print and online, to building virtual communities. Amy Bruckman is a pioneer in the field, and teaches a course on "The Design of Virtual Communities" at Georgia Tech University. Her Website contains her course syllabus and other useful references. Amy Jo Kim teaches a class on "Designing Online Communities," and has a useful Website at www.naima.com that includes her essay, "Nine Principles for Community Design."
12   "Revenue Prospect for Online Chat," New York, Jupiter Communications, Consumer Content Group, September 1997.

CHAPTER

FIVE

Internet
Advertising

Paul Lewis, Vice President, Sales Operations, iVillage, and
Leslie Laredo, President, The Laredo Group, Inc.
Whether seeking advertising as a revenue source or simply looking to
increase traffic to your site, an understanding of Internet advertising
opportunities and tactics is a crucial competency. Both Leslie Laredo and
Paul Lewis were pioneers of online advertising at Prodigy. And they have
become two of the most respected experts on Internet advertising.

Advertising has always been the commercial lightning
rod of the Internet. In 1994, when the scientific and academic network was taking its first tentative steps toward consumer and business use, two lawyers from the Southwest dared to solicit business
through a posting in a newsgroup. Their transgression earned the
couple a folder full of hate e-mail (a practice called "flaming") and
the enduring enmity of Internet purists who wanted to keep the
network free of commercial interests.

We've come a long way since 1994. In fact, since late 1996, the
business world has been fascinated by the possibilities of Internet
advertising. Spurred on by the exponential growth of the Internet
audience and exciting technological advances, industry analysts
have forecasted three-digit annual growth in Internet advertising

expenditures, fueled by massively scaled one-on-one marketing, highly personalized ad delivery, and accurate and detailed account-ability. In fact, most of the best-known brand-name sites on the Internet, including Yahoo!, Excite, MSNBC, and ZDnet, derive almost all of their revenue from advertising sales.

But what most people don't know is that online advertising has actually been in development for nearly eighteen years. Starting with the earliest attempts to create and use interactive media as a new marketing medium, a significant body of learning and tech-niques has been developed that can be employed by businesses today. And when executed properly, Internet advertising can deliver superior results for the sales of products and services, whether the target is the consumer market or business-to-business.

The History of Interactive Advertising: Prodigy or Pariah?

The first consumer online trials (then known as "videotex") occurred in the early 1980s as major newspaper companies (Knight Ridder and Times Mirror) set up tests in Southern Florida and California. These videotex experiments provided access, via modem dial-up, to menu-driven information pages, graphics, and databases. Keep in perspective, back in the early 80s, modems were essentially unheard of and most people who saw the first online demonstrations of these services were afraid they would break their phones if they unplugged them and then plugged in a modem. These systems used relatively crude vector-drawn graphics to display pictures and the maximum number of menu choices on any one page was limited to nine. To put this in perspective, modems operated at 300 baud—1/150th of today's most common speeds—and hypertext linking would not be invented for at least another ten years.

During the early 80s, consumers often accessed these systems from their living rooms, through TV set–top boxes and via public-access videotex systems running on the first IBM PCs. A few years later, telecommunications companies attempted to reach consumers through their television sets via interactive cable systems.

By the mid-80s, subscription-based online services such as CompuServe, Genie, and Delphi were gaining thousands and in some cases hundreds of thousands of subscribers. These services were based on "pay-for-use" models, charging a monthly access fee plus hourly connection rates. While these services did not carry advertisements, they offered the first online shopping programs, and were the forerunner to Internet e-commerce.

The first company to develop a model that used advertising as a major revenue source was a company formed by CBS, IBM, and Sears in 1984, called TRINTEX, which later was renamed Prodigy. In 1986, Prodigy launched the first service to use a flat-rate monthly charge for unlimited use, and it counted on advertising and trans-action fees to play a major role in the revenue model.

In another attempt to attract advertising dollars, Prodigy was based on a primitive graphical presentation language called NAPLPs. NAPLPs offered limited fonts and colors to display infor-mation and relied on vector-drawn graphics. The screens looked "cartoonish," but they were the best the technology could offer in the late 1980s. Each screen in the Prodigy service contained adver-tisements called "leader ads." It is interesting to note that Internet banner ads, today, have many of the same attributes as the Prodigy leader ads in terms of position on the page and targetability. These ads were held in a fixed position on the bottom of each page. Clicking on a leader ad led the user to a series of custom-designed screens and other interactive modules (such as dealer locators, mortgage calculators), created in Prodigy's proprietary development environment for the advertisers.

From its inception, Prodigy struggled to sell advertisements and e-commerce solutions. They were selling "the future" of media inter-active because their customer base was still small and production costs per capita were very high. Most advertisers waited on the sidelines.

Still, by 1992 Prodigy was earning $25 million annually from advertising and e-commerce. Unfortunately, these revenues were not enough to support Prodigy's massive technology, telecommunica-tions, and human-resource infrastructure. Prodigy was also slow to adapt new technologies, improve its user interface, and respond to users' desire for a faster service. By the mid-1990s, it was losing con-siderable market share to America Online® (AOL), to Internet browsers, and to Internet access providers. And yet as late as 1995, neither AOL nor any publishers on the Internet had significant online advertising or e-commerce revenues. The change began in 1996.

INTERNET ADVERTISING BECOMES SOCIALLY ACCEPTABLE

By late 1996, advertising was a key ingredient in the business models for Web publishers. While some publishers tested the waters with subscription services, consumers were reluctant to pay to access Web sites. The only revenue stream available to most Web sites was advertising. By 1997, the Internet advertising tsunami was under way; advertising revenues grew from $267 million in 1996 to almost $1 billion in 1997.

What was behind this dramatic growth? There were several factors and trends that contributed to the acceptance and growth of the Internet as an advertising medium.

The first trend was audience growth. More than 50 million Americans over 18 years of age are online today. By the end of 1998, various sources project the number of Internet users will range from 44 to 80 million. Calculating this growth puts one new user on the Internet every 1.67 seconds. Advertisers simply cannot ignore an audience of this size and this growth.

These online Americans have higher incomes ($55,000 median household income), are better educated (43 percent graduated college or higher), and are younger (thirty-seven years old) than the general U.S. population.[1] These are target demographics for many

Figure 5.1: U.S. Internet households

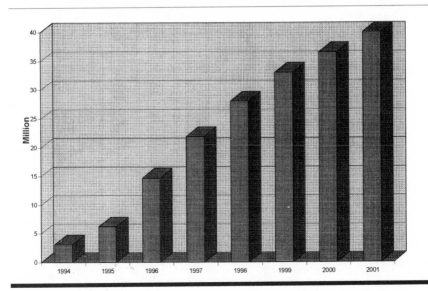

Figure 5.2: U.S. Adults Online

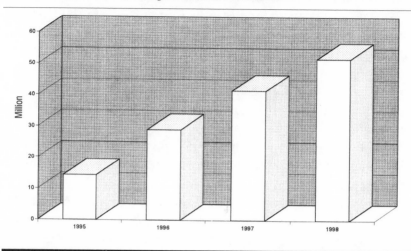

major companies in ad categories such as technology, finance, and automotive. Furthermore, 1998 saw dramatic growth in the number of women on the Internet. Fully 42 percent of the total Internet population is now female, up from 24 percent in 1995. Consumer-products and package-goods advertisers now realize they can effectively reach women through this medium.

The second factor in the growth of advertising was that online usage was increasing. The average Internet user is now online 5.4 hours per week, with 23 percent spending more than 11 hours a week online.[2] And most are accessing the Web daily—85 percent.[3] As a result of this high usage, online consumers are spending less time with traditional media. Accordingly, if advertisers want to reach a target demographic (e.g., high income, male, professional, ages 35–50), they will have a harder time reaching it through TV or print. According to a *Business Week*/Lou Harris Poll conducted in 1998, 48 percent of Internet users report spending less time with television, and 26 percent report a decline in time reading magazines and newspapers.

The third factor was the growing standardization of Internet ad units, measurement, and research. In 1996, an industry trade organization, Internet Advertising Bureau (IAB), was formed by Web publishers to help promote the Internet ad industry. One of the first tasks of the IAB was to recommend standard ad units. Now, across the Web, the "banner ad" is usually one of the IAB eight recommended standard banner sizes. This standard helped create greater acceptance by ad agencies as less creative resources were spent on designing dozens of versions of the same banner ads (often just a few pixels different) to run on different sites. The IAB is currently working on recommendations for measurement and research standards. Once these are in place, the advertising agencies will have a much easier time making apples-to-apples comparisons and evaluations of ad campaigns running across multiple sites.

Finally, Internet technology has dramatically changed how the advertising unit works and is delivered, and has vastly improved the delivery of advanced creative ideas and backend processes. While standard banner-ad units have been accepted, advertisers are

Figure 5.3: Ages of Web Users

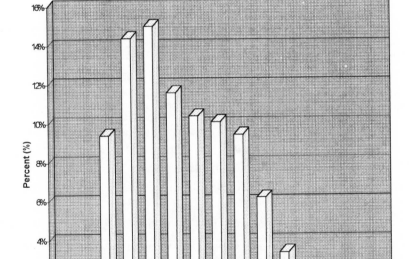

Figure 5.4: Frequency of Internet Use

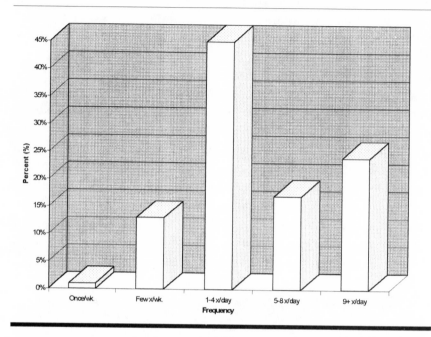

making the banner space work harder by employing these technologies. During 1998, we saw banner ads that included streaming
video (from TV commercials) and audio, as well as animation and
other "interaction" elements. By utilizing applets programmed in
Java and animation produced in Shockwave, advertisers have created banner ads that allow a user to play a Pong game (Hewlett
Packard), play golf (shooting an olive into a Tanqueray bottle for
points), fill out a consumer survey (P&G), or order a product (candy
from Godiva).

In addition to banner ad units, new ad units called "interstitials" and integrated ad programs in the form of sponsorships are
giving advertisers many options for creating unique branding
opportunities, selling direct, and linking traditional media components. And while technology has driven the creative and campaign-
strategy side of the equation, technology has also given advertisers
more sophisticated targeting tools to ensure their messages are
delivered to the right audience, with the right frequency.

The remainder of this chapter will explain why the Internet should be a vital part of any advertiser's plan and media mix, and will provide guidelines for making optimal use of the Internet medium.

Internet as "Super Media"

Internet and new media insiders have long been surprised that more advertisers have not embraced interactive advertising. The most common reasons cited by media buyers include unfamiliarity with the genre, lack of measurability and accountability standards, and various other misconceptions about this new medium. The fact is that Internet advertising is not entirely new, although it does have some new elements never before available via other media. In fact, Internet advertising has *all* of the elements of traditional advertising . . . and then some.

Print—Anything that can be written or shown in a print-media format, such as magazines, newspapers, flyers, and the like can be presented in an Internet ad as well.

Figure 5.5: Quarterly Internet Advertising Spending

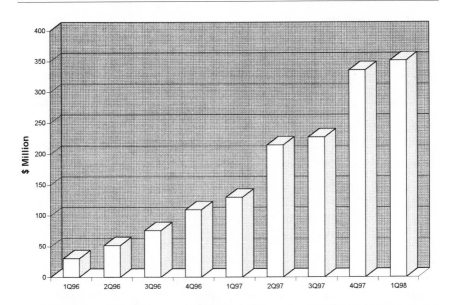

Audio and Video—Streaming audio and video technologies, together with new and faster machines and delivery channels, make the presentation of sound, music, and visual imagery (both static and full motion) as easy as in television, and increasingly as easily accessed.

Branding—When consumers see an Internet ad, whether it's a banner ad, interstitial, or other identifier, that impression stays with them as much as if they had seen a billboard for the product in Times Square or beside a local highway, or as if they saw the TV spot built to create brand recognition.

Reach—While it was true in the earlier days of the Internet that the reach was both short and very limited in terms of demographics and psychographics, it is now the case that the Internet is accessed by mainstream people all over the world.

Targeting—The Internet can be used more efficiently than direct mail or other targeting techniques. It can often be augmented, on many sites, by user-supplied data in the form of memberships and preferences.

Direct Response—Just as Direct TV and other methods solicit a direct and immediate response by the consumer, so, too, can the Internet. And the Internet can often more efficiently automate the ordering and fulfillment as well.

Immediacy—Internet ads can be placed and changed as quickly and often as radio and local newspapers.

And, in addition to all of the capabilities of traditional media, it also has . . .

Interactivity—Internet ads can involve the consumer in ways that no other media can approach. From nonlinear story lines and pitches, to surveys and even game play, the Internet can allow a consumer to move through the ad at their own pace or just sit back and watch.

Context Sensitivity—Internet ads can be delivered based on related content as sought by the consumer. This provides a greater level of mind-share benefit and selectivity, making the placement of ads on the Internet potentially more efficient and productive than traditional media.

Dynamic Customization—Internet ads can even be changed and modified in real time, as the user profile, or other factors, indicates.

This ability provides for greater efficiency and effectiveness of advertising.

Duration—Most media allow only a limited time or space for the brand interaction to occur. Online, the duration of the interaction can be very long, depending on the creative and other interactive features employed.

So, with all of the above considered, it can truly be said that Internet advertising offers all of the features and benefits of traditional advertising and then much more. As a result, it is likely that any campaign can benefit from having an appropriate portion of Internet advertising in the media-plan mix.

How to Organize Online Advertising Programs

In the early days of the World Wide Web, companies were quick to build massive corporate Web sites, expecting that the hope of *Field of Dreams*—"build it and they will come"—would be fulfilled. Those hopes were quickly dashed as Web traffic to corporate sites disappointed many Web masters and marketing managers. Fortunately, companies quickly learned that online media programs could drive traffic to their Web sites. In addition, corporations started to realize their URL was as important as their 800 number and began to place their Web information in their offline promotions (for example placing the company URL on all product literature, packaging, and in radio and TV commercials). Furthermore, recent ad-effectiveness research has shown that the ads themselves can greatly influence brand awareness and purchase intent.

Whether the target audience is the consumer or other businesses, Internet advertising offers three major benefits that make it particularly attractive to advertisers:

1. The ability to make *highly selective buys* through choice of targeting, content/context, and frequency.
2. The ability to *optimize level of expenditures* on creative asset and on media through testing.
3. The ability to *build brands*, in addition to the obvious direct-response benefits.

Let's look at each in detail.

Figure 5.6: The Targeting Continuum

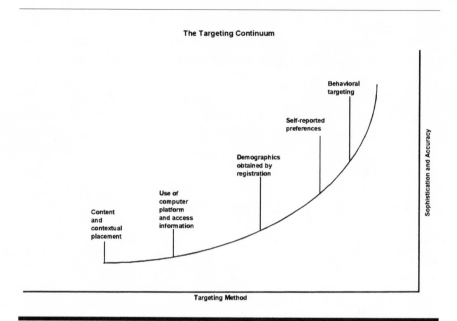

The Targeting Continuum

Highly Selective Buys

In no other medium do advertisers have as great a number of techniques at their disposal to pinpoint the audience they want to reach, present their ads in a desirable editorial context, and/or control the number of times each ad is seen by a person. Technological and marketing advances are constantly increasing these options as well.

Well-chosen targeting can not only improve the click rates—the percentage of users who, when presented with a banner ad, "click" on it to see more—it can also improve the awareness and perception of the brand as well. Advertisers can target their audience in a number of ways. They can select a site based on its overall content (e.g., golf equipment manufacturer advertises on golf Web sites), or select a specific contextual area within a site (e.g., a financial-software company's ads appear in the finance channel of a search engine). For more highly tuned targeting, an advertiser may purchase several keywords from a search engine. By doing so, anytime a user is looking for something closely related to the advertiser's products, its ads will appear (e.g., the user types in "computer" as the key word and a Dell ad appears above the results list).

Editorial or contextual targeting increases the likelihood of interesting a potential customer, since the user views the ads that are related to the subject matter at a time when the user is more likely to be in a frame of mind to make a decision regarding the product. For example, users would be more likely to respond to an ad for a discount broker if it is seen while they are looking at the performance of their stock portfolio than if it is seen while they are looking at the baseball scores. Targeting by editorial content is used extensively by ad networks, such as DoubleClick. Ad networks are companies that sell ads for an aggregation of Web sites, usually hundreds of sites. Advertisers can buy the "run of network" or a selection of sites in the network based on their content category, e.g., sports or financial sites.

Directory listings are another option, especially for small businesses serving a local market. These listings are organized by geography and/or content category. Some national directories are also available for manufacturers to list their businesses or their local franchiser. Some manufacturers (many automotive companies) might also provide dealer locators.

Geographic targeting can be achieved by placing ads adjacent to content that is only of interest to people living in or near that area. For example, sites showing TV listings that ask for the user's zip code to be inputted in order to get the correct listings for the cable system serving the area can sell ads separately for each zip code. In addition, sites that provide maps and driving directions will sell geographic listings; for example, a hotel company was able to highlight its locations on maps requested by business travelers.

The second most frequent targeting criteria is information from the user's browser. The browser contains information about a computer's platform and access information. Based upon the data passed from the browser to the servers, ads can be targeted to a particular browser (for example, Netscape Navigator or Internet Explorer); operating system (Windows 95, Windows NT, Unix); platform (PC or Mac); domain name (.com, .net, .org, .edu); or address of the sending server computer (expressed as an "Internet

Provider (IP) Address"). From that data, inferences can be drawn to target further. The IP address (yourname@ipaddress.com) can be mapped to a specific geographic area, and certain domain names might reveal companies or industries. For example, several years ago, a clever Silicon Valley Mercedes-Benz dealer was able to target ads to newly minted millionaires by discovering the domain names for the high-tech companies in the area that had recently completed Initial Public Offerings.

While most Web sites don't have registration data, those that induce users to provide personal information enable the site to deliver even more targeted ads. The *New York Times* has had great success requiring user registration and selling highly targeted ads on their site. Along with better targeting criteria, The *New York Times* Internet site can also justify higher ad rates. In addition, ad-serving companies such as AdForce are partnering with the companies that maintain giant direct-mail databases such as MetroMail. AdForce will take a user's address and append other data (e.g., household composition, income, marital status, automobile registration) and allow targeted advertising based on this user's newly enhanced Web profile.

Behavioral targeting is the most sophisticated technique in use today. Advanced technology vendors such as NetPerceptions have developed sophisticated algorithms for inferring or predicting online behavior. NetPerceptions uses a targeting technique called "collaborative filtering," which takes users' preferences and identifies the user with other users to predict or recommend content or ads. Generally, this information is gathered by either asking visitors to rate products, services, or information or by observing their behavior on the site and drawing inferences from it. Ads can then be targeted to individuals based upon the conclusions drawn from this analysis.

Database marketing is surely the targeting method with the highest probability of success. Targeting your advertising to individuals or companies who have expressed interest in your product or service can be accomplished by building a database of e-mail addresses of these interested parties. This will be discussed in greater detail in the chapter to follow on Internet Direct Marketing.

As will be made clear there, the key to avoiding precious e-mail advertising being viewed as just another piece of "spam" (junk e-mail), is to make certain permission (either implicit or explicit) from the names in a database has been obtained. One company that is building a business around database marketing is the Sales Marketing Network: www.info-now.com, which brings buyers and sellers of business-information services together. At this site, advertisers place their full-sized display ads adjacent to a high-quality, how-to article of specific interest to their customers. Sales and marketing executives come to the site to read these articles. These executives must register and give permission for Sales Marketing Network to use their names. In return for sponsoring an article, advertisers get (among other things) a monthly report that includes the name, title, address and telephone/fax information of the executives who have read their article. The advertiser can immediately add these highly qualified names to their own marketing database. There are several companies offering a form of database marketing through incentive-based programs such as CyberGold, NetCentives, and Yoyodyne. These programs get users to register and give them incentives to read ads. Once signed up, they receive daily to weekly e-mails for promotions of products by interest categories.

The ability to target ads based on frequency is another major feature of Internet advertising. Web sites and ad servers can limit the number of times a particular visitor is exposed to the same ad. This is accomplished through use of an Internet technology called "cookies." A cookie is information that a server places on the user's hard drive in response to a browser request. This information enables a site to remember the browser (user) in future transactions or requests. Only a server in the domain that placed it can read the cookie. Users can accept or deny cookies by changing a setting in their browser preferences.

Limiting the number of ads shown to a user is known as "frequency capping." If advertisers are trying to maintain a high click-rate average, they need to understand the mechanisms and benefits of frequency caps. Studies have been done that indicate the opportunity to get an additional click on a banner will decrease dramatically after the ad is viewed three times by the user. Therefore, advertisers who are looking for high click-through rates might request that the publisher set the ad system delivering the ad to not show it more than three times to a single visitor.

In addition to cookies, ad servers such as NetGravity provide Web sites with other advanced schedule and management capabilities. In addition to frequency caps, ad servers can schedule the delivery of sequences of ads, show new banner content once a user has clicked on an advertiser's ad, or not show any more ads from the same advertiser at all.

Powerful Testing Capabilities

The online medium gives advertisers new tools for testing creative and media plans. With a well-designed test plan, advertisers can optimize their level of expenditures on ad creation and media. Ad management systems give advertisers real-time access (password-protected reporting area) to their ad campaign's activity. With feedback on banner click throughs, the advertiser can judge the performance of each ad and request new ads or schedule changes. In addition to click rates, some of the variables that can be tested regarding the ad itself are the following:

- Ad copy
- Ad graphics/animation
- Media property
- Targeting of buy
- Size of ad
- Position of ad on the page
- Web site design/navigation
- Specific product offers

Advertisers can change the target of an ad, so as to test changes to the Web site or mini-site, using a measure of purchase (response rate or order rate) or of traffic (average number of screens viewed) to gauge success.

Internet advertisers can also analyze log files from their site to determine what sites the users are coming from. By using referral URLs, the Webmaster can look at the sites that drive the highest traffic to their site. These should be analyzed before, during, and after an online campaign is run.

Using cookies to track site usage, the medium can also test the Web site ad by "tagging" individual visitors. When they respond, the users' activities can then be analyzed after the initial click. In addition, accessing the results of the clicks from individual ads can enable the advertiser to make adjustments to the ads and their mix of media vehicles. This data can also be used to direct improvements to the design of the site or the marketing of products or services offered on the site.

Believe It: The Net Has Brand-Building Benefits

Businesses have been quick to understand the benefits of using the Internet as a medium for direct marketing. But the advertising community is just beginning to understand the power of this medium for brand building. Studies to determine the effectiveness of branding through Web ads suggest that the online environment has tremendous power to build brands. In a landmark Online Advertising Effectiveness Study in 1997, done by MBinteractive for the IAB, a test was conducted to measure the impact of an exposure to a single Web ad banner compared to a control group. After just one exposure, online banner advertising was shown to significantly increase brand awareness, enhance product perceptions, and improve product-purchase intent. The study found the following:

- Advertisement awareness (measured by asking respondents if they recall seeing an ad in the past seven days) increased 30 percent with one exposure.
- Web advertising boosts awareness of advertised brands. On average, it observed a 5 percent increase in brand awareness—with results being significantly higher for relatively new brands.
- Online advertising provides significant ability to improve brand perceptions. For example, after being exposed to a single Volvo banner, there was a 55 percent increase in those who thought "Volvo is a good automobile," a 44 percent

increase in those who "have a higher opinion of Volvo than other automobiles," and a 57 percent increase in those who thought Volvo "offers something different than other brands of automobiles."

- After the first exposure, online advertising is more likely to be noticed than television advertising. Television is a passive medium that doesn't require attentiveness on the part of the viewer. With online, the viewer is actively engaged and attentive.

Designing Your Online Media Plan

How Much to Spend?

Before deciding how much of an overall media budget to allocate to online advertising, it's important to define its objectives. Is the intent to build brand awareness, sell products, generate leads, or direct traffic to a Web site? With each of these objectives, there are different media strategies. Branding campaigns may take larger budgets for greater reach across the Net. Direct response campaigns need to calculate the value of a response and the cost per lead. If the goal is direct selling, mechanisms need to be created to track sales and pay the advertising site for each completed transaction originated from a user clicking on an ad.

Types of Internet Advertising

The most common Internet ad unit is the full ad banner (468 x 60 pixels), which is usually purchased by the number of impressions for a set price (CPM or cost per million impressions). According to Coopers & Lybrand's ongoing study of Internet advertising revenue (for the IAB), in the 1st quarter of 1998, banner advertising accounted for 55 percent of the spending on online advertising. Banners are relatively inexpensive to create (static or animated banners) and they are reusable since virtually all Web sites conform to IAB standards for banner size.

Sponsorships are the second most common form of Web advertising. The Coopers & Lybrand report found that 40 percent of Web-advertising spending was for sponsorships. In a sponsorship, the advertiser's brand is either linked to a specific feature, an area of a site, or is presented as a primary or exclusive endorser of the page or site. Sponsors generally receive banners as part of their sponsorship. Sponsorships take on a wide variety of components such as exclusive co-branding, the development of original content, contests, surveys, and games integrating the product. Most Web sites are very interested in putting together highly targeted and sophisticated sponsorship programs for advertisers, so if a significant media budget exists, it is recommended that sponsorships be pursued in addition to banner programs.

An excellent example of an effective sponsorship came from Moët & Chandon champagne during the 1997 Christmas season. Moët's agency developed a branded content area that was promoted from the Starchefs.com home page and included a Q&A quiz about champagne, a profile of Moët & Chandon's Chef Dance, and a weekly recipe area with preferred Moët pairings for each dish. Starchefs also asked users to share their most memorable champagne experiences to stimulate discussion of champagne during the campaign. For example, one poster wrote, "We love to break out a chilled bottle of champagne when it's unexpected. The baby said her first word. The dog sat when told. The car started in the rain. It's the little things that are worth celebrating."

The agency commented, "In the end, Moët & Chandon's sponsorship on Starchefs delivered something much deeper than impressions and page views. It provided a forum for education and discussion of champagne and Moët & Chandon amongst an audience of food and wine enthusiasts and industry professionals, delivering a level of brand interaction only possible in this medium."

The third type of ad unit, still not widely accepted across Web sites, is the interstitial. Interstitial literally means "something in between." Online, it is typically a page that is inserted in the normal flow of content between a user and a site. An interstitial ad is an "intrusive" ad unit that is delivered when a user requests something else—usually editorial content. Interstitial ads are usually full page or small daughter window sized—or pop up ad—that appear over the content.

According to the Coopers & Lybrand's study, 5 percent of ad spending in 1998 was on interstitials. Interstitials have always been a double-edged sword. Without question, these ads generate the most impact of any advertising impression; on the other hand, that impact is not always positive, as viewers may find the ads so intrusive as to be objectionable.

When Honda introduced the redesigned Accord, their agency, Ruben Postaer Interactive, ran an interstitial campaign in conjunction with Honda's print, television, and radio ads in order to raise awareness and generate excitement. The Accord introduction was a huge event for the automotive industry, and Honda felt banners and sponsorships did not capture the level of excitement that this launch required. Indeed, after showing the interstitial 12 million times, Honda found that the results were far better than they had anticipated.

Who Are You Trying to Reach?

Just as with any other medium, before selecting the Internet sites or networks to buy, the audience needs to be considered. What is known about people likely to be interested in this product? What are the target demographics and psychographics? What percent of this audience is online? Is the product recognized or sold regionally? What other media is being used to reach this audience?

Types of Pricing

Most Internet advertising is offered on a cost per thousand (CPM) impressions basis. Usually a CPM buy will guarantee the advertiser a number of ad impressions for a fixed amount of money over a

CHOOSING YOUR SITES

In choosing sites to advertise in, the following should be considered:

- Common sense combined with the provider's own Web-surfing experience.
- The use of search engines (AltaVista, Yahoo!, Excite, Infoseek, and Lycos) to find leading sites within product categories.
- Utilizing Market Match: www.market match.com and/or other companies that offer a service permitting the search of a database of more than one thousand Web sites to determine the best fit for a campaign.
- Speaking to reps from the rep firms and ad networks. These companies represent hundreds and thousands of sites and have a very good understanding of what sites are available to meeting a specific demographic target.
- Checking Standard Rates and Data Services (SRDS) and *Adweek* published directories that list media properties and opportunities, including consumers and business sites arranged by category.

specified time period. For example, the advertiser might buy a campaign for 2 million guaranteed impressions at $20 CPM costing $40,000. If the guaranteed impression level is not met, the advertiser will usually receive a make-good from the site. In some cases, Web sites will exceed their guarantee and the advertiser gets bonus impressions at no charge.

In general, the more targeted the audience, and the more focused the content, the higher the CPM. As of October 1998, typical CPMs for sites by different categories are:

Search Engines	$10–$50
Keywords	$20–$70
Top 100 Sites	$25–$100
Local Sites	$20–$80
Niche Sites	$40–$250
Ad Networks	$10–$70

Alternatively, the advertiser may be able to buy on a performance basis. There are several categories of performance-based pricing, the most common is Cost Per Click (CPC). On a CPC deal, the publisher takes the risk that the ad content works—if it doesn't work and the visitors don't click on the ad, the advertiser doesn't pay. For example, changing our example above to a CPC deal, the advertiser could buy 20,000 clicks for $40,000—a $2.00 CPC. Cost-per-click deals may be compared with equivalent CPM deals by considering the implied click rate. In our example, for the two deals to be equivalent, the ads would need to have a 1 percent click rate. If the click rate were higher than 1 percent, a CPM-based deal would be superior; if lower, the CPC deal would be better.

The other category of performance-based pricing is the direct response model in which advertisers and merchants may be able to negotiate a deal attributed to the actions taken by the visitor *after* they click on the ad and are at the advertiser's site. For direct-response advertisers, this action, called Per Inquiry (PI), is usually generated by a lead; for example, by filling out a questionnaire. For merchants, the action is called Per Transaction (PT), which usually means the purchase of a product or service. In deals of this sort, the dollar amount is usually variable—it depends upon the success of the campaign in generating business. Needless to say, this pricing is preferred by advertisers if response is their goal, since they only pay when an ad performs. Many Web publishers are reluctant to take the risks inherent in this form of pricing, since they don't control the banner content or the offer. Accordingly, if a banner doesn't work and gets a low click through, the publisher takes the revenue hit. To minimize the risk, some publishers are cutting deals that are part CPM and part PI/PT.

Making the Buy

Once a decision has been narrowed to particular Web sites, it is time to contact the salesperson at the site or network representing the site. Alternatively, if a large number of sites are being considered, a Request for Proposal (RFP) could be sent to all the sites. The following are a few topics to discuss with a salesperson.

Traffic Analysis—How many visitors does the site get? How many ads are served on the site (normally measured in pageviews per month)? Has it been growing, and is it expected to grow in the future? Is the site audited, and if so, by whom? Major auditing firms are I/PRO, ABCVS (a subsidiary of Audit Bureau of Circulation), and BPAI (a division of BPA). While many smaller sites are not yet audited, advertisers and agencies do consider the availability of an audit as a factor in their site-selection process. Some agencies will not buy from a site unless it is audited.

Audience Research—What can the salesperson provide about who visits the site? He or she should be able to offer a detailed demographic profile on the audience along with the source of that data. Also, the salesperson should know something about the psychographics and buying behavior of the audience as well as their Web usage and online buying behavior. Audience research can come from companies that provide data from their syndicated research panels such as Media Metrix, Inc.: www.mediametrix.com and from companies that conduct custom, site-based research, such as The Laredo Group: www.laredogroup.com.

Product Options—If what is desired has not been determined, ask what advertising products are offered, what targeting options are available, and what type of banner technology is accepted. Find out about the size of banner used, where the banner is shown on the page, and technical specifications. Lastly ask for deadlines and details on how to submit the content.

Reporting—How are results viewed and how often are they updated? The most common options are to receive results on a password-protected Web site or via e-mail. When conducting a lot of testing, frequent updating is necessary.

Post-Buy—At the end of the ad run, it is desirable to get a post-buy analysis from the site, detailing the results of the buy. Ask if this will be done, and detail any special requirements. Also, auditing firms provide (at a cost of $50–$100) an audit of an individual advertiser's campaign on a site. These reports can be far more useful than a regular site audit.

Negotiating Price

Media buyers believe all rate cards are negotiable. However, several Web sites that have had great successes selling their inventory may not need to negotiate. The type of negotiation will also depend on the time of year. For example, many sites are near capacity in the fourth quarter and are less likely to negotiate at that time. Negotiations are also possible around the volume of impressions being bought and the time frame and length of campaign.

Buyers should inform the sites about their budget, preferred pricing (CPM or CPC), reporting and creative requirements. Feel free to ask a lot of questions and demand a high level of service. On the other hand, remember that the salesperson's job is to bring in revenue—do not ask for a "free sample" or an extraordinarily high level of service such as personally e-mailing results with a one-paragraph analysis every four hours.

When negotiating a banner buy, look for sites that offer banners *above the fold* so that visitors will not have to page down to see your ad. If a banner is *below the fold*, seek a discounted rate. Also, in general, the larger the banner, the greater the awareness and the higher the click rate. When buying half-banners or buttons, the cost should be proportionately less then on a CPM basis.

Measuring the Medium

Online advertising is the first medium to be able to accurately measure the ad opportunity and the response to the ad. While many believe this ability makes the Internet a "completely measurable" medium, there are many fallacies and drawbacks to making this type of claim of the medium. First, measurement methodologies vary from company to company. Second, the definitions and basic terminology are not standardized.

A simple but technical description of what happens when an ad is clicked is as follows: A user requests a page from a Web site, this request is recorded in the log files on the site's computer (called the "server"). This user request for a page may also initiate a request to an ad server for a banner ad. These requests for content and ads are measurable events. In addition to the request, the servers can "read" information from the requesting browser and target either content or ads based on this information. For example, a browser with a .edu domain name may get an ad targeted to college students.

This fact alone sets this medium apart from traditional media. When an ad is shown on TV or played on the radio, there may be nobody watching or listening. When a magazine is bought, the reader may not look at the page with an ad on it. When a direct-mail piece is sent, an envelope may never be opened. But when an ad is shown in a Web browser, someone requested that page and will likely see the ad. It is impossible to measure if a user actually saw the ad as users may click past the page or take other actions that may prevent an ad from being displayed (hit the stop or reload buttons on the browser).

However, the banner click through is an accurate measure of the response to an ad. With further testing, the advertiser can also measure the branding impact of the banner ad. As measurement and research methodologies evolve and standardize, more testing and ad effectiveness studies will help prove the viability of the Web as not only a direct response and selling medium but as a powerful branding tool for advertisers to reach the masses of online users.

Internet advertising is simply the most dynamic and fastest-growing medium for talking to customers and potential customers—

and having them talk back in an instant. For those who are willing to learn the nuances of Internet advertising, and stay current on its fast-changing landscape, there are tremendous opportunities to develop new customers, maintain the loyalty of existing customers, and reach new audiences in a memorable and effective way.

■　■　■

1　CyberDialogue, 1998.
2　eStats, 1998.
3　GVU-8.

Internet Direct Marketing

J. Brent Wilkey, Entrepreneur, and Regina Brady,
Vice President, Acxiom/Direct Media

Brent Wilkey and Regina Brady are Internet direct-marketing pioneers. In this chapter, they provide a basis for understanding some of the details of direct marketing and its specific Internet applications. This information is vital to anyone marketing products via their Web sites.

Scanning **the recent news on CNET.com, a** thirty-eight-year-old consultant sees a beautiful South Pacific island scene on an ad banner proclaiming that she could be the winner of a palmtop computer. She clicks on the gently swaying palm tree in the ad and is immediately taken to a high-tech marketing site. A contest registration form questionnaire appears, and she is asked to fill in the appropriate information to register for the drawing: name, address, e-mail address, a few details about her PC, and her Internet preferences. When these are complete, a screen notifies her she has been duly registered to win the palmtop computer.

One week later, she receives an e-mail thanking her for her contest entry. Along with the thank you is a specialized offer for the company's newest product, a digital reader. Embedded within the e-mail is also a hotlink that when clicked takes her directly to the marketer's site for information about the reader. Because she is a "preferred customer" she is also being offered a special discounted price. It is an offer she can't refuse. She purchases the digital reader and is taken to a secure site for her credit card information. While she is filling out the information, she is told that by clicking on a field within the form, she can elect to receive notification of other offers designed to her needs. Also, the next time she enters the site, the site recognizes her and may have automatically entered her into another promotional giveaway. She has just experienced the innovative world of Internet Direct Marketing (IDM).

Direct to the Consumer

Direct marketing (DM) means marketing directly to the customer or prospect with the goal of eliciting a specific response. In addition, DM means capturing response information into a database for use in future decision making. DM has long been considered the workhorse in any marketer's arsenal. Its primary function is not to build brand but, rather, to drive sales in a measured and accountable fashion. This is a very sophisticated and mature industry, one in which success, like batting averages in baseball, is measured by increases of tenths and hundredths of percentage points. This is not to say that building brand is not important; but rather that the ultimate goal of direct marketing is to generate measurable sales. In today's environment where marketing dollars must work harder than ever before, direct marketing is an important part of the overall marketing mix.

Direct marketing has often been called database marketing. The marketer applies the intelligence learned from a market effort or sale into their marketing system in order to build on those successes and failures to help plan future efforts. It is a process of continually refining what creative approach, what advertising medium, what offers, or what targets generate sales activity, and then analyzing those results to build future efforts.

In the traditional world of DM, this means testing which space publications, broadcast spots, mailing lists, or other media promises the most in combination with creative and offer presentation. Typically, results are measured down to a Cost Per Order, a Cost Per

Subscriber, or a Cost Per Inquiry. If a particular mailing list is marginal, a direct marketer will attempt to refine his or her selections within the list to see if there are subselections of a list that will be profitable. It is this constant refinement that brings success. The marketer will also look at the "lifetime value" of a customer. It may be possible to bring in a new customer at a slight loss *if* the marketer knows that the average customer stays with them for a number of years and buys additional products or services. While the marketer may lose money on the initial acquisition, they know they will be ultimately very profitable.

Imagination Is the Only Limit

The Internet is changing these traditional delivery channels by providing a whole new canvas upon which to ply color and creative form. And with this new palette, marketing artists are discovering that the range of results that can be achieved is limited only by the marketer's ability to create and innovate. It is important to add, however, there is nothing magic about direct marketing on the Internet. Expecting miracles would be like saying, we've got this great new tool, a telephone, and by calling people up, something inconceivable will happen. The reality is when the Internet is used appropriately, the opportunities to create significant gains, replacing one-tenths of percentages with whole percentage points, are limited only by the imagination.

Let's illustrate this point with two simple examples—a look at ad banners and e-mail messages both designed to drive e-commerce. These examples show that by being prepared to measure results, rewards can be reaped.

There are many techniques that can be used with ad banners to increase the amount of click throughs. CatalogLink.com, a site where consumers can select from a broad array of free catalogs, has experimented with animated banners that help the ads stand out from a straightforward, static approach that touts "hundreds of free catalogs." The animated banners drove 35 percent more traffic than the straightforward approach; but the straightforward approach generated significantly more orders. CatalogLink tracks consumers all the way through to ordering. Because CatalogLink is prepared to measure results, they are in the position to capitalize on the marketing intelligence gained from their ad banner experiments. While they continue to experiment with animated banners, they are dedicating most of their placements to standard banners.

To give an e-mail example, Astrology.net wanted to e-mail those who had registered at their site to see if they would like a daily horoscope delivered via e-mail. They mailed five different approaches on the morning of day one to segments of their registrants. By noon, they analyzed results and saw that two of the creative tests were far surpassing the other approaches. By midafternoon, they retested the two winning messages and a new third one, which was based upon looking at prior results. By that evening, they found that their newest message was the winner. The next morning, they rolled out the winner to the balance of the list. Sign-ups for the daily horoscope went from an average of 29 percent on the first round of mailings to 43 percent with the final winning approach. It took just one full day to get the marketing feedback to refine the efforts in day two.

Marketing Pioneers Are Often Leaders

Many leading marketers were early adopters of the Internet, using various utilities such as e-mail, Web sites, and push-technology under the banner of "the ideal medium for direct marketing." Many of these early efforts, however, did not produce results in the traditional return-on-investment approach of direct marketing (gross profit divided by cost of effort). What these early adopters did gain was more valuable in the long term: the beginning of an organizational understanding of the unique characteristics of a fast-evolving medium.

The Direct Marketing Association recently released a study of companies that were successful on the Internet. One factor that helped dictate success is the length of time the marketer had been on the Web. Experience helped marketers to learn from their mistakes and focus their efforts for maximum payoff.

The Internet's Characteristics Are Ideal for Direct Marketing

To understand Internet-based direct marketing requires an underlying understanding of the interaction between customers, providers, and sellers of products and services. With IDM, the customer controls when the communication generated is consumed, both in terms of time of day and day of week. A direct-marketing piece delivered through "snail mail" arrives at what the marketer has decided is the most opportune time for its arrival. On the Internet, there may not be as much control of when a prospect enters a marketer's Web site. In both instances, consumers can easily end the interaction if they do not like any aspect of it. Remember, the mailing piece is a tactile, tangible package that the recipient can see and feel. The first hurdle is to get the prospect to open the piece and then the material inside is all crafted to explain the offer and to underscore the importance of ordering today. When a prospect arrives at a Web site, there are literally seconds to capture their attention and to get them to interact further with a site. The path the prospect takes when they travel through a site cannot necessarily be controlled.

One of the advantages of using IDM is that prospects or customers can be encouraged to interact with the site. Too many sites are organized for passive browsing. The consumer can point and click his or her way through a site . . . but this is *not* interaction. A good direct-marketing site creates a dialog with the consumer and encourages the consumer to provide some information. There are many ways this can be done; for example, having the consumer register at the site, enter a contest, add themselves to a mailing list, or fill out a survey. In each of these instances, the marketer will now know something more about its customers or its potential customers—and this information can be added to a database for future targeted marketing efforts.

Another advantage of using IDM is that there is a greater likelihood that a happy customer could become a marketer's best asset. A positive encounter could translate into the customer recommending products and services to his or her peer group by sending a quick e-mail or making a bulletin-board posting. These communications from happy customers are far more leveragable than with paper-based media. Of course, since customers have the shield of anonymity, it may make them more frank (even aggressive) if they are unhappy. And, likewise, they can share their unhappiness with other potential customers in a public digital forum, and that unhappiness can multiply faster in the digital medium than in paper media. Another reality is that unhappy customers have easy access to competitors with a few keystrokes. Even though there are technical techniques such as framing to encourage a customer to come back through a marketer's links, the assumption is that a value-added reason for a prospect, or customer, to return to a Web page must be provided.

A real benefit of this new medium is that a sale can be consummated online with no direct human involvement. Advances in secure servers and increasing trust with electronic commerce are enhancing this selling option for both seller and buyer. Many companies are finding that customer-service costs can be sharply reduced because various Web technologies allow self-service, automatic order confirmation, order tracking, and the ability to obtain additional information easily and quickly. Studies have found that the average cost of handling a customer service call is a minimum of $1.70. If a company is able to offload 250,000 annual calls because all the information is available on the Web, that is a savings of $425,000 or more! And, that is money that falls right to the bottom line.

A Change in Behavior

Additionally, many companies now integrate their Web order taking directly with their fulfillment operations. Orders are seamlessly pulled into their systems and shipped, resulting in dollar savings and time savings. And with current advances, if a product can be delivered digitally, such as information and music, a marketer may be able to fulfill the product order online by simply e-mailing the product directly to the customer or allowing the customer to download directly from their site.

It is important to understand that any marketing activity on- or offline that requires a change in customer behavior will require a large marketing investment. Do not be fooled into thinking that IDM will transmute this fundamental marketing truth. There is a general impression that doing business on the Internet is automatically more cost-effective. It's only cost-effective when used properly. Consider the case of Amazon.com and Barnesandnoble.com. Amazon enjoyed the distinction of being the first major bookseller online; plus, they used all the best of possible techniques available on the Web to customize and personalize the book-buying experience. Barnes and Noble got a late start. As this book is being written, Barnes and Noble has announced a major loss for the quarter and that it plans to spin off its online store in an IPO (initial public offering). There are many factors that contributed to this situation, but it has learned that marketing online is significantly different from the traditional retail space. Additionally, the online book-buying consumer has different demographic and psychographic characteristics.

As pointed out in Chapter 16, the travel industry faced a similar situation in trying to have its customers purchase tickets online. People quickly discovered the convenience of gathering flight information and costs via the Internet, but they were uncomfortable making purchases anywhere except through traditional channels. If the cost to change people's behaviors in this instance were to be amortized from inception to routine purchase, online ticket purchasing may not be as cost-effective as when first conceived.

Lifetime Value of Customer Is the Goal

The ultimate goal in using direct marketing in a substantial way is to increase the lifetime value of a company's customer base. This means that a company creates an ongoing series of communications with its customers. This concept was introduced earlier but it bears more attention. One marketing adage is that it costs five times more to get a new customer as it does to retain a customer. The cost to acquire a customer is usually high because response rates are relatively low. Once a consumer has a relationship with a company, they are usually more receptive to subsequent offerings; therefore, marketing costs become significantly lower. For example, a first-time magazine subscriber is more likely to renew after receiving the magazine for a year, and if they have subscribed for more than two years, they are statistically more likely to renew. A catalog buyer who buys one item from a company is much more likely to buy more items in the future.

So, keeping track of customers is of paramount importance. The dynamic of the changing address has had a major impact on traditional direct-mail marketing but may not prove to be as problematic on the Internet. In the United States, a rough rule of thumb is that 20 percent of a company's prospects and customers' postal addresses will change in any one year. At one time in the online industry, due to a cascade of new server offers, customer churn had been as high as 40 percent, but that has settled down considerably. Consumer marketers have found home-based e-mail addresses on commercial online services are not changing nearly as often, because a user does not need to change an e-mail address just because a physical address has been changed. This will be increasingly true as online account churn decreases even further, and as personal domain names become more common. Domain names such as human-name@domain-name.com are inherently portable when compared to phone numbers, which typically are service-area dependent. Internet business-to-business marketers are likely to continue to see dynamic changes with work-based e-mail addresses. Professionals change companies, change job functions within their companies, and change responsibilities. Business addresses are normally tied to a company name, and with worker mobility increasing, a home e-mail address may prove to be much more predictable than those at work.

There are currently a number of services under development that will allow the marketer to enhance their existing customer databases with e-mail addresses. Many marketers are just beginning to aggressively collect e-mail addresses from their customers and consequently have large gaps in their internal databases. To truly take advantage of the opportunities in e-commerce, they are looking to jump-start their efforts. The new appending services address both the consumer and business-to-business fronts. By 1999, expect to see several such services flourishing.

Executing an Internet Direct Marketing Program

PLAN STRATEGICALLY

A good Internet-marketing company has a strategic plan in mind even before their Web site is built. They have identified target audiences and their needs, and how they are going to reach these targets. Once a target audience has been defined and segmented, and a core objective for a marketing program developed, it is time for the imagination to take over.

In creating innovative IDM, it is important to look for synergies with traditional tactics. Do not overlook integrating paper-based and broadcast media when planning IDM activities. This allows greater exposure for a Web site, because if prospects do not know it exists, it will do nothing but gather cobwebs.

The first consideration of any marketer operating in both the traditional and cyberspace worlds is to include the site's URL prominently in every ad, every traditional direct-mail piece, every catalog (and on every other page of every catalog), and every piece of collateral material. And this does not mean a simple mention in small type. Make sure the URL is featured. And, if possible, give a reason why the Web site offers additional value. For example, a publication might tout additional editorial on feature stories on their Web site. A cataloger might showcase their latest merchandise and their clearance sales on their Web site.

Many marketers are following up traditional direct-mail campaigns with e-mail efforts. They are finding that the two marketing efforts have a powerful combination effect. This is being seen particularly with high-tech marketers who are likely to be ahead of the curve in collecting e-mail addresses on customers and prospects.

When integrating programs, ask: What habits do prospects and customers have? We've now seen ads for ordering Saturns online advertised on television and targeted at the college market. An online investment service such as DLJ.com advertises with multi-page ads in investment magazines. Negative-option book and music clubs provide an area on their Web sites where members can opt out of the current month's automatic selection. A PC gamer who purchases a joystick in a retail store may find collateral material with their purchase that promotes a multiplayer Web site.

Another important aspect is to maximize the power of search engines. Search-engine registration may be a good starting point, but it may not be enough to simply register. This is comparable to having an 800 number listed in a phone book. A company may be listed, but customers and prospects have to think specifically that they want to find the company before they will happen upon the listing.

Using search engines might require the purchase of banner space identified by specific words or phrases. Finding the key words that identify a potential customer for a targeted IDM message can improve responses significantly. For example, an immigration lawyer buys space with a search engine on the word "immigration." Every time someone searched the word "immigration," the marketer's banner ad would appear. The response to this targeted tactic can produce click-through rates, equivalent to someone opening a direct-mail letter, of over 8 percent. Traditional direct-mail campaigns are considered successful when they return 1 to 2 percent. For this particular lawyer, an average client will spend about $5000 on the procedures necessary to immigrate. It doesn't take many clients to break even with this kind of IDM.

Use Tactics That Support a Goal

E-MAIL MARKETING

The first and perhaps the most powerful of IDM applications is e-mail. It is an incredibly robust tool when used ethically and responsibly. Do not be afraid to use e-mail as part of a marketing strategy, provided, of course, it is in tune with prospects and customers. E-mail marketing is a good way to enhance customer loyalty if initiated and handled properly.

The most effective e-mail marketing today includes hotlinks or hyperlinks within the e-mail message that drive customers and prospects directly to the marketer's site. These links should not necessarily take the reader/responder to the home page; but rather should drive them directly to the offers being made. Companies make major investments in their sites, and e-mail is an effective way of driving targeted, action-oriented traffic.

Additionally, e-mail marketing comes closer to one-to-one marketing than most other vehicles. In traditional direct-marketing efforts, it is generally more cost-effective to produce mass quantities of an ad, direct-mail campaign components, or other communication. E-mail marketers are not bound by the same cost considerations. For example, rather than producing one major effort of 250,000 pieces, consider how effective it can be to create 10 smaller, more targeted communications of 25,000 each. Each smaller group can hone in on various segments of the overall market.

INCREASING RESPONSES

One major marketer of modems wanted to introduce an upgrade of one of their popular models. They sent e-mails to past customers and told them that by clicking on a link in the message, they would be taken to a free upgrade area. An unbelievable 66 percent of recipients took advantage of the upgrade! This same company sent e-mails to prospects promoting this same new modem but customized each message to direct the prospect to one of four resellers' sites as part of a cooperative marketing arrangement.

E-mail marketing can provide an alternative contact method to initiate live callbacks. Customers often have additional questions about some aspect of the product, billing, or delivery. E-mail provides another method to contact customer service. Some marketers even offer a live human callback, or fax, instead of an e-mail response. It may be counter-intuitive to think anything other than an e-mail inquiry must beget an e-mail response. But consider that it is much easier to ask a complicated question with a few written words, than to provide a complicated answer in a few written words. An e-mail response system allows the provider to respond one-to-one, on a customer-service- and/or prospect-inquiry-based system. By training a team of customer-service or sales professionals to handle such responses, e-mail can be a safe and value-added way for an organization to use this powerful tool as part of its marketing mix, even if live phone callback can't be justified.

If economics don't support the human touch, consider using a carefully designed and professionally maintained electronic dialoging system, an expert system that uses a "decision tree" approach. And don't fake it. Position it for what it is. It's not necessary to be apologetic about not providing human callback. Position it as efficient and convenient, but provide a method to get a human in the loop, even if it is something as unelectronic as instructing the customer to mail a question to a specific address, or to call a specific telephone number during specific hours in a specific time zone. To a customer or potential customer, there is nothing more frustrating than to have no means for resolving an inquiry or problem. Even if the method or solution is less than ideal, the fact that it is available is better than having no perceived avenue for resolution. To give an example from the interactive world, several of the online services were taken to task by the FTC because it was too difficult for customers to cancel. Most of the services alleviated the problem by posting clear instructions for specific contact information online.

If e-mail is being used simply as a method of providing dynamic product data such as changing airline ticket prices or weather-, time-, or inventory-dependent recreational services, then consider providing a Web site where prospects and customers can provide their e-mail address to receive updated product information on a daily, weekly, or monthly basis. And by all means, provide an easy way for customers to remove themselves from the service.

AVOIDING UNSOLICITED E-MAILINGS

Many marketers have avoided using unsolicited e-mail marketing (colloquially called "spam") for fear of customer backlash. If a firm is not equipped to do the careful planning required, then it should not use e-mail marketing. E-mail marketing is permission-based marketing. If you do not have the permission of the consumer, you should not mail to them. Even with a "house file" (the marketer's own customers) it is important to give the consumer the choice to opt out of receiving future e-mail messages—and this choice should be given in *each and every* communication to customers. And, if a consumer indicates they no longer wish to receive e-mail from a marketer, it is of vital importance that they never receive future communications. This means the marketer (or their service bureau) must immediately build a file of all opt-outs that is used as a suppression file against any and all future mailings. That is the beginning of "Netiquette" (Net etiquette). When marketers mail their own customer file for the first time, they will typically see between 1½ percent and 2 percent opting out. In subsequent e-mailings, these percentages fall dramatically.

Marketers interested in prospecting and sending specific marketing information to a carefully defined audience should consider targeted e-mail. Seek professional advice before doing this.

Some General E-mailing Tips

Do a culture check first. In today's world of e-mail marketing, it is important that marketers act ethically and responsibly. If a marketer wants to mail beyond its own customer base, only opted-in e-mail lists should be used. Opted-in lists mean that the individuals on that list have already said that they wish to receive additional promotional efforts within a given subject of interest. There are many lists on the market today that are not clearly opted-in. Work with a professional company that can do the research for you to ensure that you are mailing responsibly.

The reality of e-mail marketing is that no matter how carefully and well intentioned your project is planned, it will inevitably upset someone. At a minimum, an easy and fast method for allowing any e-mail recipient to permanently remove their e-mail address from a mailing list must be provided. In removing them, it is wise to create and maintain a list of these e-mail addresses in a "suppression file," colloquially referred to as a "nixie" list. This suppression file should be faithfully run against all future e-mail marketing efforts to assure compliance with customer wishes.

Test a small audience before a rollout. Send the e-mail campaign to the smallest statistically significant sample size on an e-mail list. Once a response has been received, carefully analyze it. With this in hand, a decision can be made to refine or cancel the rollout, based upon the test results.

Include an opt-out provision for prospects in the mailing. This allows the recipient to indicate that they do not want to receive any additional solicitations from the marketer.

Remember that the header of the message—"From" and "Subject"—is the most important piece of copy in the entire message. The reader is looking at the message in his or her e-mail box and immediately looks at whom the message is from and what the message is about. Even if a service bureau delivers your e-mail, make sure your domain/URL is listed as the sender. And, make sure there is value in the message header.

Include multiple calls to action in the e-mail. To maximize the effectiveness of a communication, include more than one marketing hotlink; but put the most important message first. Remember that all recipients may not want the primary product offering but might very well be interested in another product or aspect of service.

Personalize your message if possible. Omaha Steaks, a direct marketer of quality meats, tested two different salutations in a letter: "Dear Barbecue Enthusiast" and "Dear <First Name> <Last Name>." The personalized message outpulled the generic header substantially. And don't just personalize the salutation; deliver selective content. For example, all new customers might get one offer in the first paragraph, all multibuyers another offer, and all former buyers a third offer.

Track who clicked on what link and reappend that information in a marketing database. There are service bureaus in the e-mail arena that can track e-mails down to the individual letter and the individual link within the message. The more a marketer can know about the interests and activities of customers and prospects the better equipped the marketer is to move from mass marketing to one-to-many marketing to one-to-one marketing.

Use e-mail to create an ongoing dialog with customers and to drive repeat business. Marketers need to test how often these communications should occur.

Using Banner Advertising to Drive Responses

One of the earliest advertising concepts implemented on Web sites and search engines, and discussed at length in the advertising chapter, was banner ads. Banner ads that have a click-through feature and lead a user into a "call to action" are a form of direct marketing. If no click-through feature is included, this would be considered brand building. For interactive direct marketers, banner ads are only as good as their placement, their content and their ability to attract the right target audience. The "call to action" can be compelling but will only be effective if the right audience sees it. A marketer who decides banner ads are a part of the media mix should obtain as much site-audience data as possible. Construct the ads and "click-through call to action" once the audience is understood. Above all, be prepared to measure activity and not just click throughs. There are various capabilities available today that can help a marketer measure beyond the click through, such as Linkshare and others. Be sure to investigate all tracking possibilities.

Today, several companies offer capabilities that allow the consumer to consummate a transaction directly from a banner ad. Orb: www.orb.net launched an ad banner campaign for Clinique cosmetics. When consumers clicked on the banner, they were immediately taken to a registration form where they filled out a quick survey, gave their name and address, and received through the mail a coupon that entitled them to a free gift at retail locations for any purchase of $15 or more. Within two days, Clinique had over four thousand completed registrations. This can be an effective way of building a targeted list. ImpulseBuy: www.impulsebuy.net places ad banners for individual deep-discounted products across the Web. Transactional banners can help increase a marketer's presence and boost awareness across the Internet.

Combine Tactics to Create Programs

If planned correctly, IDM can become more than the sum of its parts. Assembling various tactics into an overall program may be an effective marketing approach. Early in the strategic-planning process, it is important to be more innovative and think at a "higher level" in terms of customer loyalty, promotional concepts specific to the market, continuity approaches to selling, and what to do when things go wrong unexpectedly.

SALES PROMOTION

Imagination and creativity should reign supreme when implementing a sales promotion on the Internet. One approach is to target customers with prizes that have a synergy with the product or service being promoted. The prize should be considered as another means of enhancing the overall message or promotion. The key is to think about what motivates prospects and customers. A prize might be identified that the customer and only the customer would care about. This may take more planning but would likely yield a better result. Using one or more unique characteristics of the Internet, such as hypertext links in a Web site, or e-mail enclosures as described in the opening of this chapter, can also be effective.

The small business and office supply direct marketer Quill knows how to effectively use sales promotion and premium offers. It wanted to find a way to drive repeat traffic and repeat buyers to its site. In banner ads posted on its own site and other Internet sites, it typically gives a premium with every purchase over a certain dollar amount. Quill found that it needed to change the premium it offered every three weeks. This encouraged repeat visits and repeat sales because customers wanted to take advantage of receiving a new gift.

One of the best online services to combine discounted promotions with a variety of Internet capabilities is Amazon.com. It is one of the most customized and personalized sites on the Internet. Amazon learns and builds database information about its customers based on their behavior. A customer can register his or her own preferences. For example, he or she might be a John Grisham fan. So, the next time a Grisham novel is released, an e-mail arrives announcing its availability. Amazon.com will also recommend authors based on a request for a given genre. At the bottom of most title, author, or subject searches is a list of other similar titles in which the customer might be interested.

Amazon has done one of the best jobs on the Internet of true database marketing, combining ad banners, promotions, and customization of its site. When a second-time user arrives at the site, he or she is recognized. After the first purchase, all pertinent information is retained so that a customer doesn't have to re-enter it. When requested, the customer periodically receives personalized preference e-mails, which builds customer retention, and Amazon has prompt customer service, including follow-up messages about the status of an order and information about further promotions.

Sales promotions can also be a way to generate leads. For example, 1-800-Flowers might run a contest in ad banners promoting that one out of every hundred randomly drawn e-mail addresses received by July 1 would receive a free bouquet. This is a good way to drive traffic to their site and a good way to build a prospect e-mail database from all the registrants in the contest.

Of course, the complexity of a lead-generation program could also be much more elaborate. Typically, a self-selected prize or premium can be included, as well as other means to qualify and segment the leads. The more money spent on qualifying good leads means the less money wasted trying to convert poor leads to sales.

It is important to note that if a sales promotion involves any type of contest or prize giveaway, contact a lawyer or other professional familiar with the laws covering sweepstakes. As discussed in the chapter on public policy, carefully consider the fact that a promotion may be accessible by individuals in areas where a promotion may violate local laws.

BUILDING CUSTOMER LOYALTY

IDM can also be used to build customer loyalty just by using the Web's soft marketing capabilities such as order taking, order fulfillment, informational inquiries, and product questions.

Another method of building customer loyalty is to implement a specific loyalty program. A loyalty program has at least two driving characteristics—duration and goals. If a typical sales cycle is one month, consider running a loyalty program for six months or making it an ongoing part of a marketing mix. Evaluation points should be included so that the program can be turned off gracefully if it does not produce the results desired.

There are several companies who have developed Web-based loyalty systems such as CyberGold, MyPoints, and BonusMail. Registered users can accumulate points based upon specific actions taken. Marketers may consider including participation in these programs as part of their direct-marketing arsenal.

Internet Direct Marketing Tactical Tools

The Internet adds a few tools for direct marketing not available in paper-based direct marketing. Each Internet tool has its own particular features and potential pitfalls. Some general advice: Just because it can be done, does not mean it should be done—both from a strategic and an ethical standpoint. The following are some general parameters to consider:

ONLINE USER PROFILES FOR MARKETING

As pointed out in the public-policy chapter, the United States has liberal privacy laws compared to some other countries such as Germany, specifically, and the European Community in general. To implement an Internet direct response program internationally, evaluate the privacy laws of the countries being marketed to before beginning program planning. This is an evolving area that is constantly changing. It is important to seek up-to-date professional advice before proceeding.

GENERAL ONLINE SERVICES

Some commercial online services, as well as other Web portals like MSNBC and Yahoo!, provide a method for subscribers to complete, online, a profile of themselves. This profile might include the subscriber's name, address, interests, and hobbies, which were originally intended to be used by other members in getting to know each other online. Mining these profiles may be difficult, impossible, unethical, or even illegal. Many of the larger online services have taken positions that these user profiles may not be used for marketing, without the expressed permission of the individual providing the profile.

If they are used, it is essential to consider how to test for and filter out unusable e-mail addresses and profiles that are not completed properly or do not fit the necessary criteria. Again, this final list should be run against a suppression file to remove the e-mail addresses of individuals that do not want to receive unsolicited e-mails.

Once again, it is critical to ensure that what is being done is both legal and ethical.

BOUTIQUE WEB SITES/TIGHT COMMUNITIES

Some Web site producers provide an area on their Web site for the user to register as a user and complete a user profile. The Web site producer may take a position on how, and if, this information may be used by third-party marketers. A number of trade associations recommend, and some governmental jurisdictions may require, that the Web site contain a privacy statement. A marketer should do nothing to violate the terms of the privacy statement neither with nor without the Web site owner's involvement.

If there is no privacy policy featured at a site, it can be relatively easy to construct one. The Direct Marketing Association has a simple program available on their site: www.the-dma.org in their privacy area that allows a marketer to step through a series of questions and construct a privacy policy on the fly.

USING WEB TRAVEL PATTERNS FOR MARKETING

There has been a good deal written about "cookies," which are quite controversial and in some areas may even be illegal. One form a cookie can take is to track the Web-travel patterns of the user's

USER PROFILES FOR MARKETING CHECKLIST

1. Does the designed marketing program fit within the Web site owner's privacy policies?
2. Does the quantity of the user profiles available justify the marketing program?
3. What data is available to confirm that users have completed the profiles accurately?
4. Is a planned use of the user profiles legal in the absence of a privacy policy?

computer on which the cookie has been installed. Conceptually, if there were an organized method to collect this cookie data in a standardized format, process it into something intelligent, then analyze that intelligence in terms of a specific marketing goal, then using Web-travel data for marketing is conceptually possible and powerful. For example, Dell may examine the path a user takes through its site, and if a customer is in the midst of building a PC and does not finish the configuration it may be useful for Dell to identify the customer so that it can remarket to him or her via other means later.

To use cookies properly is a tall order, and most of the elements are changing so quickly that this is unlikely to be an effective method for general third-party marketing in the foreseeable future. Once this process becomes logistically practical, the ethical question of appropriateness will still be an overriding issue. As stated previously, all marketers should respect customers' and prospects' privacy. All marketers should fully disclose these types of programs, allowing an easy "opt-out" or, even better, an "opt-in" approach.

USING ONLINE PURCHASE PATTERNS FOR MARKETING

Marketers can examine the purchase behavior of their online customers for future marketing efforts. For example, if a cataloger sees that a consumer always buys discounted items, it makes sense to make sure that consumer know about every sale. If a customer orders certain office supplies every three months, the marketer can offer a discount off the next two shipments if the customer orders in advance. If a customer orders a particular apparel item, the marketer may want to cross-promote accessories that would go with the item.

It is also possible to purchase offline data from providers of complementary products, or even competitors, that contain the e-mail or postal addresses of likely online buyers. Do not discount the power of using offline direct-marketing methods to contact prospects that will benefit from online offerings.

Establishing Responsibility

It is important to assign responsibilities for an Internet direct-marketing campaign. This will, of course, vary greatly based upon an organization's overall size and structure and decisions on what to outsource and what to do in-house. However, a number of key responsibilities need to be assigned.

An IDM manager needs to assign the following areas of responsibility in building a team:

Strategy Development	Develop an overall plan that achieves the IDM objective.
Database Management	Source prospect lists, analyze lists acquired, process the data into a usable form, maintain user profiles and suppression filter, and track usage data.
Creative Direction	Supervise the art, copy (text), and other content resources used.
Applications Development	Programming resources will need to be managed if a marketing program requires functionalities to be developed that are unique.
Applications Integration	Coordinate the creative and applications teams so that the marketing creative execution is consistent with any online software modules developed for specific purposes.
Digital Operations	Ensure that whatever Internet functionalities used will be up and running as expected, on an ongoing basis.
Media Resource Management	Legal acquisition of art and other digital resources such as news feeds and third-party databases.
Program Management	Keep everyone working on the same schedule and set of goals.

Fulfillment Management	Ensure that the information, premiums, products, and services ordered by customers are provided to them in a timely manner.
Electronic Dialoging System	Manage who answers which e-mails, how, and when.
Online Hosting	If a program includes real-time response to customers, it will need to have staff available as appropriate.

The Global Market

An enormous myth exists that goes like this: The Internet is any business's gateway to the world. This is no more, or less, true than repeating the same sentence but replacing the word *Internet* with *telephone*. Simply because I can call someone in France doesn't mean that I'll be able to market my product there. I would still need to make sure that I had instructions in French, distribution, the right safety codes, the appropriate calculations, power source, or even that my product is legally salable in France. Most of the issues we confront in satisfying prospects and customers over the telephone internationally will exist with Internet direct marketing, in addition to other challenges.

Cataloglink.com is a site where a customer can order free catalogs. However, a lot of U.S. catalogers want to ship only to customers in the U.S. What Cataloglink.com has encountered is that when an international customer comes into the site, they sometimes find something they really want but are unable to order it. They then try to fool the system and order it anyway, by placing their address—like Katmandu, Nepal—in the fields reserved for city and state. Cataloglink.com ends up collecting invalid international orders, which does a disservice to both the catalog owners and the international customer.

The obvious incompatibility issues we must deal with in international marketing of any kind are spoken languages and wide variation in style and culture around the world. Add to this the variance in computer products and protocols worldwide, and we have a lot to think about. Sure it is relatively easy to retrieve a Web page or e-mail anywhere, but printers in Europe, for example, do not use 8.5" x 11" paper as a standard. A simple thing that could have big implications, if we do not plan for it.

But planning can reap rewards. A software discounter who participated in CompuServe's Electronic Mall, a hub site for merchandising, analyzed its orders and found that 43 percent of all orders came from beyond U.S. borders. They had decided to advertise on CompuServe because of a higher percentage of international members in the total membership base. Their strategy worked.

In addition to the many things that might enhance or detract from the success of a marketing effort outside of the primary domestic market, it is important to consider public policy, legal, and taxation rules. For example, some countries will hold the employees traveling (even if just on vacation) in their country personally liable for the omissions and transgressions of their employer. Before offering goods or services for sale worldwide, contact a professional who knows the rules in the markets being entered. If not, there may be more to worry about than a simple return on marketing investment. To give an example, a pharmacy marketing online found out that a shipment of Vitamin E ordered by a person in Japan was refused at the border. The pharmacy broke the order into several smaller shipments and the order then met customs requirements.

Asking the Right Questions

In closing, here are some questions a marketing team could ask themselves when beginning an Internet marketing effort:

Are your prospects and/or customers online? Is the size of the potential audience that is online large enough to justify aggressive marketing efforts? A business-to-business marketer who sells high-ticket services may be very well served if only a thousand of its key prospects are online—and it can find ways to reach them. A niche marketer may fall into the same scenario. A consumer marketer may need hundreds of thousands of the right prospects online.

Are your online customers different from your traditional customers? Direct marketers take the magnifying glass to their customers and profile different segments of their customer base. Many Internet marketers who also operate in traditional space have found that the profiles of their Web customers differ significantly from their offline customers. For example, *Reader's Digest* finds that it is attracting a younger demographic through the Web. Internet direct marketers must take the time to profile their Internet customers and compare them with their traditional customers—the differences can lead marketers to consider different marketing strategies. In the *Reader's Digest* case, they must be aware of the differences of generational marketing to ensure success with this new customer base.

If your prospects and/or customers are indeed online, then what is the nature of their connectivity? For example, do they use their account for personal use only, business use only, or both? Is their e-mail account associated with a domain name other than at a commercial service? If so, is this domain personally owned by an individual, or is it owned and operated by the individual's employer? Answers to these questions will help you determine the general tone of communication (commercial versus retail perhaps) and what other online messages and activity your online communications will be competing with to get the attention of your customers or prospects.

What connectivity bandwidth do your customers and prospects typically have? Are they typically using old, slower modems; newer, faster modems; ISDN; cable modems; wireless modems; or what? Answers here will determine the size (and hence download or delivery time) of your graphics that enhance the consumer experience on your site—hint: It is generally safer to provide a quick low-density graphic, than to force a prospect to wait for a higher density graphic.

Can your prospects and customers be described by a set of demographic parameters (such as age, gender, and household income) and any of an infinite number of psychographic parameters (such as they like certain music, sports, and on and on)? If so, are there targeted media (such as Web sites or e-mail lists) available that are sorted by these parameters? Answers here will determine if the targeting that is available online will logistically allow you to do cost-effective targeting for your goals.

What do your prospects and customers do when they are online? Do they use their connectivity primarily for e-mail? Do they Web-surf, buy products/service, do research, play, chat, entertain themselves or others, build communities, educate themselves or others, do charity work, read news, or make news? Answers to these questions will help you understand the "time-constrained context" that your online marketing will exist in. In other words, your customers and prospects can be spending their precious time online experiencing your online message, or doing whatever it is they otherwise would like to be doing online.

How much money should you invest in Internet marketing? This will depend entirely on your goals, which sounds trite but is a profound and essential starting point.

What is your organization's internal and external level of expertise in dealing with Internet-based programs? What percentage of your company's sales and marketing staff are wired themselves? Do you have an Intranet, perhaps to use a means of educating your sales and marketing staff prior to launch of an Internet marketing effort? What level of expertise do your marketing partners, your outside advertising, sales promotions, and direct-marketing service providers have in dealing with the Internet? Keep in mind that "dealing with the Internet" in the context of this question is much like asking someone if they can play the saxophone. The sax is actually quite easy to pick up and make noise with. However, it is quite difficult to actually make music come out.

#### SEVEN

Corporate Communications and Public Affairs: Using the Internet to Communicate Ideas

Sam Simon, President, Issue Dynamics, Inc., and Link Hoewing, Assistant Vice President, Issues Management and Corporate Relations, Bell Atlantic

The Internet has as its heritage the exchange of information and ideas. This makes it ideally suited as a tool in both Public Relations and Corporate Communications. Smart companies are increasingly using the Internet to gain an edge in communicating their story. Both Sam Simon and Link Hoewing have been at the forefront of their profession in the creative application of Internet technology, and they share here their expert advice both on what to do and what not to do.

According to historians, the first presidential telephone was installed on President Herbert Hoover's desk in 1927. By that time, the telephone network had been in existence for half a century and millions of Americans had phones. Yet, presidents before Hoover's time had spoken on the phone only from a booth outside the executive office, and the president himself was unsure exactly how he would use the new device.

Just as the telephone has insinuated itself into all aspects of life, so, too, has the Internet become an essential way of communicating in today's world. It is going to be even more important tomorrow. Millions of people use the Internet, and it is on the verge of becoming a legitimate "mass" medium.

Despite the seeming ubiquity of computers and "the Internet," a person walking down the halls of Congress or in the executive suites of most major corporations, will find the "newest" technology on the staff's or support persons' desks, not on senior executives' desks. And while it might have been fine to take fifty years for the telephone to make it to the president's desk, it isn't going to be all right for our presidents or any CEOs in America to be "off line" for much longer.

According to Moore's law, computing power doubles every eighteen months. The Internet itself is doubling even faster than that, whether it is counted in the number of subscribers, number of computers offering services (Web sites), or the numbers of messages transiting the wires. The Net itself is becoming an international phenomenon with little or no ability for nation-states to control what, who, or how it is used.

The Internet is, first and foremost, a way of communicating ideas. Simply look at any television commercial, advocacy advertisement, or corporate communication today for evidence of the growing realization of the importance of the Internet. They are almost always accompanied by a Web site address. And while the Internet is currently used to complement the traditional channels in a communications strategy, the day is not far off when use of the Internet alone will create the desired impact on an issue or a strategic communications plan.

While in the early 1990s it was impossible for a public affairs or public relations specialist to get management interest in the Internet, today it is likely that management will be asking for an Internet-based strategy. More importantly, they are likely to be offering a budget. In most instances, the initial introduction of the Internet as a communications and public affairs tool is an added cost. We believe that the Internet will prove to be a cost-effective alternative to traditional channels when used and implemented properly.

Using the Internet to Influence Public Policy

Why incorporate the Internet into a public policy campaign strategy? Because the audience you want to influence—Congress, the media, activists, and the public—is using it on a regular basis to keep informed, to make their own views understood, and to find information—information that might only be provided through an effective Internet policy strategy.

The public at large is also beginning to rely on the Internet for its political information. For example, the Public Affairs Council, a trade group representing public affairs professionals, points to a 1992 survey examining where the public most often obtained information on presidential and congressional elections. The survey found that an overwhelming majority relied on television, with smaller numbers consulting newspapers and the radio. The Internet did not even figure in this survey.

Just four years later, in 1996, more than 10 percent of those surveyed indicated that they used the Internet to get their information on the elections. Substantially fewer were using television and radio, but more were reading newspapers. According to Robert Samuelson of *Newsweek*, four years ago almost 60 percent of all Americans watched TV news to keep up to date. By mid 1998, that number fell to only about one-third of Americans. The evidence is that many of them began using the Internet to get the news and information they wanted.

Politicians responded to these facts. Until 1994, when Senator Edward Kennedy put up the first congressional-member Web site, no legislators and few regulators or officials, at any level of government, used the Internet to inform the public and the media on public-policy developments. By mid-1998, of the nation's 100 senators, 98 had Web sites, and only about 100 of the 435 members of Congress were without their own sites. Virtually all congressional committees have Web sites, and while revised bills are not always available on the Internet the day after a mark-up, they seldom fail to appear within forty-eight hours.

It is not just federal legislators who are actively using the Internet. All fifty states have Web sites in which the executive and legislative branches post information. All fifty public utility commissions have Web sites, too; many of which are very sophisticated. Every major federal cabinet agency; hundreds of federal agencies, including perhaps surprisingly the CIA; and most independent federal regulatory agencies, such as the Federal Communications Commission, do as well. Thousands of towns and town governments have gone online, and by mid-1998, over one hundred national governments had Web sites.

Many of these agencies and governments are beginning to do more than merely post information on their activities. Some are beginning to accept comments on proceedings, others encourage e-mail inquiries or consumer complaints, and still others are allowing citizens to register for activities and even apply for licenses. Most do not respond to e-mails on public policy questions, but many do allow the electronic filing of comments in proceedings.

The media is also among the heaviest users of the Internet. Many of the nation's largest dailies are online, and reporters often access the Web sites of the industries or activists' organizations they cover to gather information, get background for stories, or post questions.

How the Internet Can Help Spell Success in Public Policy Debates

Like any tool used to influence public policy, the Internet is only one of many tools that must be considered in developing political strategies. Aside from the fact that policy makers are using the Internet more aggressively than ever before, there are a number of reasons it simply cannot be left out of policy-influencing strategies.

To achieve success in public policy, getting there first or shaping the way an issue is viewed is key. Historically, issues have gone through a fairly definable set of steps, from issue identification to issue resolution. It often took years for an issue to progress through this cycle, and there were plenty of points in the time line where interested parties could influence outcomes.

In many cases, this is no longer true. One of the important factors in the speeding-up of the issues cycle is the impact of the rapid diffusion of information, made possible in great measure by the Internet. People simply know more about issues today, or can learn more, much more easily, than they did in the recent past. They know about a development surrounding an issue almost as soon as it happens and can get engaged rapidly to influence its development through the use of e-mail and other Internet-based tools.

Policy development in a democracy involves debate. The Internet, unlike earlier modes of information distribution such as television, allows for genuine debate among parties. It encourages new ideas from a wide range of sources and even allows those who do not know each other to exchange views. By using the Internet, those wishing to influence policy can refine ideas, identify potential drawbacks of proposals, and even float trial balloons in a manner never possible before. Ideas and positions on issues can be shaped and refined by the manner in which issues are discussed, debated, and examined on the Internet.

But the successful positioning of an issue requires not just information, but understanding. Traditionally, such understanding has come about through media analysis, press releases, and public speeches. The Internet and its many debate and discussion sites add a new and important dimension to this process, one policy advocates can utilize to advantage in achieving successful political change.

Coalitions of often varied interests and organizations are a key means of advancing issues and ideas. *The Internet is perhaps the greatest single organizing tool ever developed for the creation of coalitions.* Not only can people be kept informed about a new development on an issue; new supporters can often be identified through the Internet. Coalitions are most effective when they take coordinated action as quickly as possible when a policy changes or takes a different direction. The Internet can be an important tool in ensuring that everyone in a coalition has the latest information, has it in more detail than has ever been possible with traditional media, and is able to put together targeted responses on a rapid-fire basis.

Because of its speed, the breadth of the information it transmits, and the fact that opinions and reactions accompany new developments almost simultaneously, the Internet influences and shapes policy more directly than the traditional media in some cases. Often times, issues are first broached on the Internet, in discussion groups or in some chat forum, and then transits to other media forms such as newspapers and television.

The Internet is influencing the manner in which public policy issues develop. Used effectively, it gives those involved in the policy process new ways of effecting the debate on issues and allows for earlier intervention in the issues cycle. It is critical for companies and policy advocates interested in the policy process to have a better understanding of how the Internet is being used today to have an impact on issues.

What Works in Using the Internet with Policy Makers?

Ninety percent of congressional offices surveyed in 1998 used e-mail to communicate with stakeholders, ask questions, and gather information. And government agencies at all levels have access to the Web and have Web sites of their own. It is tempting to think that an effective use of the Internet can be achieved by simply putting together an expensive, colorful Web site touting a company's or an organization's position; developing an e-mail system that would flood congressional or agency offices with electronic missives; and participating in prominent news and discussion groups. But there are rules and protocols for dealing with government when promoting positions and influencing policy debates, and the Internet has not fully insinuated itself into government processes.

When initiating an Internet policy debate, it is not only important to consider how to manage the communications and in what form they should be generated, it also pays to be sensitive to how the legislator or agency views a particular method of communication. For example, faxes sent in large quantities during working hours may well be viewed as in very poor taste by the receiving offices. The message that is intended to be conveyed may get lost amid the anger generated by this approach.

How Companies and Organizations Are Using the Net to Shape Public Policy

The Internet is being used in a variety of ways to influence public policy and shape issues. Each of the methods that follow are in use by many organizations and policy leaders.

E-MAILING CONGRESS

One of the current difficulties in addressing government agencies and officials is that fewer offices have organized formal processes for responding to constituent e-mails. Hill offices do not respond to e-mails from constituents, in part because it is difficult to know where the communication originated. Further, Hill offices still like to use formal approval processes for communications, obtaining the review and sign-off of their member of Congress before letters are sent out.

To make it even more challenging, the different branches of government all have their own way of dealing with these issues. The oft-quoted comment of former Speaker of the House Tip O'Neill still rings true in the electronic world of today, "All politics is local." Further, legislators, government officials, and regulators have information hierarchies that must be respected. A constituent who, in their view, abuses communications techniques, whether it be the Internet, the phone, or the fax in an effort to reach them, can put them off.

Political offices in the executive branch, such as a governor's office or the White House, are often more solicitous and responsive to constituent e-mails than Hill offices, in part because they have a national political focus. Government agencies, especially regulatory agencies, are increasingly willing to take e-mail comments and letters on issues; although because of the volume of responses, they can rarely respond directly to any comments they receive. They often have formal mechanisms for receiving comment on pending regulatory matters.

It is fair to say that there is a hierarchy of communications for outside parties and constituents that governs how politicians and elected officials react. In using an Internet-based strategy, it is well to keep this in mind.

Direct phone calls from constituents who live in the member's state or home district are probably at the top of the list. Next come letters, which tend to command a

EDUCATING STAKEHOLDERS ABOUT AN ISSUE

Because the Internet allows viewers control over how much or how little they want to see on a particular site, it invites exploration and helps ensure that material will be tailored to meet the needs of a vast audience. Education can take many forms, including how to lobby on an issue, what the issues are, who needs to be contacted, what others are saying about an issue, and providing links to other sites with more information. A good example of an educational site, with information both on the issue and on how to lobby it, is the Leadership Conference on Civil Rights (LCCR): **www.lccr.org**. The information on the site is extensive, and background on key "hot" issues is organized so as to be readily identifiable. Once the button related to a key issue is clicked, brief background information is provided, and a set of *Q*s and *A*s that the user can access in more detail is provided.

great deal of attention, and again, when written by constituents from the member's state or home district, tend to have maximum impact. Fax communications still tend to be considered relatively "urgent" and are treated much the same as letters. Far down the list are e-mails.

While this list provides a good rule of thumb, Internet strategies may well vary depending on the issue, the stakeholders involved, and the time-sensitive nature of the issue. If an issue is pending in a congressional committee, it may well be that a mass e-mail campaign to targeted congressional offices makes sense. Mass fax campaigns—focused and based on people who come from the member's state or home district—can also be effective, especially in time-sensitive cases.

The Internet, however, is also developing as a vehicle to enhance the traditional and most effective tools. Today, a live call to a member of Congress can be delivered on almost any issue by use of technology such as phone banks and patch through. While often controversial,

these techniques are widely utilized because the companies that use them believe they are effective. But they are also expensive, sometimes costing a company $30 to $40 per successful live call generated. The Internet is on the verge of offering this same capability for a fraction of the cost and with a more genuine flavor. Integration of a Political Action Committee database, with e-mail and a registration system can result in highly targeted e-mails to very interested supporters. The call to action can also be facilitated through the Internet, with new technology that automatically connects a constituent with his or her congressman or other policy maker for that matter.

What this demonstrates is that sensitivity and careful planning need to guide how an Internet-based campaign is structured. Further, what holds true for the Hill may well be viewed differently in executive branch agencies, especially regulatory agencies that have national responsibilities and formal, rule-driven processes for receiving and considering outside comments

ENCOURAGING INVOLVEMENT IN AN ISSUE OR ORGANIZATION

The Internet is very effective when organizing coalitions, encouraging involvement in an issue, and asking for support. Advocates, policy leaders, and corporations are all using the Internet to attract support and build coalitions. Compared to more traditional organizing efforts such as grass-roots contact programs, cold calls to individuals and groups with a possible interest in an issue, and contact lists developed through painstaking research and surveys, the Internet is an amazingly efficient organizing tool. More importantly, those who respond to a plea on the Internet are self-selected and much more likely to become deeply committed to an issue or cause. This strength, however, is also a weakness because those who use the Internet are only a small sampling of those likely to have an interest in an issue.

The California Alliance for Consumer Protection has organized an extensive Web site at www.consumers.com that solicits supporters, outlines key issues, provides information on key lobbying efforts, and even requests that lobbyists who contact the site contact the group to discuss issues.

Asking for Immediate Involvement Through E-mail, Letters, or Fax

Because of the enormous speed and reach of the Internet, it can often be one of the most efficient means for reaching large numbers of possible supporters in:

- the event of significant action on an issue,
- a major change in course on an issue,
- or an unexpected move by those on the opposite side of an issue.

In these situations, those working to influence an issue or organize opposition or support can often call for support in the form of e-mails, letters, or faxes from activists who use the Net, and increasingly from the general public. Recent implementations of this phenomenon include the Christian Coalition and the Leadership Conference on Civil Rights. Web sites can also be organized so employees or affiliated stakeholders can sign up to get updated e-mails on key issues, complete with hypertext links back to an action site that will take them through the process of sending an e-mail, fax, or letter. Since all information on the Web is digital in nature, it can be reorganized and reformatted easily to be sent in virtually any form that makes the most sense.

ASKING FOR HELP IN RESEARCHING, DEVELOPING, AND REFINING AN ISSUE

The old-style Internet culture in which those on the Net shared with each other, helped out whenever possible, and were very honest and sometimes blunt with each other remains alive. It is still possible to send out an e-mail to one of the many newsgroups on topics such as politics, regulation of an industry, or consumer issues and get back many helpful responses. Many are using the Internet today as a means of floating ideas in an environment that is tough and honest but still enough out of the mainstream to avoid widespread notice of a position or trial balloon.

MONITORING FOR EMERGING ISSUES AND NEW DEVELOPMENTS

Newsgroups, the UseNet, and the many media, academic, and business sites that exist today provide a wealth of information on emerging issues, new developments, and possible issue trends to watch. It is not uncommon to first catch wind of an issue in a newsgroup discussion. It is also not out of the ordinary to find information on a budding issue on a Web site based halfway around the world.

ADVERTISING YOUR VIEWS OR POSITION

Because of the growing popularity of the Internet, it is becoming more important to have a vocal presence on the Web, to let people know where an organization stands on an issue, and to gain information on late-breaking issues of importance. If a Web site is well constructed, many activists are not concerned that the information they are using is coming from a corporate site. Many large corporations, today, devote entire sections of their Web sites to public policy and explaining their position on an issue. These sites are often visited repeatedly by opponents as well as friends because the information is accurate and well organized. A well-run Web site becomes an advertisement in the policy world, saying "I want to talk with you and hear your thoughts."

Uses of the Internet by Companies to Conduct Public Relations

THE INTERNET FOR DELIVERY OF NEWS

Among the earliest users of communication technologies have been reporters. They were among the first to utilize laptop computers to take down and transmit stories. Reporters also were among the first to utilize word-processing terminals for entering their stories.

Today, almost every corporation is utilizing their Internet Web site to display their press releases. Some even have separate "newsrooms" for reporters to visit.

The power of communication technologies, however, is its ability to deliver the right information to the right reporter at the right time. Some of the more common tools that exist to achieve these goals are the broadcast fax list, the e-mail broadcast list, and the various purchased news wire services like PR Newswire and Business Wire.

The newer capabilities, however, adapt the power of delivery push technology with database development. The Internet can automate and focus the media-release function of any public relations department, with significant effect.

Bell Atlantic, for example, lets a reporter sign in, provide a profile of the geographic and subject issues he or she is interested in, and then receive only those releases of specific interest. Over fourteen hundred people have registered at that site, over four hundred of them reporters.

An automated Internet press system also allows press releases to be sent in html format. This means the release looks to the reporter in full living color just like the press release as it is printed. But since this is the Internet, the release can be hyperlinked to other information, including pictures, that reporters can simply click on and drag into the stories they are preparing.

INVESTOR RELATIONS

It isn't just the media-relations departments that are using the Internet. Investor relations increasingly are sponsoring high-end, sophisticated Web sites targeted at the analyst and shareholder communities, particularly institutional shareholders.

These companies are using the Internet to publish their annual reports, to provide answers to the most "frequently asked questions," and to automate the delivery of routine financial releases.

A number of Internet tools exist that facilitate the delivery of financial information. For example, a company's real-time or near-real-time stock price can be offered on the site, and others can be permitted to link to that information. Similarly, links to regulatory agencies such as the Security Exchange Commission are possible (required filings, such as 10-Ks). Bottom line, corporations want their own Web sites to be the first place people, especially analysts, go on the Internet to get information about their companies.

BRAND AND REPUTATION MANAGEMENT

Increasingly, companies and organizations are using the Internet to promote their brand and reputation and to enhance their general advertising. Most national advertisements today include an Internet address within the advertisement. The Internet sites then become an integral part of the overall positioning, marketing, and brand-management strategy. They offer the opportunity to enhance the message and cost-effectively provide extensive additional information not previously possible within the constraints of purchased media.

Companies are also finding new and different ways to utilize the Internet to expand their reputation and to partner with key allies. Most corporations today have foundations that provide grant money as part of their corporate responsibility function and their reputation management. The foundations are increasingly utilizing the Internet as a place to provide access to their giving record.

In other instances, some corporations are finding it helpful to partner with national organizations with which they wish to foster stronger relationships. Bell Atlantic provides a good case history in this regard. A new priority for the corporation was to emphasize its diversity program and to increase public awareness of its commitment to diversity. It was approached by the Leadership Conference on Civil Rights, a coalition of the nation's leading civil rights organizations, to support their Web site. Instead of a cash grant, Bell Atlantic worked through a third-party vendor to donate the entire Web site development and hosting capabilities. It coordinated this work with a senior relationship manager who coordinated the Bell Atlantic commitment with LCCR's overall objectives, which included working with the White House on its efforts against hate crimes.

The result was a win-win-win solution. LCCR created, with Bell Atlantic support, a Web site devoted to information on how to combat hate crimes. The Bell Atlantic logo was exclusively carried on the site for one year. The White House endorsed the site and a major news conference on the launch of the site included the participation of the Secretary of Transportation, a letter from the President, and the CEO of Bell Atlantic. Subsequently, this initiative, along with several others in this area, has resulted in Bell Atlantic being listed as among the nation's leading corporations in fostering diversity.

The Internet can also help in crisis management. Many companies today are beginning to understand how a Web site can provide detailed information to hundreds of thousands of people with relatively little advance work. When compared to a press conference or even national advertising, the Internet can be very cost-effective.

Using the Internet for Employee Communications

As explained in Chapter 10, "Using Intranets and Extranets to Gain Advantage," Internet technology can be linked to internal databases to enable companies to effectively communicate with their employees in a way that is convenient, easy to use, and easy to maintain.

During the Bell Atlantic/NYNEX merger, the two companies spent a great deal of time putting together a joint merger site that company employees could consult on a daily basis for updates, new information, and corporate positions on issues. The company realized that its own employees were among the best ambassadors it had when it came to spreading the word about the merger's benefits and importance.

Regular features of the employee merger Web site included updates on government activities, organization charts, announcements, FAQs, and responses to late-breaking developments. Employees in both companies would know within a few hours how the company felt about a decision by a regulatory agency, and they could be prepared to respond to questions from neighbors or policy leaders.

The site also included copies of crucial letters or public documents relating to the merger, quotes from key organizations supporting the merger that employees could use to buttress contacts with others, and informative media clips.

Emerging Strategies

The Internet is revolutionizing the speed, access, and depth of information when communicating ideas. Further, the cost of using the Internet for communications purposes when compared to alternative strategies can be very effective. Although today, the Internet is still largely an "adjunct" to other media, including traditional radio, television, print advertising, and marketing services, it will inevitably emerge as an effective channel in its own right.

But as use of the Internet expands and it becomes an even more cluttered and complex place, it will be harder and harder for users to find material. It also becomes more difficult to make sure that information gets to the individuals it needs to reach. There are a number of emerging strategies that can help ensure that a message gets to its intended audience.

- *Immediately begin to collect e-mail addresses.* There is perhaps no more important goal than to have a qualified list of e-mail addresses to reach a preferred group. If the desire is media related—to communicate with reporters—then correct e-mail addresses are essential. If a corporation wants its shareholders to react to a public policy that could hurt its stock price, it needs e-mail addresses to reach them immediately. If a membership organization wants to reach its members, it needs e-mail addresses, too. How to begin? Start by collecting the e-mail addresses as an integral part of any database that a organization maintains. Conduct an audit and ensure that an e-mail section exists. Addresses can then be exported into various Internet tools, and messages targeted based on the record. Interestingly, many state and local governments have understood the importance of this process and have begun to request e-mail addresses on tax forms!

- *Internal considerations.* It is critical that the various departments in an organization develop an expertise in the Internet, both technically and strategically. The Internet works best when both the content and the technology are fully understood. Too often, corporations and large organizations designate the MIS department to manage and run the Web sites, and the various substantive departments (Public Relations, Public Affairs, and Marketing) are brought in as advisors. In television, the phrase "the medium is the message" might have been true. In the Internet, the medium and the message are one. The best Web strategies develop when the department responsible has the ability to understand the technical capabilities and how they can be applied to the objectives and messages to be achieved.

- *While there are obvious needs to ensure organizational integrity, this can be accomplished by standards.* Organizations that try to centralize and standardize the Internet and the Web will probably not succeed. The intent requires flexibility, speed, and, most importantly, creativity. Organizations should reward innovation in applications and uses and minimize directives and inflexible rules.

- *Monitor the Net.* Whether the goal is crisis management, public relations, or public affairs, it is going to be increasingly important to know what is happening on the Internet. While there are a number of automated monitoring services that utilize key word searching, that technique will not yield the highest and best information. If a company wants to know what is being said about it, its products, or its issues and by whom, sophisticated search techniques are required, as well as an understanding of the issues and fields or disciplines within which a company is operating. Depending on the organization's visibility and needs, consideration should be given to incorporating such a process inside the company or contracting out for such capability.
- *Become the "site of record."* Bottom line for an organization or an association, is to become the place of record on the Internet. If an organization doesn't, someone else will. Thus, a comprehensive information site about a group or company and its products and services is essential. It needs to be adequately indexed on the major search engines, and it needs to be kept up-to-date.
- *Lead with strategy, not technology.* The business purpose for using the Internet is often lost in the fascination with glitzy graphics, sound, and video information, as well as the vast amounts of information available through the Internet. A company needs to make sure the ideas it wants to communicate are always clearly presented.

#### EIGHT

E-commerce and Merchandising

Elaine Rubin, President, ekrubin inc., and Director, iBaby.com, and Lauren Freedman, President, the e-tailing group
Both Elaine Rubin and Lauren Freedman are nationally recognized experts in e-commerce.

There was a time when it seemed like the worst sort of hyperbole was to say that the Internet would revolutionize the world of retailing. Not anymore.

Selling products and services through the Internet is altering forever the way business is conducted in the retail marketplace. The immediacy and reach of the online medium is changing the very physics of buying and selling, making moot the rules of the retail game just as fundamentally as eliminating gravity would change the game of baseball.

Consider the following:

- Manufacturers are creating relationships directly with customers.
- Customers are buying from and communicating directly with manufacturers.
- Publishers are becoming direct marketers.
- Creative companies are finding new, intermediate roles between buyers and sellers through the use of interactive technology.

Virtual retailers have turned up the pressure on traditional merchants and existing brands, heating up the e-commerce landscape in a way that no one would have predicted even a year ago. And traditional retailers, who never entertained the possibility of selling directly to consumers anywhere but in their stores, are finding the allure of e-commerce irresistible, though their progress is noticeably slower than that of direct marketers.

Entering the fourth quarter of 1998, the Internet had more than 2 million Web sites, with an estimated 10,000 transactional sites, both business-to-consumer and business-to-business. The sites ranged from mom-and-pop businesses, to the new breed of virtual brands, to established brands and traditional retailers.

The online retailing dynamic is evolving every day, with the virtual best of breed battling it out with traditional players who are now coming to virtual space. These will be some of the most interesting contests as the e-tail space evolves.

Our goal in this chapter is to explore the current state of merchandising online, to offer a perspective on the past, and to provide a road map for the future. This chapter will provide the information, tips, advice, and firsthand experiences to help guide a successful e-tailing effort. We call companies that sell online e-tailers, short for "electronic retailers."

E-tailing Is Exploding

Before talking about the keys to e-tailing success, it's worth documenting the size and scope of the online marketplace. In 1997, online holiday sales outpaced most merchant expectations, doubling over the prior year with sales reported of $2.5 billion (source: Forrester Research). More importantly, Forrester estimates that nearly 30 percent of the 35–40 million online users (about 12 million users) had shopped online by the end of 1997.

Projections for 1998 estimated consumer Internet sales in the range of $5–10 billion. Forrester also estimated that U.S. businesses would exchange an estimated $17 billion in goods and services on the Internet. While the growth rate is enormous, e-commerce is still in its infancy. E-commerce represents a microscopic share of the $2 trillion U.S. retail economy.

At the time of this writing, only 20 percent of the Top 180 specialty and general merchandise retailers and 54 percent of the top revenue-producing catalogers were selling over the Internet. Nonetheless, there has been a shift in the mindset of established brands that somehow transcends the numbers. E-commerce is real. People who want to shop online will continue to do so, and in even greater numbers as the Nintendo generation comes of age. Consumers are coming onto the Internet and looking for their favorite brands. If they don't find them, there's the chance they will find a new brand for their loyalty.

For the retailer or manufacturer, an online presence has become essential. The Internet provides the ultimate way to get in touch with customers, to conduct market research, and to establish loyal relationships with individuals. For the consumer, it has introduced a new way to shop; a global selection of product and brands; a convenient, simplified shopping process; cost savings, time savings, and availability twenty-four hours per day. The online store is never closed.

Defining the Art of E-tailing

E-tailing is the art of blending traditional retail methodology with online techniques and technologies to sell electronically, directly through the computer. E-tailing over the Internet is a discipline with less than four years of history. E-tailing pioneers have been experimenting with selling online since 1985, but the practice really only began to gain traction with the general public's acceptance of the World Wide Web in 1995.

In the traditional environment of brick-and-mortar retailing, merchandising is the art of displaying goods for sale. Successful merchants know how to create an image through merchandising and visual display, thereby enticing consumers to purchase. Their image or brand delivers a promise to the customer, and they spend countless years and resources upholding and enhancing their brand.

Successful e-tailing requires a set of competencies that includes those of traditional retailing, direct marketing, and interactive technology. Take the aspects of a traditional retailing business—sourcing of goods, inventory, warehousing, real estate, store design, merchandising, and advertising—combine them with those of the traditional catalog business—sourcing of goods, inventory, warehousing; pick and packing; shipping, customer service, telephone, and mail operations, producing a catalog, and merchandising on paper—then add the interactive technology component—site design, hosting, database and other software, online merchandising, marketing of the site, customer acquisition, customer-retention programs, online and phone customer service, online ordering, and privacy and security policies—and you have a recipe for success in an e-tailing operation.

What should be obvious by now is that e-tailing is considerably more complex than traditional merchandising. But the payoff—in increased sales that result from reaching new markets, and increased profits that result from realized efficiencies—are well worth the learning that must be undertaken by most companies.

Online merchandising is defined by the site's look and feel; its functionality, including site performance and customer shopping options; and the total customer experience from a visual, functional, and performance point of view. Online merchandising involves the following:

- Product presentation
- Site navigation—how the user gets around the site
- Online ordering—shopping cart to checkout
- Functional use of technology—search, personalization features
- Customer Service—on phone, online
- The Backend—order processing through shipping
- Programs fostering Customer Loyalty and Retention

The primary focus of online merchandising during the early days of e-commerce has been confined to the technological aspects of front-end design, the part of the Web site that the user experiences, and the integration of the backend, which is how the results of that user interaction—the order—are handled to execute the fulfillment of the product. However, as online merchants become more sophisticated in the setup of their operations, the entire online merchandising process will become the true differentiation—just as it is in the traditional world of retailing.

Becoming an E-tailer

While the world of e-commerce and all its complexities is exciting for those who thrive on challenge and change, companies who are only now considering an e-commerce initiative may have understandable doubts and questions. Whether a company is aggressively pursuing a category leadership role in the e-commerce arena or simply interested in establishing a small presence to test the waters, the same basic marketing questions must be addressed:

- What is the right strategy to employ?
- What is the size of the investment required?
- What additional resources are necessary?
- How many employees must be dedicated to the effort?
- What is the best way to utilize the existing infrastructure?

Defining Objectives

There is no substitute for developing a strategy and business plan for a potential e-tailing venture. As with any business start-up, understanding the current competitive landscape online and offline will be essential in defining objectives. It is critical for merchants to understand the upside and the risk associated with e-commerce. Most individuals and companies need to justify their online efforts and investments, particularly when senior management must be convinced of the efficacy of the initiative.

There are many reasons to become an e-tailer, but the decision to participate requires a level of introspection and a firm understanding of reality regarding reasonable goals and objectives. The following objectives should be thoroughly explored to understand how they fit into an overall business strategy, including how they might cannibalize or grow a company's current customer base:

- Revenue generation
- Brand building
- Customer acquisition
- Customer retention/loyalty
- Preempting competition
- Cost savings
- Global marketing

Defining the Company's Digital Advantage

When developing an e-tailing strategy, the most important questions to answer are: What is the digital advantage? What makes an online destination or product better than what exists in the real world today? What makes one site better than all the other related sites in a business?

Once a digital advantage—or the advantage that will be an attainable goal—has been determined, an online strategy can be developed. Based on defined objectives, the strategy must first focus on the customer. Studies have shown there are several motivating factors for a customer to shop online. These factors can be used as a reference in determining a strategy and digital advantage.

- Convenience—including 24-hour access, direct delivery, and automatic replenishments
- Detailed information—more than is available in a store
- Cost savings—often attained through auctions, name-your-own-price selling, and last-minute purchase and fulfillment programs
- Entertainment value—providing a fun way to shop
- Selection—no display or inventory constraints
- Unique—hard-to-find items
- Personalization—custom fit, custom made for an individual

Learning from Experience

While the world of e-commerce and e-tailing is in its infancy, there are many merchants and early online-marketing pioneers who have been experimenting and learning how to sell online for years. Their experiences can provide valuable lessons for today's e-tailers.

THE EARLY DAYS

In February 1985, CompuServe launched its electronic mall. More than sixty merchants participated, including American Express, Bloomingdales, BMG, Waldenbooks, and Tiffany's. CompuServe's proprietary network—less than 1.5 million at the time—was the universe of shoppers. Not surprisingly, most of the participating companies viewed it as a marketing experiment. No internal investment in technology, operational infrastructure, or staff was necessary. Most of the participants offered only catalog requests, with only a few selling goods directly to the customer.

Within a few years, dozens of merchants and major companies were intrigued with the electronic-retailing channel. They participated in a variety of new technology ventures, all of which promised to provide the answer for electronic shopping, as it was often called. There were interactive television trials, proprietary online services, CD-ROM catalogs, and hybrid CD-ROM/online systems (in which the products were displayed from a CD but the order occurred via modem through an online service).

However, it didn't take long for many of these early marketers to dismiss the online marketplace. Most merchants turned away from these trials because of the small audience size. Another problem was the narrow demographics of the online user; simply stated, most were men in their late 30s and early 40s. Finally, there were significant limitations with the technology, such as slow modems, poor, if any, graphics, and clumsy software. So, while there was valuable learning obtained from these trials, most merchants were turned off by the limited results and the difficulty of figuring out how to market online.

DIRECT MARKETERS TOOK THE LEAD—REPURPOSING YOUR CATALOG

The first e-tailers to taste success were the direct marketers who put their catalogs online. It was a fairly simple conversion for catalogers to develop online sites, using their existing images, copy, and creative people. Many direct marketers assumed selling online would be a duplicate of their current direct-to-customer business approach. Unfortunately, they were wrong. They learned that repurposing catalog assets does not necessarily deliver value to the customer.

Today, almost all catalogers have redesigned their sites to take advantage of the medium, for instance, by providing sophisticated searching of their inventory or automatic reminders to reorder consumable products. They are also adapting their product mix and merchandising strategy to the new breed of online shoppers. Merchants who have succeeded online are those who continually reinvent and reapply their traditional business experience with new ideas and new approaches to deliver real value to online shoppers.

THE ONLINE MALL

As recently as a few years ago, many electronic shopping pioneers promoted online malls as the answer to successful e-tailing. The online malls seemed like a logical approach to many, leveraging the real-world phenomenon. Aggregating storefronts in one Web location made a lot of sense to both the mall operator and the merchant. Several computer, cable, and telecom giants spent millions of dollars developing the online mall concept.

But very little, if any, value was delivered to the consumer, and nearly all of the malls failed early on in their development. Why? The reasons are similar to those that caused the failure of the initial online catalog ventures. Online mall shopping was simply not the same as traditional mall shopping. Traditional malls succeed, in part, by overcoming distance—having dozens of stores in close proximity is convenient and creates an experience. But since there is no distance to overcome online, all stores—whether part of the mall or not—are just a mouse-click away.

Online shoppers have demonstrated themselves to be destination shoppers. They know what they want and where to get it. They are seeking out brands or sites that offer a value proposition. This value might include search functionality, which appeals strongly to today's directed shopper, or a wish list and registry service, where customer preferences can be stored and remembered for each subsequent visit to the site.

PROS	CONS
Anchor tenants help create traffic draw	Revenue share % may be high, as are up-front participation arrangements, particularly on heavily trafficked sites
Initial investment covers "common area maintenance" costs, including consumer advertising for mall	Difficult to establish unique point of view and maintain this through the mall's own marketing and merchandising efforts

PROS	CONS
Way to "test" the online waters before plunging in	Not enough emphasis on individual stores to drive significant business for all individual tenants
Up-front technology costs lower and shared by "tenants," allowing participating merchants to benefit from the "latest and greatest"	Most cybermalls do not have the infrastructure in place to offer timely service to merchants on a critical-needs basis
Ability to leapfrog on strong promotional campaigns	Lack of flexibility, with individual merchants unable to do their own thing when they need to spark sales
Ideal testing ground for learning more about online shoppers, how to best handle customer-service issues, and the day-to-day running of an online store	Limited control of graphic and interface design issues, and difficult for most participants to establish or maintain a distinctive online identity

LESSONS LEARNED FROM ONLINE MALL VENTURES

Look to the Leaders

It is always useful to look to the leaders in an industry to help develop your own online e-commerce strategy. We are offering a look at these businesses in many different ways, including the number of products and number of employees working to implement the specific strategy. Simultaneously, given the importance of traffic and distribution online, we felt it was important to know who a company's existing partners are. Additionally, we considered what merchandising features they employed that distinguished their company from others in the pack.

Keep in mind, we have selected the leaders in the industry. There are different levels of commitment to selling online. Not everyone can or wants to commit the resources and focus that these leading e-tailing companies have, but their experiences lend perspective for evolving your own online strategy.

1-800-Flowers—$32 Million in Online Sales in 1998

Name of person surveyed	Donna Iucolano
Title	Director, Interactive Services
Date company established	1990
Date e-commerce began	1992
# interactive employees Day 1–today	½ in 1992, 25 in 1998
Online advertising budget	Total Budget $30 million-plus for 3 areas—stores, telephone, & online
# major redesigns	1 major/ year, 2–3 minor/ year
# products	Approx. 200–250 live products at any given time, or 2,000+ skus per year
Online revenue	Estimated at $50 million in 1998
Current partners	AOL, Fry Multimedia, Excite, Kirshenbaum Bond & Partners, Microsoft Corporation, Microsoft Network, Order Trust, Switchboard
Merchandising elements	Featured products on home page, best sellers, merchandising within an editorial context via "how-to" areas, contests, gift reminder service, add-on messages to order confirmations, e-mail marketing, & newsletters
# affiliate programs	50 in August 1998 and plans to grow to 500+ by February 1999.
Biggest mistake	Believing the first salesperson who told me his software was an "in the box solution!" My experience has been—there is no such thing—it always takes longer and it always costs more!
Biggest payoff	Investing in people! Growing our team has enabled us to have greater control over our own destiny and develop a world-class team of Interactive/ online sales, marketing, merchandising and operations professionals! Also—Integration! By leveraging the operational and marketing infra-structure to support all of our customers regardless of how they purchase—in store, over the phone, or on-line—we have been able to offer them the highest level of service and offer them the ability to cross-channels at their convenience.

Eddie Bauer

Name of person surveyed	Judy Neuman
Title	Divisional Vice President, Interactive Media
Date company established	1920
Date e-commerce began	10/94
# interactive employees Day 1–today	2
Online advertising budget	None from 1994–1997, under $250,00 in 1997, under $1 million in 1998
# major redesigns	3 major redesigns with 2 major enhancements per year
# products	Started with 50 on AOL, 200 in 1996, 1500+ in 1997
Online revenue	$10-20 million in 1997
Portal partners	AOL, Microsoft Plaza & Site Server e-commerce Team, Side Walk
Merchandising elements	Commerce-driven software, gift finder, extensive search functionality, thumbnails, upsell & cross-sell, iDream Home, EB Exclusives, wishlist
# affiliate programs	
Biggest mistake	Thinking that anything having to do with technology will meet its deliverable date. "If you say 7/15 it will be 9/1." Not enough expertise to know milestones
Biggest payoff	Growing staff from 1997 levels and utilizing core competencies for marketing and merchandising.

Cyberian Outpost

Name of person surveyed	Larry Berk
Title	Vice President, Marketing
Date company established	May 1995
Date e-commerce began	May 1995
# interactive employees Day 1–today	1–120
Online advertising budget	$5 million-plus internal site advertising available which is significant revenue streams; started 3 months post start date
# of major redesigns	3; average per year =0; Larry says none; business is evolutionary not revolutionary
Current partners	AOL, Lycos, Bertelsmann; StarMedia; CNNet; Infospace; Excite and Webcrawler; have paid money; metacrawler and The Globe; Goto Net
Merchandising elements	Contests, Special Purchases; deals, overall pricing, Rebates, Newsletter, Using Broadvision going forward
# affiliate programs	20,000+ inbound links growing exponentially
Revenues	25 million; 1997
Biggest mistake	Challenge; understanding relationship between true technology and selling product; pair of handcuffs and attached to CTO ; ways for marketing and technology to work together for better or for worse
Portal partners	AOL
Biggest payoff	IPO; August 1998

The New E-tailing Models

Learning from the pioneers of online retailing, and from firsthand experiences, merchants have become more experienced with online selling. The old models of retailing online have evolved and given way to several new e-tailing business models. While no clear winning strategy has emerged, there are several approaches that are worth evaluating to determine the right e-commerce model for a online business.

THE SPECIALIZED MALL

While online malls have had their troubles for a number of reasons, new types of malls are emerging. The specialized or targeted mall caters to a specific audience or demographic. An example would be an antique mall, in which a collection of Web stores offer antiques for sale. This plays to the strength of the Internet, taking advantage of co-locating content, sites, and stores that appeal to a targeted audience or demographic.

PORTALS

One of the biggest trends in 1998 was the creation of portal sites, which is a spin on the mall approach. A portal site is not really a new concept. It is typically a site acting as an online entry point for a large group of people; aggregating content, information, commerce, community sites, and traffic under one roof. A portal site is usually the first Web page consumers see when opening their Web browser. It can be a destination site, as in the case of search and directory companies.

PORTAL-BASED SHOPPING

Pros

- Credibility through adjacencies with other brands and stores
- Consumers offered selection and choice of stores to shop in
- Access to a large number of potential customers through the aggregation strategy
- Traffic generated from other stores' visitors

Cons

- Initial presentation of brand and design limited to the template and design of the portal
- Limited control over promotions and merchandising techniques
- Lack of control over the technical performance of the portal Web site

AOL.com and Yahoo are two leading portal sites. Ironically, many of today's portal strategies were influenced by the lessons learned from the mall and catalog attempts of the early and mid-90s. The portal phenomenon affects all Web-based businesses, not just e-commerce sites. For the purposes of our e-tailing focus, we will address the commerce and merchandising aspects of the portal mall.

The Portal Mall

Portals are jumping on the e-commerce bandwagon in a major way. All the portals are attempting to be the leader in the Internet space, and e-commerce seems to be the direction in which many of the portals are spending resources. Each portal has created a shopping area or mall where they aggregate links to stores. A competitive fight for prime real estate on the main portal pages developed what people in the industry called "the land grab or distribution wars." Virtual retailers and major brands paid several million dollars to have an anchor position on the portal home page and shopping areas. Additionally, many portals have invested in comparison-shopping and personalization software so consumers have a better online shopping experience when they shop at the portal sites. Additionally, many portals have acquired e-commerce software solutions to assist those companies that want to sell online but do not have the capability to do so. The portal sites want to become the conduit for companies to reach online consumers. Here's a look at the pros and cons of participating in a portal mall.

COMMUNITY-BASED SHOPPING

The Internet is known for allowing groups of like-minded people across the world to congregate at a single site and share ideas, conversation, and advice. As we discussed in Chapter 4, "Virtual Communities," these communities have become a powerful force representing the needs and concerns of consumers. So, while online merchandising is a fairly new approach, selling within a community allows for targeted marketing and selling to occur. The theory is that greater sales can be realized from product offers made on a community site; because the offer is better targeted, the consumer has a greater interest and a higher propensity to purchase.

COMMUNITY-BASED SHOPPING

Pros

- Capitalize on the traffic from the community site
- Ability to target products and offers to a prequalified audience
- Allow the shopping experience to be augmented with community features such as chat and bulletin boards
- Community members accustomed to sharing thoughts and ideas (product and store testimonials and loyalties shared will help promote sales).

Cons

- Community members may not be interested in shopping. They come to the site for interaction with other members and information and resources.
- Potential customer base limited to amount of traffic community site provides

DESTINATION SHOPPING SITES

Most merchants and major brands have realized that the Internet is an important way to communicate with customers and therefore have developed their own destination shopping sites.

A destination site is a stand-alone store, where the merchant has his own independent storefront, URL, and e-commerce platform (software). This merchandising model delivers great advantages of control but, conversely, requires the greatest commitment of resources. Building a unique identity, supporting a brand, and developing core electronic retailing competencies are the main reasons that marketers are building their own retailing initiatives.

CONTEXTUAL SELLING

Contextual selling is not a new concept. In the world of publishing, contextual selling is called editorial adjacencies. In the world of e-commerce, it is the most targeted way to merchandise. Fundamentally, being able to place targeted goods and services within the context of a site's editorial material is very powerful. If a poker player is on a poker player's site looking for tips, the likelihood that he or she would be interested in a new card shuffler would be high. Through contextual selling, the merchant is able to pinpoint appropriate products based on the content and audience.

Contextual selling is already happening online. C/net, a site for computer and technology news, has software.net and download.com

DESTINATION SHOPPING

Pros

- Absolute control over the presentation of a brand, and how to merchandise products on a site
- Overall site reliability and site performance in the company's control
- Ability to distinguish a store with proprietary features, functionality, and technology
- Complete control over the order process and customer service
- Ability to maintain individuality and uniqueness

Cons

- Management of all aspects of an e-commerce business such as hardware, software solutions, systems integration, hosting, reporting and tracking, site performance, operational procedures
- Need to have substantial resources to develop and implement a marketing and distribution plan to bring traffic to a site

built into its site. Parent Soup, an online community for parents, has iBaby.com, an online store for baby products, offered within their expecting and new-parent areas. We anticipate seeing many new and innovative variations of this concept proliferate in the next few years.

Evolving Trends in E-Commerce

As merchants gain more experience in selling directly to online consumers, and as new technologies and operational efficiencies are introduced, e-commerce will continue to evolve. The latest trends in e-tailing all focus on reaching out to the customer, making it easier to find a merchant's store and products online, and ultimately, enabling a quick and convenient transaction.

A lot of resources and a good deal of focus have been placed on how to drive traffic to a site and how to buy key real estate online. Several leading online commerce sites have spent millions of dollars on distribution deals with the key portal and community sites. However, the majority of companies online cannot afford or justify this type of marketing expense. As discussed in Chapter 5, "Internet Advertising," banner ads and media buys online are one way to drive traffic. Affiliate programs, whether they be private or through a network, provide all online marketers the opportunity to reach out and attract a larger number of potential customers. Affiliate marketing allows a retailer to reach a larger audience, get greater exposure, and generate a new revenue stream for his or her company.

AFFILIATE PROGRAMS

Today, more than ever, many e-tailers are looking outward to affiliate programs through which partners help drive total revenues. It is estimated that Amazon.com in fact derives 11 percent of its revenues from such a program and has over one hundred thousand affiliate sites linking to its site and selling its products. Affiliate programs cross over many categories and include such companies as eToys, CDNow, BarnesandNoble.com, AutoWeb, and Preview Travel, among a host of others.

Most of these companies have a revenue share in common with participating merchants, some level of co-branding on partner sites, and a sharing of functionality and features that is accomplished through linking scenarios. We see a trend toward affiliate programs when companies are trying to develop well-merchandised initiatives that encourage partners to better integrate their content offering with a merchant's product to maximize sales results. This might include a series of seasonal promotions, or even templates for market segmentation to multiple customer bases, as well as brand boutiques for shopping variety.

AFFILIATE NETWORKS

While several merchants have opted to build their brand and market share through establishing their own affiliate programs, there has been an emerging trend toward affiliate networks that already have a number of relationships with content sites. In this scenario, the merchant does not have to manage any individual partnerships. The network typically has built the software, manages the technology, supplies access, tracks and reports customers and transactions, and introduces and develops network relationships with as many content and community sites as possible. The power of the affiliated network is in its members, on both the merchant and site-owner sides of the business. By joining the network, the merchant is instantly introduced and affiliated with hundreds, if not thousands, of participating sites. The site owners and merchants communicate via an internal network that allows them to accept or reject product offers and place them on their site for their members to transact. The merchant gains distribution for their merchandise, and the site owner takes a commission on the transaction, providing the site owner with a new revenue stream.

AFFILIATE PROGRAMS	CATEGORIES	# MERCHANTS	BUSINESS MODEL
Amazon.com	Books	40,000	15% of sales for featured items. 5% on all other referred sales. Amazon only pays for the first referral; if any products are added to a customer's shopping cart after the customer has entered the Amazon site, it does not pay a fee.
CDNow	CDs	20,000+	7% on sales under $500, up to 15% for sales over $17,000.
N2K	CDs	500+	5% royalty off any purchase made by referred customers at the end of their Music Blvd. session
BarnesandNoble.com	Books	1000+	5% to start. 6% after $20,000 in sales. 6% after $1 million in sales.
Reel	Movies	300+	5% on all sales generated from visit. Negotiate for high-traffic sites.
Artuframe.com	Art prints and framing services	N/A	6% on each purchase. If you refer another affiliate, you receive 2% of that affiliate's billings for the first 90 days.
AutoWeb	Autos		Pay $2–5 on a per-request basis. For each vehicle ad placed they pay $5–10. Other opportunities with accessories and related products.

Buying real estate, gaining distribution, and building brand awareness online is a business for which most retailers have little experience. Merchants typically know a lot about merchandising, marketing their products and brands, buying real estate, and managing stores, but are unfamiliar or unprepared to build a business-development staff to manage all the disparate affiliations necessary to create a presence online. For these e-tailers, the affiliate network is a powerful business tool. The Linkshare Network, **www.linkshare.net** is the leading network that offers its services to merchants and content sites alike.

COMPARISON SHOPPING

Comparison shopping sites are a trend to watch as database technology and customer access to information improves. We have already seen the introduction of comparison-shopping search engines that deliver great value to those customers who are in the market for a particular product. For the customer who has decided on the specific product or brand to buy, online comparison shopping will provide an invaluable service that no retailer or cataloger in the real world can match.

STORES ON WHEELS

The concept of bringing the product or store to the customer instead of the customer going to the store is a brilliant application of the online world. One of the major problems with shopping on the Web today is the vast number of sites available, which makes it difficult to quickly find the product or store of choice. The stores-on-wheels concept addresses this issue by allowing a merchant to place a specific product or storefront within a banner ad or link on any Web site. This allows the merchant to target specific sites and customers.

The transactional banner allows the user to purchase directly within the link, without ever having to leave the Web site of their choice. From a customer point of view, there is no interruption to their online surfing experience, because they are presented with an offer on the page they are visiting. This allows them to place an order and seamlessly return to where they were originally visiting.

New software and new capabilities continually are being introduced in the marketplace. One example of an innovative new service is the Impulse Buy Network, a combination of television home-shopping, broadcasting, direct-marketing, cross-sell, and up-sell techniques. Impulse Buy Network has made arrangements with highly trafficked sites to place products directly on their sites and sell direct to the consumer. The merchant provides the product, and the network automatically distributes it to a multitude of sites, pre-sumably increasing sales and sharing in the sales commission.

Don't Forget You Have a Store

Once an online presence has been established, a strategy deter-mined, and a site or product message distributed, it's time to mer-chandise the site on a daily basis. Having an online store is like having a store in the real world. The store must be opened for busi-ness every day. Someone needs to greet the customers as they come in, and the window display and store merchandise must be current and constantly rotated. Ultimately, the most successful e-commerce sites will be the ones that have mastered online merchandising . . . the art of selling products online.

We couldn't have an online merchandising chapter without addressing the "merchandising" angle of retailing online. What fol-lows is a discussion of online components and programs that have proved successful in the online world.

Key Merchandising Components

The enhanced capabilities of the online world will allow savvy mer-chants to experiment and discover the next big customer applica-tion to retain customers. The online store gives a merchant more flexibility and greater customer-communication tools than those available offline. It provides a great opportunity to get to know cus-tomers, make relationships, and begin to build loyalty. Offline retailing has typically been limited to Frequent Flyer and Rewards programs. These incredibly successful customer acquisition and retention programs are currently conducted via snail mail and tele-phone communications. There is a big opportunity here for the online world, in terms of how these programs are marketed and dis-tributed. In the online world, loyalty programs are beginning to take on many different shapes and sizes.

LOYALTY PLAYS A BIG PART

There are many ways that merchants try to create loyalty among shoppers. These truly change the merchandising dynamic of any site and are becoming a more important aspect of the site. Building loyalty can be accomplished in many ways; through e-mail marketing programs, personalized services, and points programs. The following are some examples of this strategy.

My Account

The concept of belonging and being a part of a bigger community from a commerce perspective has become a significant advantage for a number of merchants online. Some of the best examples of such an implementation can be found on CDW, where shoppers can create a My E-Account. EToys is another company that has leveraged such a program to its advantage.

At Music Boulevard they recently launched a program called My Music Boulevard and it allows the customer to submit his or her likes and dislikes. It also gives permission to communicate with them about the subjects customers might be interested in.

Frequent-Buyer Programs

The use of frequent-buyer programs is becoming more prevalent as merchants bring the best of the real world online. Companies like The Vitamin Shoppe, which has had a frequent-buyer program since the mid-1990s has found such techniques valuable in the e-tailing world as well. Companies like Netcentives and Emaginet are also introducing loyalty-based point programs.

Gift Reminder Services

1-800-Flowers and Godiva Chocolatier were among the first to make gift reminder services an industry standard in the gift-giving world. With these programs, users sign up to be reminded of key events and occasions in their lives. All communication comes electronically. It is believed that these sites find that shoppers have a three-times greater propensity to purchase when they have enrolled in such programs.

Address Books

One of the smartest strategies employed has been the use of an address book in which shoppers can store the names of friends and family. Upon completion, shoppers are more likely to return to this destination to expedite their shopping experience. L.L. Bean was one of the first to employ this strategy and many others have followed suit, including Toys Я Us.

Seasonal Shopping

The effectiveness of themed seasonal shopping should not be underestimated. Whether looking at Back to School Boutiques found on Disney; or at products available through iQVC separated by school segments; or at Holiday Hot Lists, which enable shoppers to move quickly to make a purchase during a harried shopping period, these are valuable techniques for generating sales.

Customer Service As a Merchandising Tool

One of the least talked about forms of merchandising is customer service as a merchandising tool. Communication has become crucial in serving electronic customers. Every communication with the customer is an opportunity to build a relationship. But care needs to be taken. The online customer has different expectations from online shopping than at a physical store. The customer feels a sense of immediacy when ordering online, and they expect a certain level of service, such as electronic confirmations and improved ways to communicate electronically.

ONLINE CUSTOMER SERVICE

New software is currently being introduced that allows companies to offer live customer help. Many online users have expressed the desire for live help, someone to answer a question at the time of purchase, or someone to help them navigate through the site. Either way, the comfort of knowing someone is there to help will improve the online user's confidence and their spending habits. Additionally, if customers get comfortable with the live help technology, it will reduce the need for 800-number telephone business.

E-MAIL CUSTOMER SERVICE

Every e-mail communication with the customer is a chance to reinforce the brand image. Order confirmations, out-of-stock notifications, resolving a satisfaction issue are all opportunities to build a relationship with customers. These are all marketing opportunities and messages should be carefully planned.

The E-tailing Future

E-tailing, e-commerce, online retailing, online merchandising— whatever it is called—is here to stay. When we look back over the last few years, we realize how far the state of retailing online has progressed. Yet, it's got a long way to go until it hits the maturity curve. The world of e-commerce is a moving train and new innovations are occurring every day. The latest trends to watch are online customer service, permission-based e-mail marketing, and affiliate networks.

It is no longer a question of whether or not people will shop and conduct business online. The latest figures documented the number of online shoppers growing at 8 percent per month to a monthly total of 20 million shoppers. The only conclusion to draw is that the online shopping evolution has begun. Retailers shouldn't be left behind.

#### NINE

The Internet and the Law: Putting Your Business Online, Not on the Line'

William Burrington, Esq., Director, Public Policy, America Online®,
and Edwin Lavergne, Shook, Hardy & Bacon, L.L.P.

Where there is opportunity, there is risk. Many of the legal questions about doing business on the Internet are still unanswered. And it is likely the debate will continue for some time to come. Bill Burrington and Ed Lavergne, both experienced and respected attorneys who practice Internet law, offer the reader guidance for navigating today's thorny legal issues.

The "golden" business opportunities of the Internet can seem limitless: the ability to reach new customers, build new businesses, achieve efficiencies, and capitalize on the medium's global reach and immediacy. But such opportunities often come at a cost. Because businesses operating on the Internet frequently are in uncharted legal territory, you may find yourself working in a vacuum, with no legal precedent, other than your own business ethics, to guide you. Or, you may find yourself subjected to a patchwork of conflicting laws and regulations from every corner of the globe that the Internet can reach.

Ultimately, the Internet will benefit from the establishment of uniform global standards to guide businesses and consumers alike. But until that day comes, companies operating on the Internet need to keep in mind the legal implications of the business decisions they make.

The "Old Rules" Still Apply

As a starting point, a good rule of thumb is to assume that the "old rules" still apply. In other words, in the absence of new, Internet-specific laws, the safest assumption is that the same rules that apply in the traditional "physical" business world apply to the Internet. Although it may not be possible to apply all traditional business rules to the Internet, their underlying principles generally will prevail. You should *never* assume that the Internet will provide your business with greater legal protection than it enjoys in the traditional marketplace.

For example, if you post something defamatory on the Internet, you may be subject to the laws that traditionally protect individuals from defamation or libel. Similarly, the long-standing laws that protect businesses from trademark violations and copyright infringements must still be respected.

In addition, government agencies such as the Federal Trade Commission (FTC), the Securities and Exchange Commission (SEC), and state attorneys general have applied traditional consumer-protection laws to the Internet. All the requirements of truth-in-advertising laws are still in play, as well as laws against deceptive practices, false or misleading representations, and improper endorsements. The Web sites of government agencies like the FTC: www.ftc.gov are a good place to start when you need information about these basic business rules.

Trademark Law

Trademark issues on the Internet are inextricably linked with domain names, the mechanism for identifying Internet addresses. In fact, domain names may ultimately be more important to Web site operators than traditional trademarks because domain names serve a dual purpose: they help brand products and deliver potential customers to Web sites.

Browser keyword searches and easy-to-remember URLs such as www.cnn.com enable Internet users to find information quickly and easily. Rather than having to track down an unfamiliar telephone number or street address, users may simply type in a topic or a company name to find what they are looking for.

Because of this, Web site operators are understandably eager to acquire recognizable and easily remembered domain names for their sites. A logical domain name may give you a significant competitive advantage by making it easier for first-time visitors to find your site, and then remember your URL for future visits. Moreover, the Internet is a great equalizer, because a mom-and-pop business can have the same presence on the World Wide Web as a multinational corporation. Thus a memorable domain name, such as Yahoo.com, can lead to phenomenal worldwide brand recognition.

At the same time, the global reach of the Internet can lead to new conflicts in the trademark arena. While trademarks are often regional in nature, traditional regions don't exist on the Internet. For instance, the Anheuser-Busch Brewing Company and the Bohemian town of Ceske Budejovice, which the Germans call Budweis, have been battling for decades because they both produce a beer called "Budweiser." Both have an arguably legitimate claim to the name. Despite years of conflict with no clear result, the two brewers at least operated in distinct physical markets. But now if you look for "Budweiser" using an Internet search engine, you'll turn up both companies' home pages, one at www.budweiser.com and the other at www.budweiser.cz.

A further complication is that owners of domain names tend to try to keep them as short and simple as possible. For example, the domain name "acme.com" could belong to any company ranging from ACME Aerospace to ACME Zippers. Additional confusion may occur when acme.org, acme.net, and acme.com can exist side by side as legitimate domain names and Internet addresses.

The Internet is more prone to this kind of confusion because so much of its navigation is text based, with limited cues and no room for spelling errors. In a traditional trademark-registration process, two businesses in different industries may be permitted to use similar names because there is little chance that the public will be confused. (The Lexus automobile and the Lexis-Nexis database of news stories provide one example.) But such differentiation may not be possible when the brand names are merely words on a computer screen, without additional clues as to their meaning.

If you already have a valuable brand name in the traditional world, you may need to be careful that someone else doesn't steal it for use on the Internet. These so-called "cybersquatters" make their living by anticipating which domain names will be valuable and then registering those names for themselves. Later they try to sell the names to businesses that want them—sometimes at a substantial profit.

McDonald's Corp. and MTV Networks are among the companies that have faced this problem. In addition, in April, 1998, a federal court of appeals in California ruled that these practices violate trademark law and are tantamount to extortion in a case involving a cybersquatter who had registered the domain name "panavision.com" and then tried to sell it to Panavision.[1] (Many companies are now choosing to sue cybersquatters for trademark infringement rather than settle.)

Similarly, a company may register a domain name to block a competitor from using it. In an early battle over a domain name, the Princeton Review registered a domain name that closely resembled the name of Stanley Kaplan, the name then used by one of its main competitors in the test preparation industry.

As with "real world" trademarks, the easiest way to avoid problems with trademarks on the World Wide Web is to register your brand name or trademark as a domain name as soon as you can, put it to legitimate use, and be on the lookout for infringement by others.

Web sites that use "framing" may also run into problems with trademark infringement. Framing occurs when a Web site becomes part of a larger "metasite" that aggregates links and information from other sites. Metasites function as large, centralized information repositories that make it easier and faster to use the Internet. Framing allows you to see the contents of a Web site within a smaller area of the metasite without leaving the metasite. The metasite's logo and third-party advertising messages may surround or "frame" the site whose contents you are viewing. Because the content and trademarks of the framed site may suggest that the material has been licensed when it hasn't, or an association between two companies that does not exist, this may amount to both illegal trademark dilution and copyright infringement.[2]

Some Web site operators may also be guilty of trademark infringement when they use invisible trademarks to lure users to their sites. Also known as "word stuffing," this involves embedding another company's popular brand name into a Web site. For example, the operator of two adult-oriented Web sites reportedly coded Playboy™ and Playmate™ into the sites so that they would turn up when users were searching for the popular magazines by those names.[3]

The world of domain registration is undergoing great change. Domain-name registration historically was handled by the National Science Foundation (NSF), and then contracted to a private company, Network Solutions, Inc., and its registration facility, InterNIC. However, the contract with the U.S. government has expired and an International Ad Hoc Committee (IAHC) has called for expanding the kinds of addresses that are available, adding suffixes such as ".store" to those that businesses can use. The U.S. Department of Commerce, through its National Telecommunications and Information Administration (NTIA), has proposed its own system of additional suffixes and domain-name registries. The current state of the NSI domain name–registration policy can be found at http://rs.internic.net/help/domain/policy.html. The NTIA policy statements can be found at www.ntia.doc.gov, while the IAHC proposals can be found at www.iahc.org.

It is likely that the regulation of domain names will evolve into a system with a centralized arbitration mechanism, but with competing name registries and a greater reliance on fees from users. It may be years before all the issues surrounding the use of trademarks on the Internet are resolved. In the meantime, you should always consider the potential for trademark infringement when you use a name on the Internet. You can try to avoid potential conflicts through the good-faith use of domain names, and negotiation and compromise if you discover that you share a legitimate claim to a domain name with another party.

Issues with Linking

One of the great advantages of the Internet as a communications medium is the ease with which you can link your Web site to the Web sites of others. Links can increase the usefulness of a site and provide access to additional content at no extra cost. And sometimes Web site operators will agree to exchange links to each other's sites as a way of building traffic.

Sometimes, however, such hyperlinks can connect you to controversy. For instance, you may link to a Web site that changes its content in unpredictable ways that could offend your users or, in some cases, increase your liability if the other Web site engages in illegal activities. Or, if a Web site links to your site without permission, you may not appreciate the association of their site with yours.

In one of the most extreme cases to date involving hyperlinks, Angela Marquardt, a German student activist, faced criminal charges for linking her Web site to the site of *Radikal,* a newspaper that described how to make bombs and derail trains.[4] The servers where *Radikal*'s Web site was located were outside of Germany, but Marquardt faced criminal charges under German law for linking to restricted material. She was eventually acquitted, but the case did not resolve the question of whether a Web site operator could be held liable for linking to certain kinds of controversial material.

Linking may also raise issues of trademark infringement. For example, Ticketmaster sued Microsoft for providing links from The Microsoft Network to internal pages of Ticketmaster's Web site.[5] Ticketmaster contended that by linking to pages other than its home page, Microsoft had suggested it had a formal relationship with Ticketmaster that did not exist, creating a potentially actionable claim of a trademark violation. Ticketmaster also was concerned because the link enabled visitors to bypass the advertising it had sold on its home page.

It remains to be seen whether these are isolated cases or the shape of litigation to come. Until the underlying issues are resolved, the most conservative approach is to contact the operators of commercial Web sites before creating links to their sites.

Copyright

The personal computer, digital technology, and the Internet have greatly increased the ease with which content—whether graphics, text, music, or software—can be copied and redistributed around the world. But just because something is easy to do doesn't always necessarily mean it's legal.

Companies that have spent millions of dollars developing brand names, logos, and product lines, often tied to equally expensive movies, television shows, and comic strips, are understandably unhappy when Internet users, in effect, steal their intellectual property by copying it and posting it on other Web sites or bulletin boards. Many of these companies are willing to take legal action against Web site operators who misappropriate their material, and have been working to change the U.S. copyright laws to give them tougher remedies. Some proposals would require service providers to serve, in effect, as policemen for companies whose copyrights are violated and to "take down" the questionable material when the copyright holder challenges it.

U.S. copyright law includes a "fair use" principle, which can sometimes provide a defense for those who use copyrighted material, depending on the nature of the use, how much of the work was copied, and the economic impact it has on the original. Fair use, however, is hard to define. The safest course is to always seek permission before using another person's work or the intellectual property of another company.

Copyright law is evolving rapidly, both within the United States and internationally, under the aegis of the World Intellectual Property Organization in Geneva, Switzerland. Developments can be followed on the Web site of the U.S. Copyright Office, at http://lcWeb.loc.gov/copyright.

Data Control and Protection

The online medium also provides extraordinary opportunities for businesses to learn about their customers—what they like, what they dislike, and how they shop and gather information. In addition, the Internet and World Wide Web provide opportunities for businesses to target messages to a large number of people while tailoring the message to individual demographics and interests. But with these new capabilities come heightened concerns about the potential for invasion of personal privacy.[6]

Several major Internet companies and industry trade groups, working under the aegis of the Online Privacy Alliance, have called for Web sites to display seals to help explain their policies for the collection, use, and disclosure of personal information that has been gathered online. The Council of Better Business Bureaus: www.bbbonline.org and Truste: www.truste.org have been working on programs to promote this kind of industry self-regulation. The FTC and members of Congress have threatened to seek legislation mandating such disclosures if industry does not move fast enough to regulate itself.

You can create a simple statement describing your Web site's privacy practices by using a privacy-policy tool developed by the Direct Marketing Association and available on its Web site: www.the-dma.org. But remember, once you make assertions about your Web site's privacy practices, you will be expected to adhere to them, or you could be found in violation of the laws barring deceptive advertising, or possibly new online privacy laws and regulations.

In addition, the World Wide Web Consortium at the Massachusetts Institute of Technology has been working with leading Internet companies to modify browser software so that a user can seamlessly communicate his privacy preferences to a Web site and then "negotiate" over how the information will be used. Companies doing business on the Internet should follow these developments.

Privacy is also a very sensitive concern overseas, and U.S. businesses hoping to sell to those customers need to keep abreast of how online privacy laws and regulations are developing in Europe and other parts of the world. Foreign countries often have laws and customs that protect individual privacy much more rigorously than is the case in the United States.

Many companies are finding that it makes business sense to be sensitive to their users' privacy concerns. To cite a parallel in the automobile industry, for many years manufacturers appeared reluctant to incorporate safety features into their cars, perhaps because of their cost. Over time, however, they discovered that safety could be a strong selling point and began adding features not mandated by the government, such as antilock brakes and side-impact air bags, as options on some models.

Spamming

A related privacy issue involves what has become known as "spamming," or the sending of unsolicited e-mail that is commercial in nature. The growth in the volume of unsolicited e-mail, in many cases pushing useless or possibly fraudulent products, has unfortunately undermined the value of e-mail as a marketing vehicle. Because of the volume of user complaints, many service providers have also tried to block unsolicited e-mail.

Courts have also addressed the issue. The U.S. District Court for the Northern District of California ruled in May 1998 that a bulk e-mailer who had used a false e-mail return address (a tactic spammers frequently use to avoid retaliation and hostile return mail) had probably violated several federal laws, including the Federal Trademark Act and the Computer Fraud and Abuse Act, as well as being guilty of breach of contract, fraud, misrepresentation, and trespass.[7]

Obviously, a decision to send unsolicited e-mail should not be made lightly. Aside from the potential legal consequences, a business should keep in mind the kind of negative response such a message is likely to generate. It may be preferable to send e-mail messages only to those who have requested further information or with whom you already have a business relationship.

However, in keeping with traditional industry guidelines, if you decide to send unsolicited e-mail, you should provide an easy way for users to contact you if they don't want to receive future messages—and you should honor those requests. Further, before you sell, rent, or exchange your list of e-mail addresses with others, you should remove the names of everyone who did not want their address shared with a third party.

This area, like many others, is evolving rapidly, and businesses interested in marketing through e-mail should keep abreast of any laws and regulations that may take effect. Most of these developments are tracked by the Center for Democracy and Technology on its Web site, www.cdt.org.

Publishing

One of the attractions of the Internet is the ability to publish information to a global audience at a relatively low cost. But the ease with which information can be posted and redistributed also increases the risk of claims of libel, defamation, obscenity, and indecency. Further, the damages caused by a defamatory statement may be greater and harder to remedy than in traditional media because the material can be redistributed so quickly in ways one cannot control. Unlike a newspaper or television broadcast, which can sometimes minimize damage by issuing a retraction, bad information on the Internet can be spread rapidly through e-mail, listservs, and links from other Web sites and can be virtually impossible to recapture.

Liability for defamation on the Internet has so far turned on whether one "publishes" or merely "distributes" the material. Under established First Amendment law, distributors must have had actual knowledge of the content of information before they can be held liable for distributing it. Publishers (who are thought to have greater knowledge and control over content) have somewhat less protection.

Two court cases illustrate this difference. Several years ago, CompuServe was sued over its electronic library of news publications, which was organized by an independent third party, Cameron Communications Inc. One of the available newsletters, "Rumorville USA," published what were alleged to be false and defamatory statements about a competitor. Cameron Communications had uploaded the newsletter directly into CompuServe's computers, and the online service had had no opportunity to review it. Nor did CompuServe have any contractual relationship with the newsletter's publisher.

A federal district court concluded that CompuServe had no more editorial control over "Rumorville USA" than a public library, bookstore, or newsstand would have over a print publication that it distributed. Nor could CompuServe ever hope to examine every publication that was posted to its service for potentially defamatory statements. Therefore, the court said CompuServe would be found liable only if it knew or should have known that the statements were defamatory. The court concluded that was not the case, and the online service escaped liability at an early stage in the litigation.[8]

A different fate befell Prodigy. In 1995, a New York State Supreme Court found Prodigy liable as a publisher after users posted critical statements about Stratton Oakmont, Inc., a securities firm, to one of its financial bulletin boards. Prodigy had billed itself as a family-oriented network that exercised editorial control over the content of messages posted on its bulletin boards. It attempted to distinguish itself from its competitors because of this editorial control, using content guidelines, a software screening program, and bulletin board leaders who were supposed to enforce the content guidelines. The judge concluded that by making decisions about content, Prodigy acted as a publisher and was subject to a tougher standard for libel.[9]

Members of Congress recognized that by taking positive steps to monitor its online service, Prodigy had made itself more vulnerable to a lawsuit. In response, Congress added language to the Telecommunications Act of 1996, stipulating that Internet service providers would not be treated as the source, or publisher, of information provided by another content provider or online user. Furthermore, service providers would not be held liable if they engaged in good-faith efforts to restrict obscene, lewd, lascivious, excessively violent, harassing, or otherwise objectionable content or for providing their users with software to help restrict access to that material.

This statute was put to the test in two recent suits against America Online®, Inc. (AOL). In the first, AOL was sued in 1997 by one of President Clinton's advisers after it distributed what he contended was libelous material in a gossip column called "The Drudge Report." In the second case, AOL was sued after someone posted inflammatory material about an individual on one of its bulletin boards. The Supreme Court upheld a lower-court ruling that said the law protected ISPs from liability for third-party content, as in the Drudge case, and dismissed an appeal in the bulletin board case.[10] These rulings give Internet service providers special protections from libel that other entities on the Internet may not enjoy.

Computer networks that try to monitor content should keep a close watch on the changing legal consequences of their policies. How the distinction between publishing and distributing will be made for Web site operators, as opposed to Internet service providers, remains to be seen. As one precaution, online businesses should ensure that the roles and relationships of employees, subcontractors, independent contractors, and users are understood and spelled out clearly.

Who's in Charge?

Content restrictions create one of the most daunting legal considerations for companies doing business on the Internet: the need to keep abreast of the laws and regulations of not only the federal government and the fifty states but of countries all around the world. Sitting in your office in Kansas City, for example, you could face a lawsuit in New York, Los Angeles, Rio de Janeiro, or Beijing, depending on the nature of your business. The potential costs of defending a lawsuit in another state or country could be staggering.

Since the advent of Internet business relationships, courts have struggled to apply traditional jurisdictional concepts to the nontraditional transactions and business relationships found in the online world. For instance, a company called On Ramp Internet Computer Services was registered in Nevada with a president who lived there. On a Web site that provided tourist information, the company also promoted WagerNet, an online sports wagering service it planned to launch. It invited online visitors to add their names to a mailing list to receive information about the service. Users were also given toll-free and Nevada phone numbers, and were instructed to consult local authorities about applicable local laws that might restrict betting.

A Minnesota investigator called the toll-free number and spoke with the company president, who told him that the gambling service was legal. Minnesota law, however, does not permit commercial sports betting. The Minnesota attorney general charged the company with consumer fraud, and the state court exercised jurisdiction over the company, even though no company employee had been in Minnesota.

In this instance, the court relied on four key facts. First, many computers located in Minnesota accessed the On Ramp Web site (a fact that could be established by a subpoena of a Web site's logs). Second, Minnesota computers were among the five hundred that most frequently accessed the company's Web site. Third, prosecutors could demonstrate that Minnesota residents had called the telephone numbers advertised on the Web site. Finally, the name of at least one Minnesota resident was found on On Ramp's mailing list. On that, the court concluded that On Ramp had purposefully attempted to conduct business in Minnesota. Furthermore, On Ramp encouraged Internet users from around the world to use Wager Net, demonstrating that it intended to seek customers from a wide geographic area, rather than to merely distribute information over the Internet.[11]

In another case, a California resident posted bulletin board messages about an investment opportunity on an online service provider's "Money Talk" bulletin board, sent e-mail to a Connecticut resident, and phoned the person. The California resident was forced to defend a subsequent lawsuit in Connecticut because of the combination of passive bulletin board messages and active e-mail and telephone contacts.[12] Similarly, a California court exercised jurisdiction over a New York software company, solely on the basis of e-mail and telephone contacts.[13]

In still another case, this time involving a trademark infringement claim, a Connecticut court exercised jurisdiction over a Massachusetts software company that had no offices or employees in Connecticut and did not conduct regular business there. What the company did do was advertise on a Web site and provide a toll-free number for potential customers to call. The court considered those to be activities "directed" to consumers in all states, including Connecticut, and therefore concluded that it could properly assert jurisdiction over the company.[14]

In some states then, courts will not hesitate to exercise jurisdiction over your business simply because your Web site is accessible to its residents. Other states may look to see whether your Web site merely provides information passively, or whether it actively advertises, promotes, or sells a product, or targets an audience. But that doesn't always hold true. A New York court refused to exercise jurisdiction over a New Jersey resident, even though he was actively engaged in trying to sell information services through an "electronic law office" in Pennsylvania.

Easy to understand? No—particularly when the courts can't agree. The underlying policy question is whether a person operating a World Wide Web site subjects himself to the laws of every state and foreign country. Uniform, universal standards are needed to give businesses better guidance on what they should and should not do. But until those standards are established, you can expect this area of law to change frequently and to vary from state to state and nation to nation.

Industry-Specific Issues

Companies that operate certain types of businesses have to consider some additional industry-specific laws when they operate on the Internet.

CHILDREN

According to *Consumer Reports* magazine, children purchase an estimated $15 billion per year worth of products, and influence how their parents spend another $160 billion per year.[15] Nevertheless, companies that market to children through the Internet need to be sensitive to concerns that the medium raises in the eyes of parents, teachers, and increasingly, government regulators and legislators. Many of these concerns grow out of a few—but well-publicized— incidents in which children were contacted by predators in online chat rooms or through bulletin boards and lured into offline meetings. These incidents have heightened parents' fears about what their children are doing online and contributed to a climate in which marketers may face more restrictions on their online activities than they do in traditional media. Government officials are moving more aggressively to impose legislative and regulatory solutions in this area.

To attract visitors, many child-oriented Web sites try to promote interactivity and online contributions from children. Some may conduct contests in which children are asked to produce stories or anecdotes. If you engage in such activities, be careful how you identify contributors online. Even if you know the child's full name and address, don't publish it online.

Marketers that sponsor or operate chat rooms also need to consider whether they have the resources to monitor what transpires there and whether they will be able to screen who participates. All the positive interaction children enjoy at your site may be worthless if one predator uses it to make inappropriate contact with a child. To gain a better understanding of these issues, refer to "Child Safety on the Information Highway," a brochure published by the Internet Alliance in conjunction with the National Center for Missing and Exploited Children. The brochure is available on the Alliance's Web site: www.internetalliance.org or by calling the center at 1-800-843-5678.

Web sites that are directed toward children should clearly disclose why they are gathering information from children and how they intend to use it. Web site operators should also evaluate whether they really need the information they are collecting and whether it needs to be in a personally identifiable form.

There are a number of places online marketers can turn to for help with these issues. The Children's Advertising Review Unit of the Council of Better Business Bureaus has developed guidelines for companies that advertise to children online as part of its long-standing guidelines for advertising to children in traditional media. The online guidelines assert that advertisers should make "reasonable efforts" to ensure that parental permission is obtained before identifiable information about children is collected. The guidelines also state that online advertising should be labeled and differentiated from program content.[16] In addition, the Direct Marketing Association has adopted guidelines for companies that collect information about children. Consumer groups and children's advocacy groups have supported still-tougher restrictions on companies with child-oriented Web sites.[17]

Concerns over children's access to online pornography and other inappropriate materials, and parents' and educators' concerns about the difficulty of monitoring children's online experiences have also led to the development of filtering software. Newer versions of these products incorporate the Platform for Internet Content Selection (PICS), which will enable Web sites to be rated according to criteria adopted by third-party groups.[18] The Recreational Software Advisory Council has taken the lead in using PICS to rate Web sites for children. Web sites can help promote self-regulation of the Internet by visiting the RSAC Web site: www.rsac.org to obtain a label for their site.

Educational tools of this sort, along with industry self-regulation, may enable children's marketing to grow on the Internet, albeit in a way that balances free enterprise with the critical need to protect children's privacy and safety. As this issue plays itself out in the industry and in political arenas, you should tread carefully when communicating with children online, and keep informed about policy developments.

TAXATION

Electronic commerce is fast becoming a major economic force in the United States. By the year 2002, the Commerce Department predicts that up to $300 billion worth of business-to-business commerce could be conducted online.[19]

The potential size of the online marketplace makes it an attractive target for generating tax revenues but also raises concerns that it may provide a way to avoid certain kinds of taxes. At the same time, many legislators realize that the industry is still in its infancy, and that by imposing new taxes on Internet-based businesses, they could derail an otherwise robust economic engine. This issue is further complicated by the lack of borders on the Internet that would determine which, if any, jurisdictions could tax a business.

Members of Congress and some state officials have called for a moratorium on taxing the Internet, and the creation of a congressional commission that would try to sort out these issues. Because the situation is in flux, check with your accountant or tax attorney on the possible tax consequences of doing business online.

SWEEPSTAKES AND GAMBLING

Electronic sweepstakes can be a valuable marketing device for Internet businesses, enabling them to build audiences, capture information about their visitors, and retain their visitors' loyalty. However, even if your sweepstakes is legal where your business is physically based, you may unknowingly violate other state or foreign laws when you make it available to others around the globe.

The risk lies in the fact that nongovernment lotteries are illegal in most states. Lotteries involve the payment of "consideration" for a chance to win a prize. Generally, in order to run a legal sweepstakes, sponsors must eliminate the possibility of consideration.

Unfortunately, it isn't clear what constitutes consideration in the Internet age. Clearly, if you charge a fee to enter the sweepstakes, that's consideration. What is less clear is whether purchasing a computer, paying Internet access fees, or paying certain telephone charges constitute consideration. Lawyers with expertise in this area hold differing views, and there is little case law on the subject. At least one state agency has taken the position that the costs of owning or leasing a computer and obtaining Internet access constitute consideration. This issue needs to be resolved—universally—so that legitimate businesses can avoid running afoul of the law.

If you offer a game to users, no matter where they live, you may subject yourself to the laws of every jurisdiction in which the game is available. To protect yourself, you could review the laws of every state and nation involved. Another alternative is to post a clear and conspicuous disclaimer on your Web site, limiting the promotion to persons who live in jurisdictions where you know the game is legal.

Online gambling is more problematic because gambling is even more heavily regulated than sweepstakes. The crux of the gambling issue is that it's difficult to define where an online bet actually takes place. Is it the state where the bettor's computer is located, where his Internet service provider is located, or where the servers used by the Web site are located? Is it in the foreign country where the bet is placed or all of these places?

Remember the operator of the On Ramp Web site in Nevada, who faced criminal charges in Minnesota for enabling that state's residents to gamble online? That scenario is playing out with greater frequency. In another case, a Delaware corporation doing business in Pennsylvania and through a wholly owned subsidiary in Grenada tried to offer its casino gambling services through a Web site. One service it advertised was an Internet-based slot tournament. A Missouri investigator accessed the Web site and called the company's toll-free number. He said he lived in Missouri and was told he could participate legally. Based on that information, he completed an application, sent in a payment, and received more information by e-mail.

After the Missouri state attorney general brought charges, the company was permanently enjoined from marketing, advertising, or offering its gambling services by any means, Internet or otherwise, to residents of that state, from representing that casino gambling was legal in Missouri, and from concealing the fact that it is illegal there. In addition, the company had to post a prominent notice on its Web site, stating that it could not accept applications from Missouri residents, and that any applications would be rejected and returned.[20] Note that even though the conduct in question was based on the

Internet, the punishment extended beyond the Internet: The company was prohibited not only from using e-mail but also from communicating with residents of Missouri through notices, direct mail, brochures, pamphlets, handbills, letters, or conversations.

Because of concerns over the potential for fraud and abuse and the potentially addictive nature of gambling, this issue has drawn a good deal of attention from lawmakers as well as state prosecutors. Despite concerns about its enforcement and the potentially adverse effect on electronic commerce, legislation has been introduced in Congress that would make online gambling a federal crime. Some Web site operators contend that online gaming sites should be permitted but regulated. Others simply move their sites beyond the boundaries of the United States to try to escape regulation.

Obviously, the issue is a controversial one. If you are considering getting into the online gambling business, you should consider the costs of complying with ever-changing rules and the ever-present threat of an enforcement action when evaluating your prospects.

A REDEFINED BUSINESS

Unlike other media, the Internet is both interactive and real-time. Laws will need to be rewritten to take into account the fact that information can be exchanged immediately, in both directions, between parties who may have no idea where the other person is physically located. Even traditional contract law may not apply perfectly to contracts that are executed over the Internet, leading to confusion and uncertainty until new principles develop.

The real-time aspect of the Internet allows for much faster interaction between contracting parties. This rapid-fire business environment may demand a rethinking of traditional concepts such as when an offer is made, when an offer can be rescinded, when and how an offer is accepted, and when a defamatory statement is published. Scores of other legal issues that have been worked out in other media may need to be rethought and redefined as they play out over the Internet. Companies that have already ventured into the Internet business world may be at the forefront of these legal and policy developments. Ultimately, the frustration of trying to ram a square peg into a round hole should convince someone to drill a square hole, so that businesses can realize the

Internet's tremendous potential without being hampered by ill-fitting legal principles.

The Clinton administration has entered the global debate, preparing and distributing "A Framework for Global Electronic Commerce."[21] The framework proposes a strategy through which government and industry can work together to address the issues surrounding taxation, intellectual property protection, privacy, content restrictions, and technical standards in a way that does not inhibit the growth of the Internet as a vehicle for electronic commerce. The framework also calls for governments to work together to develop universal approaches for regulating this medium.

We believe that the greatest need is to strive for uniformity, and whenever possible, industry-led, market-driven solutions. All Internet users should be subject to the same universal rules. The Internet industry must self-regulate and build consumer confidence and trust as this new global medium continues to evolve. Business managers must keep abreast of local and policy developments. Getting involved in industry groups, attending seminars, and consulting your attorney will enable you to minimize your risks of doing business on the Internet. Your prospects for mining real Internet "gold" will be strongest if you keep the old rules in mind, keep informed as new laws are written, and keep your business in compliance with the ever-changing regulatory landscape.[22]

■ ■ ■

1   Leslie Miller, "What's in a Name? Domains Caught in the Middle of a Tug-of-War on the Web," *USA Today*, May 13, 1998.

2   Barry D. Weiss, "Metasites Linked To IP Violations," *The National Law Journal*, July 21, 1997.

3   "Use of Name in Web Site Meta Tags Violates Trademark Laws, Firm Alleges," BNA's *Electronic Information Policy & Law Report*, vol. #2, no. 33, August 22, 1997.

4   Ruth Walker, "Berlin Case Posts a Win for Freer Net," *The Christian Science Monitor*, July 18, 1997.

5   Steven B. Pokotilow and Matthew W. Siegal, "Controversy Heats Up Over Whether Hotlinks Can Get You in Hot Water," *The Intellectual Property Strategist*, vol. e, no. 9 (June 1997).

6   "Commerce, Communication and Privacy Online: A National Survey of Computer Users," conducted by Privacy & American Business and Louis Harris & Associates, April 10–27, 1997, sponsored by the Interactive Services Association, American Express, America Online®, Citicorp, Dun & Bradstreet, Electronic Messaging Association, IBM, MCI Communications, Metromail, Microsoft, Netcom, NYNEX, and The News Corporation Limited.

7   "Spammers Likely To Violate Lanham Act By Using False E-mail Return Addresses," BNA's *Electronic Information Policy & Law Report*, vol. 3, no. 18. (May 6, 1998): 586.

8   *Cubby, Inc. v. CompuServe*, 776 F. Supp. 135 (S.D.N.Y. 1991).

9   *Stratton Oakmont, Inc. v. Prodigy Servs. Co.*, 1995 N.Y. Misc. LEXIS 229, 23 Media L. Rep. 1794 (N.Y. Sup. Ct. 1995).

10   "CDA Preempts Negligence Action Against AOL For Distribution of Alleged Defamatory Matter," BNA's *Electronic Information Policy & Law Report*, vol. 2, no. 14 (April 4, 1997). *Zeran v. America Online® Inc.*, E.D.Va., Civil Action No. 96-952-A, 3/21/97, printed at BNA's *Electronic Information Policy & Law Report*, vol. 2, no. 14 (April 4, 1997). James Vicini, "US High Court Sides With AOL In Defamation Case," Reuters Ltd., June 22, 1998.

11   *Minnesota v. Granite Gate Resorts, Inc.*, Minn. Ct. App., File No. C6957227, 9/5/97, discussed in "Minnesota Appeals Court Upholds Jurisdiction Over Nonresident Internet Gambling Service," BNA's *Electronic Information Policy & Law Report*, vol. 2, no. 35 (September 12, 1997).

12   *Cody v. Ward*, 954 F.Supp. 43 (D. Conn. 1997).

13   Matt Richtel, "Wide Use of E-mail Alters Jurisdiction of Courts," *New York Times*, August 25, 1997.

14   *Inset Systems, Inc. v. Instruction Set, Inc.*, 937 F. Supp. 161 (D. Conn. 1996).

15   Martha M. Hamilton, "Persuading Young Minds to Buy," The *Washington Post*, September 9, 1997.

16   See www.bbb.org/advertising/childrensMonitor.html.

17   BNA's *Electronic Information Policy & Law Report*, vol 2, no. 25 (June 20, 1997).

18   See www.w3.org/PICS/.

19   The Emerging Digital Economy. Chapter One. www.ecommerce.gov/emerging.htm *citing* Forrester Research. www.forrester.com.

20   *Missouri v. Interactive Gaming & Communications Corp.*, Mo. Cir. Ct. Case No. CV 97-7808, 5/22/97, discussed in BNA's *Electronic Information Policy & Law Report*, vol. 2, no. 23 (June 6, 1997).

21   See www.iitf.nist.gov/eleccomm/ecomm.htm.

22   The authors were assisted on this chapter by Sara Fitzgerald, Shea Thomas Hickman, and Amy E. Weissman. Sara Fitzgerald is a former *Washington Post* editor and a specialist in online policy issues. Shea Hickman is the law clerk for the Law and Public Affairs Group of America Online®, Inc. and formerly worked at Irwin, Campbell & Tannenwald. Amy Weissman is a communications associate at Shook, Hardy & Bacon L.L.P in Washington, D.C., where she focuses on Internet, broadcast, telephony, advertising, sweepstakes, and other regulatory matters.

Business-to-Business Uses of Internet Technology

While most of the attention, press, and media hype has been focused on the consumer Internet activities discussed in the previous section, there are arguably more powerful initiatives that are occurring quietly in the halls of corporate America. These are the activities that can result in a very big pay back in a very short time frame.

Insiders know that using Internet technology to produce Intranets and Extranets is the best return-on-investment bet in the interactive marketplace today. These initiatives address some of the less sexy, but very real problems facing companies, such as: managing legacy corporate databases and vast, complex, and expensive private networks, and the increasing demands of administration. The gains here through improved efficiency and productivity, thus achieving higher profits. And they can be accomplished with manageable technical effort and cost. The primary challenge here lies in education and managing change.

There are also softer, less measurable gains to be made, too, like competitive advantage, improved communications, empowered employees, and satisfied customers.

The chapter by Jim Pisz provides an in-depth discussion of how Toyota has transformed its business through the use of Intranets and Extranets. He also takes the reader through some of the recommended approaches for implementation. The chapter by Hilary Thomas takes a look at how some companies are using Internet-based technology to extend the reach of established private networks, like EDI, with vendors and trading partners, and sets the stage for the further evolution of public and private networks.

#### TEN

Using Intranets and Extranets to Gain Advantage

Jim Pisz, Director, Intranet/Extranet Services, Toyota Motor Sales, USA, Inc.

Jim Pisz has led the Internet effort at Toyota, first to direct marketing efforts, and then to address improvements in corporate processes. He offers a fascinating look at how Toyota's corporate culture is being redefined. Empowered employees, collective thinking, and improved efficiency and productivity, using Intranets and Extranets, are adding up to increased profitability. This chapter also provides valuable management advice for successful implementation.

The development of knowledge is the business battleground of the future. Knowledge is power and its development emerges from information—our ability to inform and be informed—which evolves directly out of our human interactions. When everyone builds products well, the only competitive advantage we have is our knowledge and ideas. We then bring these ideas to bear, improving our processes and our business efficiency. These are the natural by-products of the sharing of knowledge. Intranets and Extranets are the vehicles of today and the future that will allow a company to deliver its information to a broad band of constituents while outmaneuvering the competition.

What Are Intranets and Extranets?

An Intranet is an internal Web site published to your company's employees. An Intranet's content includes business information and applications and uses tools and utilities that help employees do their job. When the Intranet is connected to remote partners, vendors, or employee locations through a secure network or the Internet, the Intranet becomes an Extranet.

A corporate Intranet sets the politics of information control within a corporation aside. Information owners are encouraged to share with their colleagues. Intranets create a power shift. With an Intranet, power no longer comes to the person who controls the information; instead, it goes to the person who can create knowledge from the open flow of information. It is for these reasons that Intranets will have a profound impact on business in the future. Intranets will tear down any artificial walls that hold back new knowledge and good ideas.

Intranets and Extranets utilize Web technology with hypertext markup language (html) as the dominant programming language. Associates generally access their company's Intranet via a personal computer and browser software such as Netscape or Microsoft Explorer.

Moving Beyond Consumer Web sites

In the business world, the purpose and value of consumer Web sites have long been argued within corporations. Can a Web site create a brand? Is the best use of a Web site to generate leads? Should my Web site be about customer satisfaction and loyalty? What we learned is that all of these were possibilities. Toyota created a very successful lead generation site, as did Levi's for branding, and FedEx for customer service. Just as these companies succeeded in the fields that they applied themselves too, hundreds of other companies failed in their attempts.

What practitioners came to understand was that content is the most important ingredient in building a successful consumer Web site. The correct product, a unique value proposition, and execution consistent with the expectation of the Internet literate were part of defining Web success. The unanswered question was and is: What is the correct mix that creates success?

As the content discussion raged on, technical facts became crystal clear and have received near universal acceptance. The hyperlink, search engines, and e-mail were among the technical features common to the Internet that defined our expectation of nearly every consumer Web site. Common rules for navigation were set that allowed an information gatherer to travel from one site to the next with little confusion.

Gaining a technical trust of the navigation, search, and communication tools through the use of the consumer Internet served as a technical proof of concept for the future use of Web technology. This technical knowledge also framed an unusual paradox. Utilizing consumer Web sites produced a clear understanding that Web technology was an easy and effective logistics tool for moving information. However, determining what to say in an effective content strategy was a difficult task. This paradox was perhaps a signal to practitioners that Web technology combined with a type of content that was focused and controlled would be a successful Web implementation. This type of content is the focused and controlled information that businesses produce every day to conduct commerce. To that end, the development of Intranets and Extranets began.

A Tool to Gain Advantage

Corporations naturally produce information in the course of everyday business. For instance, the automotive industry produces and saves information on topics such as vehicles, parts, accessories, sales, profitability, customers, and dealers to name just a few. The distribution department keeps its own records on vehicle orders, inventory, and shipping. The customer-service department keeps information on vehicle warranty claims and repair procedures. The sales department keeps records on the sales of vehicles by model, grade, and series. These departments routinely share information, but in most cases, each department maintains control of their files.

Toyota strategically identifies critical topic areas and classifies them as "channels." The channel concept was originated with the inception of the corporate Intranet. Toyota has strategically identified twelve channel topics—dealers and customers are two of the twelve. The purpose of the channel area within the Intranet is to bring together all information on the specific channel topic. This is done to break down the artificial walls of information ownership where permission to access had to be requested and granted. Toyota also initiated channels as a way to begin to understand what innovations could be generated when smart people utilize information not previously available to them.

Collective thinking often produces the best ideas. Bringing together the human and informational resources of many areas to solve problems is very efficient. A corporate Intranet where the channel concept has become a mandate by management and has been accepted by associates can produce unusual advantage for the corporation. As an example, a corporate sales manager wondered what dealers would be concerned with a recommended computer purchase proposed for all dealerships nationwide. Investigating the dealer channel uncovered the fact that a significant number of dealers were located with another make manufacturer at the same retail outlet. The owners of these combined locations would be concerned about owning more than one computer to do the same function for different manufacturers. Information from another source produced the age, type, and current payment status of computer equipment that existed at each location. This information helped to determine the propensity to purchase. This and other information was analyzed to answer the sales managers' questions. The answers came quickly because the sales analyst knew to look in the dealer channel for all the pertinent information. Channel information stored centrally, developed with the same technical parameters, readily available with a simple graphical user interface changes the playing field.

In today's Internet business world, disintermediation is a major area of concern. It is a concern for workers and for organizations that don't provide value to the enterprise. As a concept, disintermediation refers to the technological obsolescence of a stage of the workflow. Disintermediation is the elimination of middlemen as a result of productivity improvements. An example of disintermediation is best seen in the retail computer industry. Manufacturers such as Dell and Gateway are disintermediating retailers such as Computer City by selling custom-built computers directly to consumers. Dell allows consumers to configure their purchases individually on the consumer Internet or with the help of a sales assistant via the telephone. Consumer satisfaction with the process ensures its continuance.

Intranets promote internal disintermediation when they perform at optimal levels. In most cases, internal disintermediation occurs because a service is valuable to a company and technology offers the opportunity to change and improve the workflow. Savings comes from improved time to market and the elimination of a resource needed to complete the original task.

When Microsoft developed its internal Intranet and created "a company store," the results were dramatic. Like many companies, Microsoft must supply the workers with the basic tools of business, such as writing tablets, diskettes, and binders. Microsoft used to stockpile an inventory of these supplies and assigned employees to order and distribute them. As Microsoft developed its company-store approach on their Intranet, it extended the solution to its suppliers. Microsoft's office-products supplier, Boise Cascade, joined this effort and became a partner in the Extranet. Utilizing Microsoft commerce-server technology, both companies developed applications to supply Microsoft with its daily business supplies.

Microsoft developed and published Intranet forms for all associates to order needed supplies. Associates entered their internal billing addresses and order information. Where necessary, they could forward orders electronically to their superiors for digital approval. On the Boise Cascade side, orders could be taken and fulfilled throughout the day. Inventory control dramatically improved.

Microsoft then extended these features to many other business functions, including conference-room scheduling and food services. In the end, it was able to reduce the direct workforce associated with these tasks from fifteen employees to just three. Microsoft's company store is a model for many other companies today.

Microsoft was able to save money by making its purchasing process more efficient. This example returned 100 percent of its implementation costs in less than six months. However, the really big gains will come when processes such as sales, marketing, and distribution are made more direct. In these departments, savings are measured in terms of time to market. Hypothetically, when Microsoft utilizes an Extranet to simultaneously distribute

Windows 2005 to all of its established customers the day after its release, then the gain will be immeasurable.

Overcoming the Cultural Hurdles in Implementing an Effective Intranet/Extranet

In most businesses, hurdles are created when established procedures change. Change is the culprit; it makes most people feel uncomfortable. Most of the change in business today is driven by competition and the marketplace. Some change associated with process improvement comes from a company's self-examination. The decision to build an Intranet can come from the marketplace or from the self-directed need to improve. In either case, cultural hurdles will arise once the decision has been made to implement web technology in business.

Many Internet-savvy, strategic thinkers within your company see a digital tsunami starting to crest. Many believe that not quickly and dramatically changing to face this oncoming wave puts the company in dire risk. There are also line-of-business executives who don't see any reason to rush to embrace the new Internet possibilities. Many of these individuals see that business will drive the need for technological change in its own time. It is often a clash of corporate culture that occurs when individuals from both of these camps confront each other with the goal of successfully implementing an effective Intranet/Extranet.

When presented with a plan to implement a corporate Intranet, top managers are likely to ask: "Will the corporate Intranet/Extranet help me sell one more widget? How will I use it to gain an advantage over my competitors?" The answer, though, is simple. A corporate Intranet is not about increasing revenue; it is about improving efficiency and productivity and thus achieving higher profits. Obtaining agreement and support of top management at this strategic level is critical. With it, resolving issues related to culture differences within the company become much easier. Retaining profit is a goal that all corporate camps understand. Retaining profit is an excellent motivator for working together to implement quickly. Profit is the glue that will form the implementation team into a cohesive unit.

A company that has a solid Internet strategy and executes it well will have an easier time launching its Intranet than one that is still struggling to define the purpose of its World Wide Web site. Providing a common vision and setting guiding principles for associates to follow is part of a solid e-commerce strategy. One of the most significant cultural issues to arise within a corporation that does not develop an e-commerce strategy is information ownership (territory protection). A corporate Intranet should be developed as a company-wide asset that crosses the boundaries of many departments and makes information available to everyone. In today's highly political corporate world, the ability to control the distribution of key information is a significant power/control issue. A corporate Intranet by its nature immediately eliminates an individual's power to control information, because it places information in a secure, but open, environment. The elimination of these boundaries may be perceived as a threat to those who now control the information. Overcoming this corporate-culture issue is a process of gaining executive-management adoption of governance that states the rules of information control. As a guiding principle, all corporate information developed by originating departments should be published, with appropriate security, on the Intranet. As these rules become strictly enforced, a corresponding change in the culture will occur.

Gaining the Support of the Workforce

While certain age groups tend to be more accepting of new technology, the ability to utilize Web tools is by no means generational. And in fact, the generation *y* programmer who wants to incorporate the newest scripting language without regard to the business objective may be as much of a problem as the executive who has never surfed the Web.

In the development of an Intranet/Extranet, there is no more challenging experience, nor one more rewarding, than turning the Web lights on for key individuals in a company. Being responsible for the moment of understanding of the potential and power of Web technology is a Web reality. On occasion, this experience is traceable as an event that changed the company.

When I taught novice automotive dealer groups about the fundamentals of the Internet, I would always start with a technical demonstration. I would ask each member of the class to name his or her hero. I would choose the most obscure hero named and conduct an Internet search on that name. The search always produced impressive results, and five minutes of information gathering paid off in enormous dividends to the whole class, particularly to the doubters in the group.

Enlightenment for top management comes with great personal effort—it seldom comes without significant one-on-one interaction. I have had the unique pleasure of turning those lights on for a number of people, both in business and in my personal life. I have found the common elements in accomplishing this task.

TOOLS FOR INDIVIDUAL WEB ENLIGHTENMENT

- Capture their imagination
- Give them hands-on experience
- Offer personalized benefits
- Nurture a vision of the future

The need for enlightenment usually comes from a lack of understanding for the depth of the Internet and the scope of Web technology. Capturing the imagination of a subject is not difficult; it simply requires that you put yourself in the other person's shoes. You can accomplish this by using the World Wide Web search tools and understanding what pushes the hot button of your student. In your first sitting, teach your student something new about a subject that they may be expert in. Even if the student is a medical doctor and I can't teach him or her a new medical procedure, I can still teach him or her about how to access journals, how to find out about experts from hospitals or universities, or how to access the research of authorities in a distant country.

This process may be hampered by inexperience with technology. This issue is becoming less of a problem as more and more people are exposed to the Internet. The changing of norms is assisted by changes to technology and ease of use. Still, placing the keyboard in the hands of the unknowing is a critical link in the understanding of the power of Web technology. A hands-on experience is powerful for all.

The dismissal of Web technology might come from not understanding the individual benefit of Web technology. Teach personalized benefits in terms that are relevant. Teaching a college student about the Internet can help him or her save time in writing a college paper or locating the best price for a new surfboard. A purchasing manager for a company can relieve the pain of internal purchase-order workflow with an Intranet, and at the same time find new vendors and new opportunities with open Internet request for purchase. The most effective tool of the four for gaining quick action is the ability to personalize benefits.

Nurturing a vision for the future will help to institutionalize the Intranet/Extranet experience within the company. To add head-count, acquire budgets for infrastructure, and otherwise plan a long-term future requires a common vision that is in tune with the strategic objectives of the company.

The most successful implementers of web technology are usually the individuals who understand the latest programming languages and utilize them when proven. Intranet success occurs when implementers use proven technology to add value to the business application.

Developing an Intranet/Extranet

To build a successful corporate Intranet, many components have to be in place. First, an organization must come up with a plan, including governance, to direct all departments on the distribution of information through the Intranet. Then, organizational teams have to be created to provide a broad synergistic expertise that will obtain enterprise acceptance and management approvals/ funding.

Next, a statement of work needs to be drawn up that will effectively outline the vision and scope of the work to be completed. Within this document, there should be a comprehensive list of the content to be developed as well as the line-of-business applications, associate utilities, informational references, and community content. For a company's Intranet to gain advantage, the right mix of content is absolutely essential. Definitions of Intranet content are as follows:

Intranet Content by Type

Line-of-Business Applications—Operational workflow directly affecting the day-to-day business of the company. Example: Expense reporting, Sales-order input.

Employee Tools—Tools that associates commonly utilize to accomplish their daily work process. Example: Company telephone book.

Informational Sites—Departmental Intranet site that describes the scope of activities that the department manages. Example: Risk Management department Intranet site explains Insurance coverage, disaster recovery planning, and modeling techniques used to analyze business risk.

Community Content—Features that associates will find useful from a personal life perspective. Example: access to a freeway traffic cam, online company classifieds, hyperlink to charity.

The strategy to develop the mix of content should include plans for the first two years of life on the Intranet. It should also be expected that there will be three or four version releases during that time. Each version if developed properly should represent a progression, allowing for the evolution of the Intranet site's personality to shift from young to mature, from occasionally visited to broadly used. This type of version forethought will changes the focus of the content to allow for maximized use by associates. This is accomplished by changing the mix of application types over a period of time. Intranet site content, just as in the public Internet, will be the primary driver of site visitations and usage.

So how do you determine what content will make a successful Intranet site? The answer comes by facilitating the customer. Start asking questions from an Enterprise perspective. What are the ten toughest things for associates to do? What simple repetitive task could be eliminated? What are the applications that affect the largest number of associates? When the answers start to come back, the results may be very surprising.

According to corporate legend, in the 1970s the executive management of the Ford Motor Company, in an effort to improve productivity among their tens of thousands of administrative employees, issued an edict that Ford would be identified only by letter "F" in all internal correspondence. That way, a typist would save a minimum of three keystrokes every time the word was written—you can almost calculate the return on investment without knowing the financials of the company.

With an Intranet, it is often the little things like that or the unexpected that produce dramatic results. As an example, corporate employees often find it difficult to change how their 401(k) savings plans are invested. Creating a simple program that lets employees review and change their investments saves them time and empowers them. Similarly, an Intranet for a company with a "cafe-teria-style" benefits plan enable employees to review their options among health-care and other benefits. Creating electronic forms for basic company paperwork such as expense reports also saves time and gives employees a sense of control. Finally, something as simple as a corporate organizational chart saves employees the frustration of trying to locate the right person in a bureaucratic maze. None of these examples involves a change to the company's basic business. Nevertheless, providing easy access to old information and processes provided a remarkably positive result. Convenience was created. A gift of time was given. Incorporating information like this is an excellent way to make the Intranet an everyday tool.

At launch, the Intranet content mix should be heavily oriented toward employee tools. This will help deliver a critical element for success, namely a broad user base willing to try out the Intranet during its first months. In addition, some content should be devoted to building community and creating the same kind of emotional attachment that Internet surfers feel to their favorite World Wide Web sites. For instance, the Toyota Intranet offers an area called "the Trading Post" where employees can list items they want to sell. This area is particularly popular at lunch time.

Different kinds of informational sites are developed in different ways. You can start by having individual departments build their own areas. Informational sites can include reference areas such as bulletin boards, shared databases, and other communication tools. After Toyota launched its corporate Intranet, Toyota Vision, it began a program to promote the development of new areas. Toyota's

Information Technology group sponsored sessions to teach employees how to use Microsoft Frontpage software to make it easier for them to build departmental Web pages. Within six months, thirty-five sites had been built by different business units.

Line-of-business applications are at the heart of the Intranet. It is the line-of-business application that will give a corporate Intranet longevity. It will also justify Intranet budgets and infrastructure enhancements. When an Intranet-based, line-of-business application is the best possible way of conducting the business, then the Intranet becomes the business. When developing the Intranet statement of work, it is critical to add the right line-of-business applications to the mix. There are delicate considerations to be evaluated when deciding what line-of-business content should be part of the Intranet launch version. For Toyota, a pure line-of-business application is its dynamic sales-reporting system that updates every three minutes the number of vehicles sold. Any Toyota employee can see the exact number of vehicles sold almost in real-time. This line-of-business application allows sales information to be seen by geographic area, by model, against objective, and historically.

Potentially conflicting goals exist in trying to launch a large Intranet. For instance, the goal of getting everyone to use the Intranet may conflict with trying to make the information valuable from a strategic standpoint. It is important to set reasonable expectations based on the available budget, staffing, and timetable.

For a start-up launch, a total of ten applications might be the extent of content that employees see. With the ability to define ten applications in a statement of work, the question arises: What do I pursue? By choosing ten employee tools in the beginning, like a corporate phone book, it is fairly certain that a large number of associates will visit and use the site. Under this scenario, the question of substance and relevance will arise. Another choice might be to go with all line-of-business applications. In a company like Toyota, with more than one hundred departments, ten line-of-business applications might be pertinent to only 10 percent of the employees. In this case, the value perception would be extremely high for the departments with valuable information, however the rest of the company may be left wondering what the big deal is all about.

In a review of all options, my experience has shown that a mix of content provides the best prospects for success in the long term. The following table provides an insight into what the mix should be at launch and one and two years later. The cumulative percentages represent the changing mix as new applications are continually added.

Intranet Content Mix

	LAUNCH	YEAR ONE	YEAR TWO
Line-of-Business	20%	30%	40%
Employee Tools	60%	40%	30%
Information	10%	20%	25%
Community	10%	10%	5%
TOTAL	100%	100%	100%

This formula will ensure that a broad range of employees are visiting the site, but also that it is becoming more important to the company's core business. This strategy will capture the support of top management.

DEVELOPING AN INTRANET—TIPS TO GAIN ADVANTAGE

For those individuals charged with developing a company's Intranet, here are ten tips that can assist in producing an excellent quality product and a successful launch.

Obtain Consensus from Key Stakeholders. In the final development of the statement of work, a small number of applications will be identified. Make sure early on that top management agrees that these are the most important areas to be launched. Early identification, discussions, and consensus with peer groups will smooth the way.

Apply Lessons Learned from Your Consumer Web site. Image is important internally. Remember that fellow employees can be positively influenced by many of the same features that work for external customers. Creating a lasting, useful name with a working metaphor, and a solid internal brand will help the Intranet team in launching, promoting, and maintaining the site.

Understand Your Core Competencies with Human Resources. An Intranet group will need people with different types of skills. In most cases, there will be gaps in needed skill sets. With limited resources it is critical to identify and locate people with the skills you will need in the future. Then hire qualified outside contractors to fill in the rest of the gaps.

Take Technical Cues from Internet Best Practice. Be graphically conservative; use proven programming languages and database tools. Thoroughly research hosting options. Ensure that network infrastructure for Intranet delivery is in place and tested weeks prior to launch.

Integrate Traditional Business Applications. Use a three-tier approach to delivering line-of-business applications. Wherever possible, take advantage of business applications on other computer platforms. The three-tier approach uses the Intranet (1) as the user interface to an existing legacy application located on a mainframe or other computer (2) with a special translating software (3) that makes sure the two systems understand each other.

Be Dogmatic about the Scope of the Project. When a statement of work is finished, steadfastly protect it from changes. "Scope creep" is the mortal enemy of a successful Intranet development. Allowing continual changes to the plan destroys budgets, timetables, and limits existing resources. When change has to occur, re-evaluate the elements of the statement of work and modify them accordingly with each change.

Create a War Room, Assemble Team Members Every Day. Communication is the key to success in any rapid application development. Sharing wins and losses, watching pivotal dates, allow the dynamics of the team to shine.

Create New Product Every Day. Do not wait for due dates to release new programs. Allow the work that is completed to be seen by all every day. Progress is a great motivator; it also points to the contributors, and identifies where difficulties may be occurring.

Gather Stakeholders and Prelaunch. Create a beta group and prelaunch the Intranet prior to complete quality-control testing. Allow different eyes to view the results. Present the near-finished product to all executives and detail the activities associated with launch day.

Create a Launch Extravaganza, Celebrate a Successful Launch with the Team. Plan to launch the site and let all employees know that the

Intranet is now available. Included in that plan should be teaser communications that build anticipation. On launch day, use printed media, posters, and video to create excitement. After the official announcement, provide demonstrations, track users, and measure results. As a team leader, prepare an appropriate celebration for all team members.

Following these steps will help an organization accomplish its goals. Although they involve a considerable amount of work, the results will change a company and the way it conducts business.

As the Intranet comes to life, the logical extension of that product is to tie it to vendors, customers, business partners, and affiliated companies. This is the process of building an Extranet. An Extranet is the culminating effort in bringing Web technology into the business environment. It can tie together the entire organization and redefine how business is done.

Extending the Intranet to Become an Extranet

When a company sees itself as a single part of a greater effort to deliver a product or service, it begins to understand a concept called "Value Chain." A value chain is a vertical group of companies whose services provide cumulative value to produce an end product. As an example, a Toyota dealership is a business that provides Toyota products and services to consumers. The consumers are the final link in the chain. How many links exist before the Toyota dealership?

Let's examine the Toyota value chain for a new Camry automobile purchased by a consumer. Each of the following companies provided a value-added service to the Camry before it was received by the consumer. The dealership provides vehicle preparation, selling, and finance services. The regional office provides wholesale selling, scheduling, and support services. The national office provides marketing, logistics, and support services. The transportation companies provide delivery. The manufacturing plant consolidates parts, provides assembly and finished cars and trucks. The stamping plant transforms banded steel into assembly parts. The foundry creates banded steel from raw materials. Each played an integral part in placing the new Camry in the customer's driveway.

With so many companies dependent on each other for their success, it would seem natural for advanced forms of communications to occur between all of them. However, the reality of U.S. business is that there is little communication beyond the next link in the value chain. The benefits of robust communications within a value chain in the automotive industry are many. If a lower-tier supplier of seat-cover materials for the Camry had direct access to the dealer or even to the end-product consumer, significant benefits could be realized. As an example, the lower-tier supplier estimates consumer demand via focus groups and internal sales projections. By connecting to actual sales, a lower-tier vendor could dynamically purchase raw materials, saving on inventory costs and eliminating obsolescence. The suppliers' Extranet would reduce costs and improve profitability. Internet technology allows every company in the value chain to be linked through the standard protocols of the Internet. This implementation is the Extranet.

Within the automotive industry, the first broad Extranet—called ANX for Automotive Network Exchange—is being developed. General Motors, Ford, and Chrysler are sponsors and part of the original team that came up with the concept. These automotive manufacturers, along with Johnson Controls and twelve of their suppliers, initiated the Manufacturing Assembly Pilot (MAP). These companies were chosen as test sites for identifying, implementing, and validating improved business processes, which then could be rolled out nationwide. If the pilot is successful; thousands of automotive-industry vendors will convert to a common set of technical standards that will allow advanced communications to spread throughout the Industry.

The ANX example is one of the most aggressive Extranet applications in the world, and it is limited to only technical infrastructure. For most companies, significant productivity gains can be achieved by connecting to just one business partner, vendor, customer, or affiliated company. Building your company's Extranet will take time, and strict attention to the many details will be necessary. Complicating issues such as security, partner relationships, and high telecommunications costs make the risks significant. However, the potential benefits to implementing a successful

Extranet are extraordinary. Included in this list is business-process improvement, improvement in time to market, dramatic improvement in productivity and profitability, and the redefinition of business operations driven by consumers that are creating a global Internet economy.

The Elusive Return on Investment

The Internet was the first step in a technical revolution that is having a major impact on society. The business use of Internet technology, specifically Intranets and Extranets, will ultimately have a similar impact on the world's economy. The purest proof is the return on investments they provide. Intranets and Extranets improve productivity and save money. They create more net income to business. As mentioned earlier, Intranets usually return 100 percent of their implementation costs in less then six months.

Unlike many public Web sites, the return on a corporate Intranet is easy to measure. With the basic Internet tracking tools, the number of visitations can easily be tracked. Benchmarking studies can determine the exact savings that the use of a single application can produce. When these tools are combined, the dollar savings on each application is easily determined.

It is recommended that an estimated return on investment be developed when creating the statement of work for the Intranet project. It is highly recommended that an actual ROI be conducted six months after launch. This study should be conducted by an internal audit or accounting group or an outside consulting firm. If a consulting firm was engaged to assist in the development of an Intranet/Extranet, they will often do the ROI analysis for no additional charge.

Do not be shocked when the results of your ROI come out to be in excess of 100 percent and in some cases more than 1000 percent. The results of Toyota's ROI came out at a level not seen in normal projects conducted in this or any organization. It is for this reason that Toyota's corporate Intranet and Extranet have become the business.

Business-to-Business Commerce: The Internet Evolution

Hilary Bryn Thomas, President, Interactive Telecommunications Services, Inc.

It is not a question of public or private networks, open or controlled environments. For large corporations, the very investment in private networks and their pervasive reach into business processes requires a careful integration with new technologies. Hilary Thomas, who for many years has advised executives in the art of integrating online technologies with large complex systems and organizations, addresses the evolution that is taking place in corporations across America, as private networks link up with the Internet.

Electronic Commerce in the Web-Empowered Enterprise

With the evolution of the Internet into a universally accessible total business-communications network, we are witnessing an event more powerful than any since the invention of the telephone. This reflects the broad scope and deep influence that the Internet will have on the way we manage our businesses, present ourselves to customers, interface with our trading partners, and relate to our employees. Designing an Electronic Business involves the total remaking of the enterprise as the Internet pervades its every form and function. And it then involves the total transformation of the way that we conduct trade. As we will demonstrate in this chapter, there is plenty of evidence that the change has begun.

In mid-1997, United Parcel Service (UPS) claimed to have implemented the largest business-to-business electronic commerce application to date. The company converted to electronic management its 60,000 vendors who collectively generate 7 million invoices annually. By October 1997, General Electric's Internet-based procurement system had been used to purchase more than $1 billion worth of goods and supplies. During that same year, three companies, Cisco, Dell, and General Electric were responsible for $3 billion worth of Internet-based electronic trade. In mid-1998, whole industries were creating electronic-trading communities, extending access to networks and services across the boundaries of competing companies. The Automotive Industry Action Group (AIAG) plans to link the big three U.S. automakers with their suppliers, dealers, and other participants in the supply chain through the Automotive Network Exchange (ANX). This Extranet is expected to result in cost savings of over $1 billion annually when all levels of suppliers in the industry are connected. Its most dramatic effect, however, may be its ability to facilitate cooperation between competitors in a way that has not been achieved before.

Web-Empowering People and Processes

The term "electronic commerce" (e-commerce) is used to describe the automation of the processes by which we conduct trade. The challenges of e-commerce are many. Although it itself is not new, e-commerce on the Internet (ECI) is uncharted territory. Its commercial users are its pioneers. This is not a role that most companies relish. Business executives are faced with a choice; begin to embrace the Internet now and risk its uncertainty, or wait until its impact is proven. We support starting now. We believe that any enterprise that plans to remain commercially competitive in the first decade of the next millennium must become Web-empowered. This requires the strategic integration of the Web into the business process at every place in the enterprise where the Internet can touch it. "The corporation must become Web-Centric," says Steven Ward, Chief Information Office of International Business Machines (IBM), who is in charge of the mammoth task of converting IBM into an electronic business. "You need to have faith. You must make a business decision that anything you do from now on will be Web-Centric."[1]

The irony is that the Internet was not built for the job. It was not designed for commerce, but for free and easy communications between academics and researchers. Now, we are asking it to facilitate a business revolution. The question is whether it is up to the task.

This chapter will investigate the opportunities and the pitfalls of e-commerce. It will conclude that it is not the Internet Network per se that is important, but rather the technical standards and business practices that will be built upon it. The vision is one of the globe cocooned in a virtual blanket of networks of many different types and technologies, linked together by a robust set of standards that will be the heritage of the Internet and the World Wide Web. It is this set of technical standards and business practices that, if truly standardized and adopted worldwide, will provide the glue to hold electronic business together.

Conducting Electronic Business

E-commerce is an integral component of electronic business (e-business), which is a broader process of change within and between enterprises. While recognizing that e-commerce involves the key functions that enable sales to be made and revenue generated, it is, ultimately, the total transformation to e-business that will unlock the promise of the Internet. Common standards of access will be found throughout all the links of the commercial chain—between manufacturer and supplier, wholesaler and retailer, and buyers and sellers everywhere. As millions of individual employees are empowered by it, the Internet will emerge as an alternative to, and in some cases a replacement for, many of the tried and true mechanisms of commercial society.

In the Internet protocols (TCP IP and its derivatives) and in the World Wide Web, we have a standard for global data communication and the tools for electronic commerce on the Internet (ECI), and it encompasses a variety of technology uses in both public and private scenarios. While consumer access to the World Wide Web is the catalyst that has spurred this growth, we believe that the real impact of the Internet over the next decade will be the impact on businesses as they restructure themselves to survive and prosper in an electronic world.

The Evolution of Electronic Commerce

In the few short years since the arrival of the World Wide Web, there have been three overlapping phases of business use of the Internet related to electronic commerce. The first phase was a frenzy of Web site development, much of which was done without much concern for strategic value or return on investment. It was driven by advertising and marketing departments and focused on the consumer. Some companies, especially those in Internet-related businesses such as equipment manufacturers, vendors, software developers, and distributors, successfully promoted and sold products to business customers.

The second phase extended the use of the Internet for an organization's internal purposes, referred to as Intranets. Information Technology managers are learning to use the Internet technology to break down internal barriers, allowing the free exchange of information among the companies' data bases as well as extend the reach of its legacy systems, such as Electronic Data Interchange (EDI), to reach broader audiences of users. EDI had been introduced in the early 1980s with the goal of automating manual systems such as inventory and order entry, to increase the speed of the transaction, improve efficiency, and reduce the potency of human error. But EDI did not result in critical mass among its audience. Despite two decades of operations, the majority of EDI proponents are large corporations and governments that use it to conduct business with large, known, and contracted trading partners. Approximately 100,000 companies worldwide use EDI; a number that represents only 5 percent of all businesses that could benefit from the technology.[2] This is due in large part to the high cost and complexity of installing and managing the operational facilities required at each EDI user's site. With only 5 percent of companies equipped to

INTERNET AND EDI— A COMPARISON

The Internet has many attributes that enhance its e-commerce predecessor, and that enable much broader adoption of electronic transactions. Some of these attributes are:

- It is global and has a base of global standards.
- It is relatively easy to implement.
- The cost of entry for trading partners is low.
- It offers flat, volume-independent and time-of-day independent pricing for data transmission.
- It is robust because it encompasses multiple alternative pathways, gateways, and interconnections.

- It is capable of providing high bandwidth for data throughput.
- It is platform independent.

It also has many weaknesses, some of which are endemic to a network that was designed for the free exchange of ideas and information between academics and researchers. Most critical of these are:

- It is insecure; sensitive data and payment systems are at risk of being compromised.
- It is based on rapidly changing, immature, and unstable development tools and standards.
- There is no clear business model to follow.
- It has few rules of engagement suitable for commercial transactions.

operate EDI, it is not surprising that by late 1996, the major thrust of business-to-business electronic commerce had shifted toward finding ways to use the Internet to leverage the investment in EDI by increasing the number of trading partners that could access large EDI operators ("hubs"). Established EDI software vendors such as Harbinger, Premenos, and Sterling began to develop interfaces that would allow vendors, suppliers, and customers access to the EDI system via the Internet. At the same time, EDI network providers such as AT&T and GEIS started to evaluate and engage the competitive threat posed by a shift of traffic to the Internet.

The primary focus of the third phase of evolution will be the development of ECI: secure, stable, and tested solutions for end-to-end electronic commerce over the Internet. As ECI gets underway, we see Intranets and the early Internet/EDI solutions joining to form Extranets, which extend the private network beyond the boundaries of the corporation to known and trusted business partners. Successful business models are emerging, based on efficient use of resources to reach business partners, faster sales-turnaround times, improved fulfillment cycles, and lowered costs. At the same time, governments and regulators are engaged in attempts to define and legislate for this changing environment. While Europe struggles to unify codes across a changing map of national boundaries, the U.S. government has proposed solutions such as a moratorium on taxes, to ensure that the Internet is not strangled by the individual attempts of fifty states to protect sources of income against changing methods of trading. The lack of a predictable legal environment is an inhibitor to ECI. The U.S. government is working with the United Nations Commission on International Trade Law (UNCITRAL) to develop a model law that will underpin commercial contracts for electronic commerce internationally.

The stage is then being set for a fourth phase, beginning in the not-too-distant future, in which many layers of differentiated public and private "Nets" will be chained together and woven into an "electronic blanket" covering the globe. These Nets will incorporate new levels of security and positive personal identification that will allow them to be accessed, under controlled circumstances, by anyone with a browser. This will facilitate the emergence of the level playing field upon which all users, know and unknown, contracted and ad hoc, business and consumer, will have access, in five or more years from now, to a singular and ubiquitous repository of commercial interaction at appropriate levels of privilege.

The fourth phase will mark the ability of enterprises and consumers to participate in true Web-enabled commerce. This will emerge from:

- the convergence of secure technologies and access discriminators;
- major investment in Intranets, Extranets, and linkages to legacy systems;
- widespread availability of high-speed, high-bandwidth delivery systems on a global scale; and
- a stable political and regulatory cyber-environment.

Increased technical and regulatory stability combined with the lessons of five or more years of Internet use will break through the remaining barriers of consumer trust and confidence and provide the basis for electronic commerce to move to the mainstream.

Electronic Commerce Set to Explode

Pundits predict growth on an unprecedented scale. ECI is growing faster than any other segment of the U.S. economy. In 1997, it grew three times faster than the economy as a whole. Forrester Research predicts that the total volume of goods and services traded between U.S. companies over the Internet will exceed $17 billion in 1998. In 2002, Forrester predicts, the total will have reached $327 billion, which represents 2.3 percent of the total U.S. business revenues. This growth has been kick-started, Forrester reports, by the manufacturing sector, which is predicted to conduct 0.3 percent of its business on the Internet in 1998. This sector will still hold the lead in 2002 (3.7 percent of its trade being on the Internet), but by then, Forrester expects the wholesale and business retail sector to be a close second, growing from 0.1 percent in 1998 to 3.1 percent in 2002.[3] Gartner Group predicts that by 2003, nearly 50 percent of all electronic-commerce transaction revenue will be derived from secure Extranets with 15 percent of business-to-business transactions using the global "public" Internet.[4]

Redesigning the Internet

Behind all this predicted growth and societal change is an infrastructure that was not designed for the task. The whole environment is in the process of being redesigned for commercial traffic, and the Internet community must deal with many issues—technical, societal, regulatory, and political—before it will be fully developed and capable of delivering the levels of privacy, security, and reliability necessary to evolve to the fourth phase. We are dealing in an imperfect and rapidly changing world that is still finding self-definition and establishing its modus operandi. The initial focus of the Commerce Department, of industry consortiums like the banking community's Banking Industry Technology Secretariat (BITS), and of many major corporations is the elimination of issues that keep consumers from using the Internet for commerce; issues such as privacy of information and secure payment mechanisms. At a different level, these same issues are defining the evolution of Intranets and Extranets.

Figure 11.1. Growth of Electronic Commerce in the United States

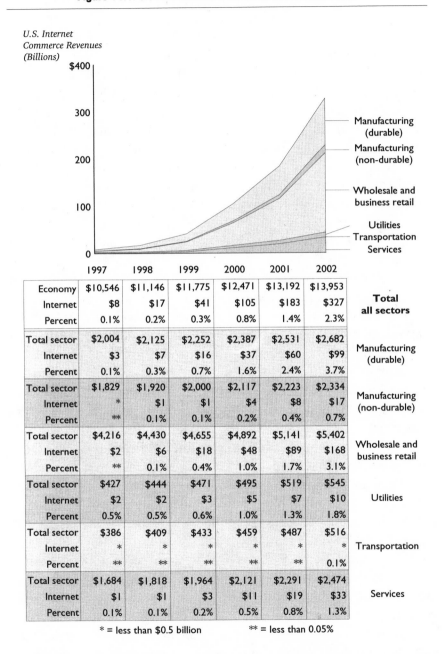

U.S. Internet
Commerce Revenues
(Billions)

	1997	1998	1999	2000	2001	2002	
Economy	$10,546	$11,146	$11,775	$12,471	$13,192	$13,953	**Total**
Internet	$8	$17	$41	$105	$183	$327	**all sectors**
Percent	0.1%	0.2%	0.3%	0.8%	1.4%	2.3%	
Total sector	$2,004	$2,125	$2,252	$2,387	$2,531	$2,682	Manufacturing
Internet	$3	$7	$16	$37	$60	$99	(durable)
Percent	0.1%	0.3%	0.7%	1.6%	2.4%	3.7%	
Total sector	$1,829	$1,920	$2,000	$2,117	$2,223	$2,334	Manufacturing
Internet	*	$1	$1	$4	$8	$17	(non-durable)
Percent	**	0.1%	0.1%	0.2%	0.4%	0.7%	
Total sector	$4,216	$4,430	$4,655	$4,892	$5,141	$5,402	Wholesale and
Internet	$2	$6	$18	$48	$89	$168	business retail
Percent	**	0.1%	0.4%	1.0%	1.7%	3.1%	
Total sector	$427	$444	$471	$495	$519	$545	Utilities
Internet	$2	$2	$3	$5	$7	$10	
Percent	0.5%	0.5%	0.6%	1.0%	1.3%	1.8%	
Total sector	$386	$409	$433	$459	$487	$516	Transportation
Internet	*	*	*	*	*	*	
Percent	**	**	**	**	**	0.1%	
Total sector	$1,684	$1,818	$1,964	$2,121	$2,291	$2,474	Services
Internet	$1	$1	$3	$11	$19	$33	
Percent	0.1%	0.1%	0.2%	0.5%	0.8%	1.3%	

* = less than $0.5 billion   ** = less than 0.05%

Although individual companies may be scrupulous in the way they handle confidential information, access to corporate applications will not be opened up, nor will transactions take place, unless all parties are confident that the information they provide is not available to unauthorized users and that the transaction will be completed correctly. One of the strengths of EDI is the ability to track the path of a message and to ensure its secure passage from end to end. This path is not clear for ECI. Concerns among businesses and consumers regarding security on the Internet still linger.

While these fears may be exaggerated by media hype and industry self-interest, there are legitimate concerns that face anyone transferring payment information or funds, whether it be between a consumer and a merchant or between a business customer and a supplier. Enormous efforts are being made to allay fears on all fronts. Firewalls are being deployed and secured servers, employing a variety of encryption techniques, are being used to create defenses around the networks to protect data from attack. New and more sophisticated server software offer additional levels of user identification and authentication of access. To be realized, the fourth phase depends on robust solutions to these concerns. And the practical considerations must be matched by sincere and demonstrable efforts to address the perceived insecurity of the environment. At this stage, user qualms are as real a barrier as the threat of physical attack.

One company that is pushing ahead in spite of these concerns and demonstrating how the Web can enhance relationships between trading partners is IBM. As a supplier of computer hard drives to customers such as Compaq, Dell, and Gateway computers, IBM is following the creed "Feed the Web." A business decision was made to put low-level manufacturing systems on the Web. The decision was made because the Web was simplest to implement and easiest to use. The unanticipated outcome is that most of the customers that purchase the hard drives can access relevant data that enable them to understand IBM's internal processes, such as how production operates, what quality-control standards are applied, and how products were tested. This increases confidence in IBM as a supplier, gives it a competitive edge, and increases sales. The information that was the subject of this particular Web-centric decision has gone from being a manufacturing necessity to becoming a sales asset positively impacting revenue and profits without incurring security issues.

Creating a Secure Payment System

In addition to corporate security concerns, significant efforts are also under way to create a secure payment system for Internet commerce. These have resulted in a wide range of proposed solutions, including:

- MasterCard and VISA's much heralded but elusive Secure Electronic Transaction (SET) protocol, which promises to secure credit-card transactions and address allowance of purchases
- Hardware-based debit-card and smart-card systems from companies such as VeriFone, ISED Corporation, and Innovonics
- Cyber-wallets, smart cards, and digital cash and tokens from CyberCash, Digicash, Mondex, and Verisign
- The use of the telephone bill or other utility bills to collect payments (e.g., eCharge™)

None of these payment systems has yet to be accepted as the standard, or even "the answer." Some are more appropriate for the consumer than for business use. In the world of Extranets, the users are known and often under contract, and/or have an account with each other, so the need to use a real-time payment system such as a credit card is less urgent. The increasing use of procurement cards, and the urge to complete the total purchasing-and-payment cycle electronically, will mean that this is a continued area of concern well into the fourth phase.

Organizations such as CommerceNet: www.commerce.net have emerged to galvanize the industry, to commission research, and to offer solutions to these issues. Mechanisms such as Truste™: **www.truste.org** have proposed security guidelines and standards to be voluntarily adopted by the industry.

Political Restraint

Politically, the Internet industry is gathering itself to respond to challenges from Washington and Europe. But the regulatory process has not yet acclimatized itself to work at the speed of the proverbial week-long "Internet year." In the United States, despite the surprisingly "hands-off" attitude adopted by the Clinton administration, and the continued efforts of groups such as the Internet Alliance: www.internetalliance.net, the industry is taking a tortuous route toward self-identification. In July 1998, Congress and the Federal Trade Commission made it known that e-commerce had "one more chance" to demonstrate that it could police privacy effectively without legislation. The U.S. Department of Commerce continues to play an active role in the thought process, publishing a number of well-researched treatises on the impact of the Internet on the economy. (One of these, *The Emerging Digital Economy,*[5] has a useful chapter entitled "Electronic Commerce between Businesses," and an appendix packed with case studies. This report is available at www.ecommerce.gov/danc3.htm. Ira Magaziner, who first spelled out the White House's restrained approach in 1997 in the Framework for Electronic Commerce,[6] continues to call for self-regulation. "Legislative action is a knee jerk reaction of the industrial age when government was expected to protect you," he said. "In the digital age, there are new paradigms; one of them is to empower people by giving them the tools to protect themselves."[7]

Under the Emerging Nets

The issues that are limiting electronic commerce today will be resolved, but it will not be by simply building new layers of technical and regulatory complexity. A more complex, layered environment will emerge. We predict that much of the information intended for purely public access will remain within the confines of the "pure" public Internet. The majority of electronic commerce will take place on secured Extranets. Globally, there will exist multilayered and interconnected Nets, each of which will have a specialized function and will be accessible only by authorized users and connected to one another in proscribed ways. Each Net will conform at the appropriate level to the same standards and protocols, be accessible from a familiar browser or network-access device, and will appear the same to the user except with regard to access privileges and application sets. Nets will be functionally linked by common authorized users. In the simplest terms, the supplier on one Extranet is the buyer on another. An automotive manufacturer supplying parts via the Automotive Network Exchange is, in another business context, a customer purchasing office supplies from a separate but compatible Net.

Different Nets will operate according to different business rules and require different levels of regulation. Although this may seem onerous, it may actually simplify the process of regulation, as each Net will adopt an appropriate subset of the rules of the whole. As e-commerce Nets cross the boundaries of corporations of states and of nations, for example, new taxation becomes an opportunity for the authorities and a hazard for enterprises. The proposed moratorium on taxation on Internet commerce will help the growth of the industry financially. It is hoped that it will provide a sufficient pause for governments around the world to realize that the new age needs new, global visions and solutions. It also needs industries to implement them.

Reaching New Audiences

Despite the visionary efforts of the U.S. automobile industry, most current examples of Extranet deployment are more tactical in nature than strategic. The majority are not being implemented at the corporate level but within business units. This is appropriate, given the complexity of the projects, the instability of the technology, and the lack of proven business models. However, one of the key tenets of this approach is that any e-business deployment ultimately should be part of an overall Web-centric philosophy. While this will not result in an immediate, robust enterprise-wide chain of Extranets, it will provide the best basis for future expansion. Applications should target opportunities to improve operations and an organization's competitive edge. They should do so in an environment that is secure, reliable, and easy enough to install and use.

One example of this kind of phased implementation is taking place in Canada, at the Liquor Control Board of Ontario (LCBO). This provincial agency is responsible for regulating the control, distribution, and sale of beverage alcohol in a socially responsible manner. The overall approach is part of the long-term strategy of the Canadian Association of Liquor Jurisdiction (CALJ), which, since 1990, has been engaged in the establishment of electronic trading standards for Canadian Liquor Jurisdictions and their trading partners.

The LCBO is growing its e-commerce market in a controlled manner, using EDI as an integral part of its existing applications. LCBO has fourteen hundred suppliers located worldwide, to which LCBO issues a total of twenty-two thousand purchase orders (POs) per year. These suppliers range in size from major conglomerates that receive over one thousand POs a year from LCBO, to small boutique wineries that receive only one PO per year. Until one year ago, all POs were sent out by fax and acknowledged by either fax or telephone. In the six months following its inception, the EDI system processed $50 million in POs with six of its largest trading partners. By mid-1998, the LCBO was trading PO data electronically with 13 trading partners, and the volume being processed had reached over $200 million. Although these suppliers represent less than 1 percent of the total number of trading partners, they receive approximately 25 percent of all the POs generated by the board. The remaining 75 percent of the POs continued to be faxed and/or mailed by low-volume trading partners who did not have EDI capabilities. In its recommendation to the board management, the LCBO's EDI working committee stated:

> In order to realize the full benefits from Electronic Commerce . . . the LCBO must expand the EDI trading partner population. Issuing a mandate to the supplier community to become EDI capable is unreasonable. We cannot expect our trading partners that receive only a couple of POs a month to invest thousands of dollars in EDI. The LCBO must provide an easy to use solution that is cost effective and accessible by the majority of our small and medium size trading partners.

Kittling Ridge Estate Wines & Spirits is one of the first to implement the LCBO's Web-based system. Its owners are enthusiastic about the improved access to sales data, and feel this Web/EDI system will allow it to access current data at any time, to assist in setting production targets, managing inventory, and assessing the performance of sales representatives. Kittling Ridge is less enthusiastic about the immediate impact of the electronic PO system.

"I understand why LCBO is doing this, but in the short term, I am not certain that I am going to benefit from receiving a PO over the WEB," says Mr. Burrows, Vice President of Kittling Ridge, "Because I do not yet have an interface to my other systems such as accounts receivable and supplies management systems. I need to pass this information directly on to other departments if it is to be truly effective," he explains. "Also, we rely a lot on human intervention to ensure that trucks go out of here full. I haven't figured out how we are going to do that electronically."

Recognizing the Benefits

As LCBO has shown, Extranets enable corporations to leverage investment in EDI and reach a critical mass of business partners cost-effectively. A successful Extranet will have direct effects on the bottom line; it will decrease communications costs, extend the supply chain, improve channel management, and increase employee efficiency. Indirectly, it can improve service and therefore improve customer relationships. An analysis of the benefits was conducted by the LCBO:

Benefits of EDI/Electronic Commerce

Source: LCBO

IMPACT	SAVINGS AND BENEFITS
Reduced clerical effort in processing purchase orders at every stage of the cycle.	Hard dollar savings from long distance charges.
Reduced merchandising time and effort.	Soft benefits from the reduction of wasted phone and fax time spread over the entire product management team. No reduction of staff but increased efficiency.

IMPACT	SAVINGS AND BENEFITS
Reduced inventory results in better service to customers.	Efficiency gains throughout the supply chain. Reduced corporate inventories. Reduced stock outs due to more accurate and timely PO tracking. Increase in acknowledged POs from 60% to 100%.
Receiving efficiencies and inventory accuracy.	Reduction of clerical keying and error resolution. Distribution clerks have more time for analysis, forecasting, scheduling, and routing. No reduction in staff is anticipated.
Expansion of continuous vendor replenishment programs from vendors or agents.	Reduced cost of storage, detention, and demurrage fees. Move closer to "just-in-time" replenishment.
Vehicle for measuring vendor performance.	Improved vendor performance and relationships
Increased sharing of information with trading partners and agents.	More informed and more responsive vendors. Increased vendor loyalty.
Automated link to EDI payment cycle.	Faster payments. Happier vendors.

"Substantial benefits have already been realized with our top suppliers using traditional EDI technology," said LCBO's Dave Collings, who was responsible for the introduction of the system. "Now, with the World Wide Web, we can expand our EDI trading partner base to any supplier throughout the world. Eventually we will have the majority of our PO's delivered using our EDI system seamlessly; they won't know they are using EDI and we won't know they are using the Internet."

Leveraging the Legacy System

Michelin North America is another company that has benefited from the implementation of an Extranet. It created a virtual private Internet to which trusted external partners gain access through a bilateral security system. Like many other corporations in phase three, Michelin wanted to take advantage of the worldwide standard but was uncertain about the security of the public Internet. Its Extranet was built by layering Internet standards and browser-based applications onto existing data networks, in this case CompuServe. The corporation leverages its proprietary legacy systems and networks (for example, its EDI system and its Intranet) and enables them to be accessed by a much larger user population—those who have authorized access from browsers.

One of the challenges facing corporations such as Michelin is the legacy of fifty years of MIS—the enormous repository of computer-based data held all over the globe. Millions of dollars have been invested in closely guarded proprietary systems that allow access only to certain privileged individuals. The Internet turns this upside down. While there is clearly a role for proprietary systems, there is increasing pressure to enable more widespread access to much of that data. This pressure is not only coming from the marketplace, but from the operational side as well: How can I use the Web to make better use of my legacy system and to reach more of my suppliers electronically and eliminate costly, inefficient paper-based systems?

The Internet has the potential to unleash this resource in an incredibly powerful way. Companies whose supply-chain management is deeply entrenched in legacy systems may find it more difficult and more costly to adapt those systems to the new, open-standards environment than a new company starting from scratch, with no legacy to impede it.

Michelin's answer was its BIB NET™, a private network that connects Michelin NA with its tire dealers and merchants throughout the United States and Canada. It does not use the Internet, but Michelin has adopted Internet standards to create more effective communications with its independent tire dealers. Michelin provides the dealer with a customized Netscape browser from which the user dials a preset number and is connected to CompuServe and Michelin's private Intranet. Michelin cites security issues as the main reason why the network has been configured this way. The goal of this network is to extend electronic connectivity into a part of the business where there was little penetration.

Electronic systems, including EDI, had been implemented in many of the distribution channels. "One channel where there was little electronic connectivity was the independent tire dealers," says Tom Hall, Manager of Electronic Commerce for Michelin NA. "We needed to improve customer service because our customers are demanding more information, more quickly around the clock." Michelin found the solution it was looking for using Internet tools that enabled it quickly to implement an inexpensive way for its small, low-volume customers to get the same service as its large customers get from EDI. "It could be argued that they get more than our EDI customers," says Hall. "Now that we have the system in place, even our largest, established EDI customers benefit."

As an example, one large West Coast dealer who uses EDI to place orders with Michelin, works on a tight schedule, turning an order around in twenty-four hours and delivering tires to twenty-three locations. Michelin's batch EDI process takes two and a half hours to process the order and costs the dealer $500 per month. Using the BIB NET system, the same order can be processed in 23 minutes and costs $25.00 per hour.

A Fundamental Architectural Shift

These examples demonstrate that within phase three, a fundamental architectural shift is taking place. Companies like Michelin are engaged in creating a new "three-tier model" to connect the customer or business partner to its core Information Technology infrastructure using the Web as the common interface. Business-applications software is distributed away from its traditional centralized location in the enterprise mainframe and is accessed on the client side via a "thin client" interface. Joe Parker of Signal Internet Technologies, which implemented the system for Michelin, proposes that IT executives take a tactical approach, moving the burden off the mainframe while maintaining database integrity and dramatically improving scalability and usability by isolating the application layer as the "third tier." The architectural shift is illustrated in figure 11.2.[8]

Figure 11.2. The Three-Tier Electronic Commerce Solution

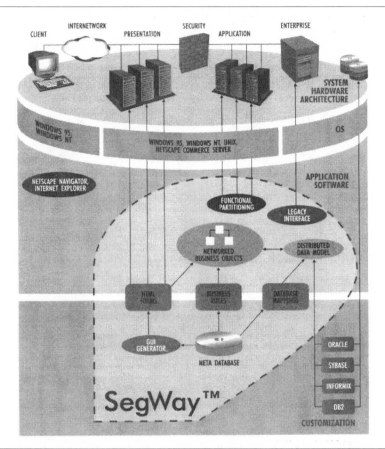

Reproduced courtesy of Signal Internet Technologies Inc.

And the Challenges

As with any technology that offers simplicity to users, Extranets are complex to implement. Reaching the long-term goal of shared intra-company communications and intelligence will take several years and require significant investment. In phase three, applications will be started without too great a concern for overall return on invest-ment. As we enter phase four, more sophisticated business processes, larger numbers, and a variety of business partners and customers will be involved. The total cost of procurement will increase and will need to be managed at a more strategic, corporate level to ensure its positive impact on profitability. In a major corporation, we recommend that management should be lead by a senior corporate executive who will soon become solely responsible for the task.

The challenge of managing a rapid increase in number of users is that there are more orders to be filled, and they need to be filled faster. Alyse Terhune of the Gartner Group claims that 70 percent of the managers of successful Extranets will fail to anticipate the rapidly increasing expectations of customers. With competing Extranets the click of a mouse away, the resulting decrease in customer loyalty could have devastating effects.

An E-Code for Electronic Commerce

To improve the chances of success in e-commerce, we recommend that managers of e-businesses follow the E-Code.

The E-Code
Feed the Web.
- Identify all the places the Web touches the company and imbue them with Web-enabling philosophy.
- Appoint a senior corporate executive with responsibility for Web-enabling your world.

Leverage the Legacy.
- This repository is your resource; Web-enable it. Stick to the standards. Outsource in the short term if you're not ready and in the long term if global is larger than your scope. Don't let Y2K distract you; look for a Web-enabled solution.

Get Ready to Globalize.
- It's a de facto global environment, but it won't happen overnight. Build functional Nets as cells that can later be chained together. Prepare your organization to think and act globally.

Build Your Web Brand.
- The domain is your brand. Power is "IBM.com." Strive to provide a single point of contact that will meet all the customers', suppliers', employees', and stakeholders' needs.

Embrace Everyone's Expectations.

■ Anticipate *customers'* expectations; offer them a convenient and familiar way to interact with you. They will expect the store always to be open.

■ Give *trading partners* all the information they need to make an educated decision to do business with you, rather than your competition.

■ Provide *employees* freedom of choice and systems to enable them to achieve the same performance more conveniently.

■ Offer *shareholders* and other stakeholders easy access to the information they need to retain confidence in your ability to pay dividends and feed your retirement plans.

Don't Wait.

■ Start where you are.

■ Learn. Copy. Plan. Leverage.

■ Outsource.

Avoid the "Inertia of Speed."

■ Twenty new Web sites are added every second.

■ Don't panic. Web *your* world.

■ ■ ■

1   Steven Ward, IBM, personal interview, June 25, 1998.
2   Hilary B. Thomas, "The Role of Electronic Data Interchange in the Evolution of Electronic Commerce," in *Interactive Services Association Strategic Briefing Book*. Vol. 2 (July 1997).
3   Forrester Research, Inc., The Forrester Report, Business Trade & Technology Strategies, Sizing Intercompany Commerce, Volume One, Number One, July 1997.
4   Alyse Terhune, "Gartner Group Impact of Extranets on EC Strategies," Internet & Electronic Commerce Conference and Exposition, April, 1998.
5   U.S. Department of Commerce, *The Emerging Digital Economy*, April, 1998. From the U.S. Department of Commerce Website: www.doc.gov.
6   U.S. Government inter-agency report titled "A Framework for Global Electronic Commerce," released July 1, 1997. By President Clinton, available from the White House Website: www.whitehouse.gov.
7   *Wired* magazine, July 23, 1998.
8   Signal Internet Technologies Inc., Electronic Commerce: A Fundamental Architectural Shift. A Technical Primer, 1997.

How the Internet Is Helping to Transform Industries

A few industries have been at the forefront in using the Internet, either because they were among the first to see the opportunity or the first to feel the threat. The five industries included here were among the earliest to experiment with online services. They have built foundations, thought through many of the issues, learned what their customers want, and determined how to deliver those desired products and services.

These chapters are personal. They are the stories and observations of the individuals who have led the change. The stories speak to the challenge and complexity of working in an emerging medium, and to the process and discipline of managing change.

Common themes that emerge include the disintermediation of traditional roles and channels; the tension between physical (e.g., brick and mortar) versus virtual; overcoming the cultural hurdles; the need to master the technology to control content; and competing against the new well-funded competition that is purely Internet based.

The "Banking" chapter addresses the sweeping changes that continue to throw open the whole notion of banking's legacy from one of branded products and services to the movement of information. It further discusses how the industry finally took the threat from companies like Microsoft and Intuit seriously and is mobilizing to hold onto its customer base.

"Brokerage" is a story from the front line. It is about being there first, then having to play catch up. "Publishing" chronicles an industry leader's emergence from one of the most successful online niche businesses to a broad Internet-based powerhouse. While the "Health Care" chapter documents an industry that is probably moving more quickly than the Internet, the marriage of the two promises significant improvements in the quality and efficiency of health-services delivery.

Finally, this section closes with a chapter on the travel industry. Travel agents are getting squeezed by the airlines, hotel, and car rental companies who are using the Internet to go directly to the consumer. This chapter discusses how travel agents are fighting back.

#### TWELVE

Banking: The Biggest Risk Is to Do Nothing

William M. Randle, Executive Vice President, Managing Director of Direct Access Financial Services, Huntington Bancshares, and Jeffrey Kutler, Executive Editor, *American Banker*

This chapter blends the personal front-line stories and perspectives of an industry leader with the keen observation of a respected industry pundit who has been following the banking industry for over a decade. It begins with Bill Randle's story of how Huntington Bancshares created its cyber-age version of a bank branch—the successes, missteps, and future strategies. Jeffrey Kutler then provides a comprehensive look at an industry in transition, its legacies, the opportunities, and the pivotal issues that will determine success for banks in the future.

In March 1995, I must admit, I publicly and confidently asserted that the Internet would not be significant as a mass-access banking channel any time soon. Fifteen months later, I had our Internet bank up and running, making Huntington Bancshares in Columbus, Ohio, the first full-service bank in the United States to provide complete interactive banking services via this new medium.

It is an easy boast to be "first," but we got there because of groundwork laid before the fact, and the launch of Huntington Web Bank was just the beginning of a lot more hard work. The fact remains that executives at this institution in Columbus, Ohio, were unusually attuned to the rapid changes in the banking landscape and were prepared to move quickly and act decisively, taking considered risks where necessary.

The Beginning: It Took Vision and Commitment

By the mid-1980s, most banks began to realize that the branch-building frenzy of the previous decade was hitting a wall. It was costly to build a new branch because it took years to see a profit from any new customers that branch might attract. In addition, the fierce competition from other branches in many neighborhoods was eroding brand loyalty: It was hard to keep a new customer in a new branch long enough to make any money at all.

While most banks continued to fiddle around with products and pricing, trying to squeeze more and more out of their brick and mortar, Huntington's Chief Executive Officer, Frank Wobst, realized that the problem was in the branch paradigm itself. The bank needed to find a way to make it less expensive to deliver services, and more convenient for customers at the same time.

"What do you predict the bank branch of the future will look like?" Frank asked me.

"Like a telephone," I replied.

From that short interchange, it was clear that we both saw the same future for banking as an information product.

The Infrastructure—Managing Change

Huntington quickly embarked on the radical restructuring of processes, products, and delivery required to transform itself into an information bank. As early as 1990, we began moving to integrate all existing systems and to maintain control of the technologies required for the direct distribution of financial services.

By the spring of 1992, we opened our seven-day, twenty-four–hour, full-service telephone bank, called Huntington Direct. Within eighteen months, Huntington Direct was producing more consumer loans than our hundreds of branch offices combined, largely because we were able to offer ten-minute loan approval by 1993, while our competitors still took days. By the end of 1998, having handled more than 20 million customer calls, the telephone banking program will have sold hundreds of thousands of loans, credit cards, and other banking products. Still, the success of this venture in itself is less important than its value as a foundation—both functional and strategic—for the information- and Internet-based transformation that would follow as Huntington prepared itself for a new century.

Functionally, we had full ownership and control of a complete set of electronic-banking applications (including a proprietary bill-payment system) for our customers, as well as the data interchange platforms and the trained personnel required to make it work—even including access to information (such as credit records) outside the bank.

From there, it was a relatively short leap to direct the flow of this information through any number of access channels that might appeal to our customers in the future, from video kiosks to Smart Phones to the Internet and beyond.

Our early start meant that no matter what access channel might appear in the future, we were ready and able to integrate it into a meaningful electronic banking infrastructure that we controlled, one that allowed us to maintain control of our customer relationships. We were positioned and ready, both culturally and technologically, to move forward faster than people ever expect banks to move.

Building Toward the Web

Based on the information foundation created for Huntington Direct, the company stepped up on a number of projects. We partnered with technology companies to develop and test new ways to deliver financial services directly to consumers—in their homes; in their offices; and for some, in a cyber-age version of the traditional bank branch, called the Huntington Access branch.

The centerpiece of these unstaffed Access offices is the Personal Touch Video Kiosk, developed in partnership with NCR. The kiosks connect consumers with banking representatives located at one of the three Huntington Direct phone centers in Ohio and West Virginia. These provide for live video banking, twenty-four hours a day.

It would be disingenuous to claim that every technology experiment tried by Huntington turned to gold. We worked closely with AT&T between 1990 and 1993 to develop a Smart Phone. Hindsight suggests that it was a concept that was not so much unrealistic as overenthusiastic. We understood that the market would require a small, inexpensive household appliance that could provide global connectivity through what is now known as a "thin client, fat server" environment.

Consumers were clearly ready for financial-services connectivity: many were even prepared to use cumbersome, rather daunting applications like early versions of Checkfree, Money, and Quicken. These required consumers to keep megabyte-guzzling applications on home PCs much less powerful than those available today.

A Smart Phone offering a simpler, easier way to connect seemed a winning combination with online financial service. But by the time AT&T delivered the prototype in 1994, the price of PCs was trending downward and the World Wide Web was beginning to demonstrate its potential. We recognized that we had been lapped by the fast pace of technology. With cheap PCs connected around the globe, a Smart Phone simply would not be necessary.

As a result, we never put the prototype AT&T Smart Phone into full production. It was a "thin client" way ahead of its time; the advent of Java and related programming languages eventually made it happen. In the meantime, the Smart Phone experience taught us a lot about reading the market for new technology, as well as about content development to create the optimum environment for success, which we put to use in a number of later projects.

In other words, it made us ready for the World Wide Web.

Market Pressures—The New Competition

By the end of 1994, the Web was taking off. It seemed to be attracting enough users to become a new locus of banking. Banks at the time were under pressure to find new, simpler, more convenient ways to deliver services to customers. Between 1993 and 1994, the

Wall Street Journal had proclaimed "the end of banking as we know it"; Montgomery Securities Analyst Richard Fredericks had pronounced banks "money mortuaries"; and Bill Gates had called them "dinosaurs."

The name-calling would not have disturbed anyone in the industry, were it not for the fact that all the statistics suggested it was on target. Banks in the United States and worldwide were bleeding assets. We were losing market shares in virtually every category, from revolving credit to business financing to new financial-services competitors.

In just two years, between 1992 and 1994, U.S. banks lost nearly half their share of wealthy customers. Where did they go? Companies like Schwab, Fidelity, and others were beginning to offer a full range of services, using computer-telephony integration and other direct-access channels. And the technology companies, Microsoft chief among them, were clearly upbeat about the potential of the home PC to give them a handle on banking and payments.

Still, in early 1995, I could not recommend any attempt to put real banking activity on the Web. Quite simply, it seemed clear that at the then-current level of technology, the necessary security was not available. Neither our individual customers nor the bank could be well-enough protected in the open global environment of the World Wide Web.

The Meeting—A True Story

Like so many important events, Huntington's move to the Web began with a serendipitous encounter.

I had been making a gadfly of myself, appearing at conferences and seminars all over the country and abroad, to present a case for fast, decisive effort on the part of the banking industry to transform itself in the face of the changing marketplace—before there was no banking industry left at all.

One such conference, hosted by Montgomery Securities, was held in Pasadena in April 1995. There, Dick "Money Mortuaries" Fredericks introduced me to James S. "Chip" Mahan of Cardinal Bancshares in Lexington, KY, and Mike McChesney of a security software company called SecureWare, who had come to talk about their idea for a secure, bank-centered system for online financial services.

Unlike Quicken, Money, or CheckFree, their system would not require customers to load special software onto their home PCs. Customers would simply enter the bank's Web site, log in a security code, and take care of business. In techno-speak, it was the "fat server, thin client" paradigm.

Back in Columbus, Huntington's Chief Executive Officer, Frank Wobst, considered the evidence, and with extraordinary speed but due diligence, put a business strategy into place, with funding by June. Cardinal, Huntington, and Wachovia Corp. of Winston-Salem, N.C.—its CEO was also in on Mr. Mahan's early presentations— were partners in a venture that had no precedent in the banking business: Security First Network Bank (SFNB).

It was the first true online bank, running on the Virtual Branch Manager system developed by its subsidiary, Five Paces Software (later renamed Security First, or S-1 Technologies), in which Mr. McChesney and Mr. Mahan were principals.

SecureWare's "trusted operating vault," the unique security technology that protected the online bank, was now owned by Hewlett-Packard Co. By October, SFNB was open for business as an independent bank brand, with no brick-and-mortar presence at all. And by June 1996—just a year after the partnership was formed and less than two years after I was saying the Web was not yet ready for banking—Huntington Online launched its initial offering.

Today, after one complete overhaul of the site, including the name change to Huntington Web Bank, as well as constant updating, www.huntington.com handles well over one hundred thousand customer accounts from all over the United States. At the current rate of expansion, approximately one of every five customers will use Huntington Web Bank by the end of next year.

The Seventh Region—Cyber-Banking

Huntington Web Bank proved that the visions of a national, even global, electronic marketplace are quite practical and workable. The customers are out there and increasing: Millions of people, physically dispersed, are eager to participate in the convenience and simplicity of direct banking.

In 1997, this customer group, defined by access channel rather than location, was accorded the status of a "seventh region" for our bank. Cyberspace—the region drawing customers from all fifty states—exists organizationally alongside Ohio, Michigan, Indiana, Kentucky, West Virginia, and Florida.

However, the Web in its current conformation, locked inside the personal computer, leaves gaps in service. For this reason, Huntington along with Battelle and Sallie Mae, established in 1996 a new company called Cybermark, to market smart cards. These plastic cards have computer chips embedded in them that have far more information capacity and are far more secure than conventional cards' magnetic stripes. We see a link between the power of smart cards and the Internet.

Smart cards can fill in the gaps in Web-based financial services because they operate as a naturally integrated electronic channel. They can carry cash, downloaded through home computers, to use any way we use change and small bills today: in parking meters and vending machines, at public telephones and public transportation gates.

The important aspect about smart cards, which I feel is central to the development of banking strategies for the twenty-first century, is that they operate best as an adjunct to Internet banking. I believe that over the next decade or so, at least, any new channels that develop will be based on a foundation of Web banking. Current predictions of the growth of e-commerce point in this direction. In 1997, Web consumers spent $1.8 billion. By the end of 1998, annual over-the-net spending will reach $4.5 billion; by 2002, consumer spending via the Web will reach $26 billion, according to some research firms. And that number is dwarfed by the predicted $268 billion in business-to-business transactions conducted over the Internet.

One must be reluctant to cast forecasts of this nature in stone, but I feel fairly safe in expecting that in 2002, half of Huntington's customers will be banking on the Net, and that e-commerce will be the most important channel for expanding the reach of our bank . . . or any financial institution.

An Industry at the Crossroads

Whoever said the Internet changes everything could very well have had banking in mind. It might illustrate both the rule and the exception, representing one of the purest examples of the clash of old ways with new technologies, diluted by banks' "exceptional" and protected status as government-regulated institutions.

Another high-technology truism also hits home in banking: The consequences of change are overestimated in the short run and underestimated for the long run. Bankers have swung with the hype cycle as much as any group. They feared in 1995 that the Internet would change every rule of their game—immediately. Two or three years later, they looked back to find not only that the basic rules had not changed, but that they were being rewarded more amply than ever, in the form of record profits, for being, well, banks.

Therein lies the rub. As Dudley Nigg, Wells Fargo Bank Executive Vice President and leader of its successful Internet banking strategy, put it: "Sure, banks are making a lot of money today. But in a few years they may no longer be around."

If ever there were an industry capable of celebrating and luxuriating in its own success, oblivious to even visible threats on the horizon, banking is it. The recent megamergers that have created banking companies of unprecedented size and scope have bankers feeling even better about themselves and their prospects for long-term survival. But reality in this business can hit hard, throwing conventional wisdom and shared assumptions into disarray. In lending, which is supposed to be their core competency, bankers have gotten burned time and again by sheer excess—international country loans in the 1970s, energy and real estate in the 1980s, Asian emerging markets in the 1990s.

Technology is no doubt one of the driving forces of consolidation. But it will be in the banker's nature to deny it if he can afford to, and historically, he has been able to quite easily.

To understand the interplay of freewheeling technological phenomena like the Internet with ingrained cultures and habits like banking's, one has to understand a bit about the banker's DNA, the industry's hardwiring. And through that understanding may come useful insights about how, where, and why the Internet eventually will change everything we do commercially.

Legacies That Impede Progress

Since modern banking was born in Renaissance Italy, bankers have been a conservative, risk-averse lot. The inheritors of that tradition walk the halls of the skyscrapers that loom over our major downtowns and manage the offices and branches on shopping streets and Main Streets in every city and town.

The banking tradition is physical and paper-bound—about as far as one could get from the boundlessness of virtual space. Historically, customers chose their banks and identified with them according to location. The physicality of it was important, hence the marble and pillars that characterize the buildings, dating back to an era when safety needed to be communicated literally. Customers' loyalty was often defined by the relationships they developed with the officers, tellers, and service personnel inside. The bank existed largely to accept, transport, and exchange paper—application forms, loan documents, letters of credit, deposit and withdrawal slips, statements, passbooks, and, of course, coins, currency, and checks.

Technology changed all that—long ago. It helped make most of those products and processes far more efficient than in the days before computers, document readers and sorters, automated teller machines, and artificial intelligence. The banking industry in the United States, controlling some $4 trillion of assets—more than half the gross domestic product—employs about 1.5 million people, or twice the number employed by the U.S. Postal Service. It is anyone's guess how big banking employment would have to be if automation had not come along.

But technology didn't change the products and processes. The fundamental definition of banking, written into U.S. law in the nineteenth century and largely upheld in the twentieth, is the taking of deposits and the making of loans. Commercial banks and their deposit-taking cousins, savings institutions and credit unions, spent years chipping away at the legal barriers that kept them out of the securities business, insurance, and even some nonfinancial lines of commerce. But deposit taking and lending still constitute the core, and senior bank executives have continually debated whether their historical "franchise," not to mention their physical legacy of more than fifty thousand branch offices (the postal service has about thirty-eight thousand), is a blessing or a curse.

Banking DNA Meets the Internet

The Internet, as a culmination of technological advances that bankers and others had been dealing with in piecemeal fashion for decades, puts basic strategic questions in bold relief. No industry is more racked by the sheer dynamics of change. No industry has seen more soul-searching about its—and individual participants'—future. In this process it became clear that the "break-the-mold" mentality of the Internet and the World Wide Web just doesn't jibe with the banking DNA.

"Entrepreneurs don't come to the Internet studying a lot of rules and regulations," said Parker Foley, Vice President of Electronic Commerce at First Union National Bank in North Carolina, one of the more experimental institutions with new technologies like Internet banking, smart cards, and virtual cash. "They 'just do it' and worry later about regulations."

Can bankers be entrepreneurs? Can they move at Internet speed? Can they change their personalities? Should they even try?

More than one industry leader has admonished bankers to change their thought processes, to become more like the people from Intel or Microsoft who are not only accustomed to the rough-and-tumble of short product cycles, unbridled competition, risk taking, and uncertainty, but who have infused the rest of the corporate world with such values.

Without falling into a nostalgia trap, there is something to be said for the unique roots and traditions that made banks and banking endure. It has to be said: Even if the Internet turns every historical assumption about services and their delivery on its head, the legacy cannot just be written off. Banks still need offices and customers still need to go to them for certain purposes. Cash and checks may eventually wither away, but they haven't yet, and in fact continue to grow despite many premature utterances about their coming demise. It's still a people and—perish the thought—a paper business. And it is one that has seen precious few groundbreaking product innovations over a generation or two—credit cards, ATMs, and Merrill Lynch's patented Cash Management Account (not strictly a banking product) come to mind.

The tension between new and old, technology and humanity, physical and virtual defines the banking-industry challenge. As the Internet hype of the mid-1990s gave way to the harsh reality of making business cases stick, banking strategists puzzled over where to strike the necessary balances. Paralysis may not have set in, but "just do it" responses were few and far between.

Gradually, though, the banking gene pool began to diversify. Bankers became exposed to other ideas, other industries. Many still have to learn, however, that the natural pace of evolution may not be fast enough.

Much has been said about the remark attributed to Bill Gates, the chairman of Microsoft Corp., in 1994, that banks were "dinosaurs." That was one of those "other ideas" that, however painfully, began to change the way bankers looked at their business.

Catching a Wave—Experimenting with E-Commerce

Some banks saw fit to partner with Microsoft in their home-banking efforts. They also worked with Intuit Inc., which Microsoft tried unsuccessfully to acquire in 1994 and 1995. Eventually, they also worked with America Online®, Excite, Yahoo!, and numerous others. A group of banks bought Meca Software, a long-time Intuit competitor; some of those banded with others in a home-banking consortium, Integrion. The new openness to strategic alliances indicated a change in the banking DNA.

As mentioned previously, Huntington Bancshares of Columbus, Ohio, blazed such a trail in a partnership with Security First Network Bank, which came together less than a year after Mr. Gates's "dinosaur" provided the proverbial wake-up call. Now banks were on the cusp not just of some nonspecific, generic technology wave, but of a fundamental change in computing and communications that could have drastic effects on market structures and on institutions themselves.

Security First was one of the smallest banks in the country and the world, but it broke new ground in terms of entrepreneurial outlook and speed to market. The point was never to create a new money-center giant. It was to prove the concept and generate sales of the underlying software and security. "Proof-of-concept" is a term more likely to be heard on Silicon Valley's Sand Hill Road than in the staid corridors of a financial institution.

In 1998, Security First was acquired by Royal Bank of Canada. Some observers said the fledgling Internet bank was throwing in the towel. They didn't get the point—Royal Bank probably did.

Structural Realities—A Bane and a Blessing

The clash of cultures, of traditional and new-age mindsets, haunts and even paralyzes the highly fragmented American banking industry. In contrast to, say, Canada, where six banks dominate the national market, some seven thousand independent commercial banking companies operate in the United States. Triple that number to include savings institutions and credit unions. The decentralization fostered a focus on local communities and markets, which in turn contributed to the dynamism of the American economy and of an entrepreneurial, small-business sector that no country with more highly concentrated, big-bank domination can match.

But paradoxically, a highly fragmented financial-institutions sector, despite its competitive nature and favorable economic byproducts, is ill-equipped to deal with some of the new, technology-driven phenomena that require more of a "collective intelligence" to make sense of, and large scales of operation to achieve peak performance. The banking industry as a whole, for example, would have been no match for Bill Gates and Microsoft if they chose to prove the "dinosaur" allegation literally. That company proved it could turn on a dime when it embraced the Internet and all its formerly hostile implications in 1995, and it still may seize that opportunity in the banking or payment-system area. Huntington's and Wachovia's coalescing behind Security First Technologies—they were later joined by Citibank and others—was a foreshadowing of the kind of collaboration that just might preserve a place for these durable but tottering old deposit-taking and loan-making engines.

There may be cause for such hope, but another paradox was at play. Despite the incursions of technologies, wake-up calls, and new entrepreneurial thinking, the United States banking industry through most of the 1990s enjoyed an unprecedented boom. There was no financial crisis, like the Third World debt crash of the 1970s or the real estate depression of the 1980s, to shake a tired industry out of its torpor and prepare it for new challenges. The sustained economic expansion yielded the biggest net profits and the widest profit margins ever. Federally insured commercial banks have been earning more than $50 billion in annual aggregate income, breaking records year after year.

Internet and electronic commerce were, at best, negligible factors in the profit performance. Banks were still making their money the old-fashioned credit-granting way, and they were hardly partaking of the success companies like Microsoft or Netscape or America Online® were meeting as society took to the Internet. By the end of 1997, 2.5 million to 3 million U.S. households were banking online, according to market-research data. But four times that number were subscribing to America Online®; five times that number were using the Quicken or Microsoft Money financial software to manage their household budgets; ten to twenty times that number had made some use of the Internet.

Bankers were not suffering financially—yet. But the dangers of inaction were becoming clear, as were the hazards of backward thinking and complacency.

During the 1980s, and in keeping with historical trends, the drive to deliver convenience meant a free-standing bank branch on practically every high-traffic street corner. At the end of 1991, a year in which 572 new U.S. branch offices were constructed, there were 70,817 bank and savings-institution locations. That meant one office for every 1,300 families. At a cost of $1 million per office, banks served their public at a cost of $362 per person. But given customer mobility and turnover rates, the average checking account stayed in place just long enough to earn the bank $33.

It was, indeed, just this obvious that building more branches was not the most effective of marketing solutions. But habits and hidebound thinking are hard to break. Banks and bankers had tied their identities inextricably to their neighborhood presence and to the convenience. The bank *was* that sign on the street.

With good intentions, bankers began to learn from retailers, a proactive change from the old tradition of building a branch and waiting for customers to come in. But the initial results were perverse. Price wars ensued as banks vied to offer the cheapest checking accounts, highest-rate certificates of deposit, and lowest minimum-balance requirements.

Like retailers, bankers learned that commodity competition, based on price and location, left them vulnerable to new modes of delivery and to "category killers" that could make up for the commodity pricing on volume. Not unlike retailing pacesetters Land's End and L.L. Bean, Charles Schwab in discount brokerage and Fidelity Investments in mutual funds used telephone services to climb to newly prominent positions on the financial industry's market-share charts, at traditional banking's expense.

Dissing Intermediation—Recognizing the New Opportunities

Like retailers, bankers also heard persistent warnings about disintermediation. This was, actually, an old banking word. When the government regulated interest rates on savings accounts, and money flowed out to the stock market or other higher-yielding instruments, that was disintermediation.

Internet people adopted a literal meaning—the elimination of intermediaries. Banks, as intermediaries between depositors and lenders, are just one of many endangered species that could be bypassed by the Net, or displaced by a savvy electronic marketer. Travel agents, mortgage brokers, and book and music stores might be in the same boat—consumers can scan certain Web sites and deal directly with suppliers, disintermediating the middle men as they go.

Scott Cook, the founder of Intuit and its popular Quicken financial-management software, was not one to jump to conclusions about disintermediation. He said a few years ago that some intermediaries might fall by the wayside, but the Internet created demand for new types of intermediaries. Mr. Cook's own quicken.com, quickenmortgage.com, and associated sites, and his alliance deal with America Online® now show what he meant by that. His message was that bankers had to rethink the way they intermediate, much like those behind Amazon.com or Travelocity did. He offered to help in the process, perhaps by sharing the "customer interface" tools that Intuit viewed as a core competency. Bankers did not have to buy completely into Intuit's vision. But they did need to take it to heart, even if they were in a difficult position to act.

Anchored to millions of dollars worth of real estate, the redundant equipment and employee base needed to run their offices, and organizational structures built to fit branches not the products and customer characteristics, a banking company was not one to take risks on barely tested technological innovations.

Banking did, however, recognize the appeal of direct forms of banking that bypassed their brick-and-mortar infrastructures. In doing so, they turned to third-party vendors to support a variety of electronic services such as bill payment by telephone. Many had done the same sort of "outsourcing" with their credit cards and automated teller machine networks. They sustained profitability by concentrating on customer service while turning over the complex backroom operations to others. But one important baby got thrown out with the bathwater, a loss that would come back to haunt them as delivery systems became more and more virtual.

Brand Critical

That critical asset was the brand. Banks for the most part failed to strengthen their name recognition and the tie it symbolizes with customers, who often established a closer psychological connection with Visa, MasterCard, and American Express than with their hometown banks. With due credit to the successes and conveniences of plastic cards and ATM networks, American consumers came to learn that access to loans, payment systems, and even cash were not necessarily related to any bank they happened to patronize.

THE NUMBERS DEBUNK SOME MYTHS

For an industry known to do things by the numbers, banking until relatively recently suffered an embarrassing deficiency in data mining. Banks had unequaled stores of information about customers' finances and financial behavior, but no way of making any real sense of the mishmash.

Advances in data-base technology began to change that in the 1990s, and this had a profound effect on retail bank marketing. Bankers learned, for example, that the vast majority of their accounts were not profitable. Their focus on making the unprofitable profitable led to new wrinkles in pricing, of which First National Bank of Chicago's $3 teller fee—aimed at people viewed as overtaxing branch tellers while yielding insufficient income to the bank—was the most extreme example. (It was maligned in the press, but it was part of a comprehensive strategy that engendered a positive customer response, higher profitability for the bank, and some defections of customers the bank was not sad to lose.)

One of the lures of the Internet is its low access cost, which can drive the cost of a transaction down to perhaps a penny, versus a dollar or more for a branch transaction and twenty-five to fifty cents for a check.

Until the data began to show otherwise, bankers widely assumed that their best customers were those who were wealthy or maintained the highest balances. The data mining revealed that no such generalizations held up; some wealthy people wrote so many checks, managed their balances so aggressively, and took up so much of a service representatives' time that they were net drains; some low-balance customers produced fee income that made them more attractive than others.

Beginning with a 1993 "Retail Delivery Systems" study by the Bank Administration Institute and First Manhattan Consulting Group, the industry began to turn similar attention to transaction habits and preferences. Many bankers were surprised to learn from that report, a compilation of data from major banking companies, that a majority of their transactions were taking place outside of branches, primarily by telephone and automated teller machine.

Upon further analysis, it became clear that transaction behavior was just as complicated as profitability segmentation. Generalizations—like the often-predicted demise of bank branches—became dangerous. The trend toward alternative delivery channels was unmistakable, but the total number of transactions was also rising— and old-fashioned branches were sharing in the growth. If too many branches were

While trying to take customer convenience and speed of responsiveness to their logical and seemingly desirable ends, financial institutions did not grasp the deeper, longer-term significance of the move toward electronic channels. When they ceded marquee billing to Visa or MasterCard or Plus or Cirrus, they did not realize that the whole script was being rewritten. By the time Intel Corp. introduced the Pentium chip in 1992, banking was no longer about a set of discrete products that the laws defined as its "line of commerce." It was all about information.

closed, good, profitable customers would be alienated.

A 1996 study by MasterCard International, following the earlier methodology of First Manhattan Consulting Group, included an eye-opening segmentation analysis according to age and channel-usage characteristics. Consumers were separated into three groups: those who used only branches, those who used only self-service, and "mixed-channel" users who used both.

The most profitable bank customers are those over 60, and of this group, the branch-only people delivered 2.6 times the average customer's profit. The over-60 self-service customers were almost as high, at 2.4 times average, followed by mixed-channel users at 1.5 times.

Bankers used to assume that branches were for old people, personal computers and ATMs for the young. Surveys like one done by American Banker and the Gallup Organization show an average of about three visits a month to a person within a financial-institution branch—up to age sixty-four. Branch visits fall off to two a month among the elderly.

A PSI Global survey indicated that PC-banking customers remained heavy branch users. They performed six of their average twenty-five monthly banking transactions at a branch; the reading for all households was seven out of thirteen.

"People will remain mixed-channel users" even as the Internet grows in importance, predicted Cliff Condon of the Cambridge, Mass., firm Forrester Research.

William Harris, President of Intuit Inc., said, "Less than 2% of the people who do online banking only do online banking." He said the brokerage industry similarly fell into a generalization trap, considering "self-directed" and "assisted" investors mutually exclusive.

Might there be similar perils in the information—or lack of it—available on Internet behavior? The Internet-access statistics are impressive. Household PC penetration is approaching 50 percent in the United States. The number of regular Internet users is approaching 50 million.

But according to a May 1997 FIND/SVP survey, 9.3 million people had tried the Internet in the previous year and were no longer using it. In January 1998, that figure jumped to 15.9 million.

No business would want to settle for that kind of attrition. What does that tell us? It's saying that people assume they have answers before they actually have them. Once answers appear, they peel back new layers revealing more and more answers. The point is to initiate research and data-mining tasks and never assume that the task is finished. In a volatile medium, awareness of the playing field is an ongoing responsibility.

When the initial stirrings about Internet banking occurred in 1994 and 1995, many bankers reflexively returned to familiar patterns. They relied on experienced technology partners to create "turnkey" systems that would interfere with established banking operations as little as possible. They should have done something similar to what Microsoft did when it saw the Internet train leaving the station without it, or what Chip Mahan did in breaking the old mold with a new, virtual banking model. Undeniably, the old branch bank could not and should not have been dismantled. But it was time for something completely different.

The Transition to an Information Economy

In describing the global transformation into an information economy as "alchemy," the futurist writers Alvin and Heidi Toffler hit on why banking will be critical to the way the economy will reorganize itself around the Internet.

As the familiar argument goes, the industrial society and the United States' post–World War II dominance of it was based on mass production, economies of scale, and a high price-quality ratio. Customization was a costly luxury.

"New information technologies, in fact, push the cost of diversity toward zero," the Tofflers wrote in *Creating a New Civilization: The Politics of the Third Wave* (Atlanta: Turner Publishing, 1995). "In a sense, knowledge is a far greater long-term threat to the power of finance than are organized labor or anticapitalist political parties."

In the 1970s, Citicorp/Citibank Chairman Walter Wriston and his future successor, the technology-savvy operations expert John Reed, spoke of money as "information in motion" and rallied their bankers around strategies based on that idea. Simply put, all commerce requires the movement of money. Given the power of the Internet to connect all buyers and sellers on a common payments platform, payment itself requires nothing tangible at all. It becomes simply a secure, protected movement of information from the seller to the buyer, from the buyer to her bank, and from her bank to the seller's bank.

What happens at each step along the way is no different from what bankers call presentment, payment, clearing, and settlement. Whether it be a loan, a securities transaction, payment of a utility bill, or a transfer of funds between accounts, every banking transaction can be reduced to some combination of these basic information transfers. In Internet or electronic commerce, currency and paper checks are eliminated.

Making Money Virtual—It Takes Time

The concept of virtual money reared its head at the very start of the Internet hype cycle. A few bankers were intrigued. Central bankers and regulators were a bit concerned about their own disintermediation—they could lose the ability to manage monetary policy, and financial institutions would be subject to out-of-control risks in a system that moved wholly or partly away from physical money.

David Chaum, an American-born computer scientist and cryptologist, had been working toward this eventuality since 1990 in a company he founded in Amsterdam called Digicash Inc. He posited e-cash, consisting of bank-issued "virtual coins" on a computer screen, which could be used to buy and sell electronically and anonymously—a true Internet cash analog. A few banks, notably Deutsche Bank in Germany, took Mr. Chaum up on his offer to test the system. Other virtual-cash alternatives followed, incorporating varying degrees of anonymity, auditability, and crossover capabilities between the physical and virtual worlds. The crossover was a major selling point of Mondex, a smart-card system pioneered by National Westminster Bank in Britain, which sold shares in the invention to about two dozen international banks and an eventual 51 percent interest to MasterCard International. Visa Cash, Cybercash Inc.'s Cybercoin system, and Digital Equipment Corp.'s Millicent are other virtual-cash proposals.

There was never any gold rush, or in this case coin rush. Just a deliberate assessment of the alternatives. Good old MasterCard, Visa, and American Express cards became the dominant payment choice for Web purchases, a carryover from the conventional retail and mail-order market. The credit-card companies developed a higher-level security protocol called SET—Secure Electronic Transaction—to make sure consumers and merchants felt absolutely safe about virtual commerce.

"It's the same old story," said Thomas Vartanian, a cyberlaw expert with Fried, Frank, Harris, Shriver & Jacobson in Washington, who has been following cybermoney from the beginning. "The technology gets over-hyped in the beginning and the long-term implications are underestimated."

"If you just read history," Mr. Vartanian said, "you get a sense of the evolutionary in financial services. People feel an emotional attachment to their money, and it takes time for them to understand and react to the new."

Mr. Vartanian, however, was not necessarily arguing that bankers do nothing. Things could change quickly—governments could do something to instill legitimacy in the new forms of payment. So far they have been hands-off, to the liking of free-marketeers.

Confounding any fears that they might get in the way, central bankers and regulators were generally supportive. A committee of the Bank for International Settlements, essentially the central bank of central banks, gave the various virtual-cash schemes a clean bill of security health. The U.S. government took the lead in encouraging the rest of the world to endorse a laissez-faire approach to emerging electronic money and banking. James Kamihachi, Senior Deputy Comptroller of the currency, the supervisor of national banks, explained this hands-off regulatory attitude: "There are not any serious systemic risks right now with respect to electronic money because nobody in this country has much of a project going."

In September 1996, Treasury Secretary Robert Rubin hosted an international conference on electronic money and banking in Washington, where the most discouraging words came from Citicorp's visionary Chief Executive Officer John Reed. He said it would be fifty to seventy years before electronic banking is truly mainstream, used by a majority of customers worldwide.

Like Mr. Vartanian, Mr. Reed was not suggesting that anyone sit around and do nothing. Citibank certainly didn't. Even before its late-in-the-game Internet banking site went live in the fall of 1997, it was arguably the most successful online bank in the world, with hundreds of thousands enrolled in its dial-up PC service since the mid-1980s. Even so, there are a number of reasons why e-cash has been so slow to be accepted. There has been a combination of strategic and marketing misfires by the pioneers of digital cash combined with the public's preference and comfort using credit cards on the Web. The advocates of e-cash maintain that just as there is a need for quick, low-value, anonymous transactions in the real world, they will be demanded in virtual space as well. Unfortunately for the vendors—Digicash Inc. and Cybercash Inc., the two most prominent—their schemes have been a bit too complicated to explain, sell, and install. They and a number of banks, including the Mondex consortium and VISA, are proceeding with a test of Internet cash. In the latter two cases, it has been tied in with smart cards. The problem still remains that e-cash is up against a couple of thousand years of habits built around perfectly convenient legal tender.

Think Checkless

Researchers versed in electronic commerce are convinced that these early stirrings are leading somewhere. Web commerce, generating $2 billion to $3 billion of revenue in 1997, is predicted by International Data Corp. to rise to $220 billion in 2001. Definitions and assumptions can vary. A lot can happen between now and then, but it may be time to begin thinking about the demise of the paper check. It is sure to be reduced to a trivial part of the payment system within the next ten years. (In fairness, it must be said that many earlier predictions of the decline of paper checks never came true.)

Making the Crossover from Atoms to Bits

Branch banking may still be entrenched, but it is equally certain that banking has become an information business, crossing over "from atoms to bits," in the words of Massachusetts Institute of Technology Professor Nicholas Negroponte. In the virtual world, bankers must consider carefully how the marketing value of their branches relates to this new medium.

In other words, whose sign is "on the door" when the customer visits a virtual bank? Who sets the standard for service? Upon whom does the customer ultimately rely for the safety, security, and privacy of transactions and account information? For reasons of history, tradition, and perception, banks owned the security "franchise" with its marbled and pillared physical world. It may not be transferable to the virtual world, especially if banks repeat the pattern of relying on partnerships with information-technology providers like Microsoft, IBM, or anybody else.

The Security First approach, adopted by Huntington and others, took full advantage of the immediacy and flexibility of the Internet. The processing load was borne by the remote bank server, not a software-laden PC at the customer desktop. In computer industry parlance, reflecting one of the controversies pitting Microsoft against many of its antagonists, the customer's computer was reduced to a "thin client" linked to a "fat server."

This is where the worlds of technology and banking can clash, with explosive results. Microsoft attracted much of the hostility even as major banks, brokers like Charles Schwab and the Internet upstart E-Trade Group, and software developers flocked to the Open Financial Exchange (OFX) standard that Microsoft, Intuit Inc., and the bill-payment processor Checkfree Corp. all got behind.

IBM offered a counterweight through its part-ownership of the Integrion network and its Gold standard. Despite the technical differences, which Integrion and the OFX group sought to iron out in the interests of interoperability, there is a sense that companies with a very different perception of how wealth is generated in an Information Age are redefining how financial services operate. There is a parallel here with the bank credit-card brands, which became stronger in many customers' minds than those of the Visa- and MasterCard-issuing banks. Microsoft Windows, Money, and their ilk are similarly in position to take center stage in brand perception. They could control and perhaps even homogenize the individual's banking experience at just the time, and in just the medium, that product differentiation becomes most crucial. Even if such technology companies do not literally compete with banks, they create a new layer of interface between the banks and their customers. Taking this view of the supposed "Microsoft threat" to its logical conclusion, the company does not need to compete with banks because it can transcend them.

Microsoft keeps entering into the discussion, but we do not mean it to be argumentative. The aforementioned scenario only serves to illustrate how far banking has come—to the point where a Microsoft is on its strategic radar screen—and how far it still must travel to make sense of online and Internet implications and possibilities. In the real world, the fortunes and future of any one company, even Microsoft, are beside the point. Banking will survive, it has been said, but whether today's banks will is an open question.

Disappearing Barriers

The real issue for banks—and for any company preparing to succeed in a radically transformed information economy—is to understand that just as the boundaries between banking and other financial services are eroding, so, too, is the difference between "technology" and "content." A company (or an industry) must be in control of its technology to be in control of its information. And information is the banks' business.

Charles Schwab, to take one instructive example from outside banking's historical confines, began in the 1980s with a basic computer-telephony integration. It then moved very quickly and took the financial services industry by surprise with a full-blown electronic delivery strategy, delighting customers with the ability to call in at any time, from anywhere, to complete a securities transaction within minutes. It was faster, more convenient, and cheaper than before. The Web service e.Schwab became a logical extension, and a far more direct and immediate threat to banks than Microsoft. Schwab single-handedly created a new set of assumptions and expectations among an important group of customers, and it reinforced those by building a brick-and-mortar branch network. In common with Merrill Lynch, which similarly has a few hundred well-selected office locations nationwide versus the banking industry's tens of thousands, Schwab viewed its physical distribution network as support for largely virtual core activities. Bankers still tend to think the other way around—that virtual alternatives support the physical plant.

Internet experts have conditioned us to think in terms of radical, discontinuous change. Fits, starts, and quantum leaps are the norm, and in banking, we have mainly seen just fits and starts. It becomes almost an exercise in linear thinking to assume that the growth in use of the Internet will continue apace, the user base will mature, and the World Wide Web will become an active hub of commercial activity. Four out of ten U.S. households have personal computers. In 1989, $3,000 bought a top-of-the-line PC with 3 MB of memory and 112K of RAM. That sum in 1997 bought 100 times the memory, 64MB of RAM, a CD-ROM drive, a 56K modem, and a breathtaking speed of 300 megahertz. Now products under $1,000 are more than serviceable and promise to widen the home PC market. New modem technology and modems combined with cable-television bandwidth—Microsoft is placing big bets in that area—promise a convergence of PCs and TVs. Who will want all this easy access, speed, power, and versatility? How would consumers use it? How will banking and financial services fit in?

Could Banking Be a "Killer App"?

In April 1994, practically the beginning of Internet time, the semi-annual GVU World Survey of Web users revealed an audience 97 percent male, solidly white and middle class, and very much tied to the academic roots of the medium.

Three years later, according to NetSmart Research, the audience comprised 10 million women, 42 percent of the total. What do the women on the Web want? More and better financial services. The NetSmart study showed women pay 70 percent of the monthly household bills. While 64 percent of women said they would be willing to bank online "when security issues are resolved," 54 percent had already bought something online with a credit card. Unlike the early-stage male users drawn to the novelty and recreational value of the Internet, women recognized its potential as an everyday "time-saving household appliance."

Scott Cook founded Intuit and built its Quicken software around the idea that banking, if not literally a mass-market-driving killer application, is the centerpiece of the financial persona. He believed it was a short step from the personal financial-management software to online banking, and he was right—from the standpoint of the early adopter market. Claiming more than 10 million users, Quicken was a big seller to the PC-owning market, but only a small fraction of those took full advantage of the direct-banking capability. The Web clearly opens up that utility to a much broader, potentially critical mass of consumers, pushing it "across the chasm," to borrow from the Silicon Valley Consultant Geoffrey Moore's book, *Cross the Chasm*. The banking industry's challenge is to design services suited to the medium and unavailable—because they are impossible to deliver—through traditional channels.

Seen as likely to fill this bill is electronic bill presentment. Imagine the working mothers who come home to face the monthly stacks of paper mail that must be sorted, opened, recorded, paid by check, and sent back in a return envelope with a postage stamp affixed.

By contrast, imagine instead that the bill payers could simply open their Web-banking screens to find all bills listed, each linked to complete details. Imagine that they could, with a simple click, arrange for a bill to be paid; the payment posted, accounted for in the check register and account balance, and on the way to the biller in a fraction of a second.

Payers and billers alike would be rid of the postage costs. Billers could cut back on their vast statement printing and stuffing operations—costs that would no longer have to be passed to their customers.

Raising the Comfort Level

The technology for bill presentment, like so many online applications, is ready for prime time. And like other good ideas waiting for a market to materialize, it must overcome the perception that the Internet is too open and chaotic to be secure. A 1997 FIND/SVP consumer survey found only 17 percent of online banking users trust the Internet or an online service. CommerceNet, the California-based corporate consortium promoting electronic commerce, said its surveys indicated a noticeable rise in trust and security concerns between 1996 and 1997. A majority of "Netizens" in the 1997 survey of the newsletter "Privacy and American Business" supported passage of a law to regulate the use of personal information on the Internet.

Reaching Agreement on Privacy and Security

If this wonderful, transformative new tool is to grow much beyond its appeal as a novel direct-advertising medium and interpersonal-communication device, it must earn public trust as a dependable way to get things done, particularly things of a financial nature. The satisfaction of getting information about books, blue jeans, or blueberries is limited if the consumer is not comfortable completing the marketing cycle by ordering an item and paying for it. To appeal to the large mass of risk-wary consumers, a seamless, reliable process must be established that moves funds reliably and securely from payers to payees. Government isn't, and shouldn't be, ready to solve this problem.

And in the banker's mind, this is not a task to be left to technology companies capable of disintermediating banking.

This point is likely to be tested and debated in the hunt for the "killer app." Technology providers are expert at moving information between host and client computers. Only banks combine a vested interest in the financial security of customers with decades of experience in handling payments, based on a well-honed sensitivity to the legal and regulatory requirements surrounding the movement of money.

A proper public perception of the Web and its security is crucial to the banks. Hence, the major trade associations came together in 1996 and formed the Banking Industry Technology Secretariat (BITS) to foster a secure electronic environment for financial transactions—and preserve a future for the industry.

Any system, to work, must address and solve three problems:

1. *Interoperable specifications and standards for the transition to electronic delivery and payments.* A variety of nonbanks develop standards and protocols, but they are designed just for the Internet. Bankers must keep in mind a multichannel future that includes smart cards, interactive kiosks, telephone-call centers, and PCs, just for a start. The look, the products, processes, and results must be seamless and consistent across all channels.

2. *Security and privacy specifications and standards.* It will be vital that the computer systems controlling payment flows meet agreed-upon, industrywide standards. A single, designated authority such as BITS could be assigned to certify and regularly check on all applicable servers in every segment of the industry.

3. *A real-time payment system with absolute reliability.* Again, it will take a central, trusted authority to assure and adequately protect the public. To leave this to chance or to a party less interested in the outcome than banks, would leave a cloud over the entire electronic-payments process.

Ultimately, the nature of the Internet itself will govern the solution to the payments issue and how banks' physical legacies translate to the virtual world. The Internet is all about connectivity, and connectivity implies interdependence. Any banking or financial-services company has manifold options for developing a compelling product mix and providing the desired level of customer service. But if the Web is to flourish and reach its potential as a basic tool in everyday living, with finances at the core, all stakeholders—banks, technology companies, the various consortia, and consumers—will have to come to some agreement on a standard for security and privacy.

The still brief history of the Information Age teaches us that the marketplace does not always wait for the absolute best technical solution. Operating systems and applications might gain acceptance because they are first, cheapest, most easily available, or simply because they offered the path of least resistance. Web browsers became widespread because they were free. Web developers constantly improve the speed, flexibility, and usefulness of their sites using free software. If something does not work well, it is not a big problem—an upgrade or a competing application will be available tomorrow.

Those luxuries and assurances do not apply to payment systems. Consumers are reluctant to make Internet payments, and their fears will come to pass unless the systems are meticulously designed and carefully controlled. Any serious breach of security that causes a major loss for banking companies or their customers will make it difficult if not impossible to rebuild public trust.

Basic Lessons—A Conclusion

Professor Negroponte of MIT, taking in the rapid pace of technological change, advises this perspective on the current state of Internet affairs: "It's just the way we live now." As much as the Net may already be changing basic aspects of contemporary life and commerce, banking may be a special case of symbiotic transformation. Assuming it lives up to its potential, online banking will affect the Web as much as the Web affects banking.

Just putting up hundreds or thousands of banking sites and hoping people come is as misguided a strategy as the "branch on every corner" was in the not-too-distant past. The missing link in the last generation was a sales and distribution strategy tied to customer needs and profitability. The electronic infrastructure needs a strong, trusted, and reliable system for payments. Banks might develop it themselves, or others will do it while relying on banks' money-handling resources. The survival of banks and banking as we know it hangs in the balance.

Asking the Right Questions

Here are some questions bankers should ask before taking the online/Internet plunge:

Does the strategy have top-management support and buy-in? Without it, it will be hard to sustain the commitment over the years necessary.

Have you identified strategic partners—and are they truly compatible with your strategy? No bank can do it alone, so the partnerships have to be smooth and actively managed.

Have you apprised regulators of your plans? Advance notice and consultation will avoid problems down the road.

Are you ready to test, adjust, and test again? No service emerges full blown and perfect the first time. It's a good idea to work with a pilot group of employees, then gradually bring outside customers into the mix.

Have you done your market-research homework? Do you know whom you are selling to? Different customers will have different tendencies to use any alternative delivery channel.

With your choice of domain name, Web site design, screen presentation, and marketing materials, have you taken care to preserve, protect, and enhance your brand? A strong brand identity cuts through clutter and reinforces the trust relationship with the customer.

Can you integrate the online service platform with core banking systems, aka legacy systems? If not, you won't be presenting consistent and fully updated account information all the time—a turnoff to customers, a challenge for marketing and analysis, and a prescription for operational confusion.

Have you addressed customers' privacy concerns? If they are not comfortable on this score, they will be reluctant to entrust financial and money matters to a Web-based entity.

Have you addressed your public's security concerns? Ditto with privacy issue.

Basic Lessons

For banks, and perhaps any other information-intensive businesses, a few primary lessons stand out:

- *It is always better to be too early than too late.* There are a lot of nonbank—or "disintermediating"—competitors out there ready to claim market territory on the Web.

- *Connectedness is the vital concept to incorporate into all strategic thinking.* It is one thing to integrate information systems, and quite another to get a corporate culture to integrate around electronic delivery. It is all well and good to offer services like bill payment, a Web bank, and a smart card, but it is a much better idea to integrate all these under a cohesive brand structure.

- *The emergence of the World Wide Web both as a delivery channel for financial services and as a major global hub for commerce of all kinds has radically changed the location of value for customers.* We are now all in the information business. Each institution has to come to grips on its own with the radical redefinition of its specific markets and goals.

Based on those lessons and on the evidence of emerging trends and merging banks, one prediction follows: Any bank that does not have a clear, integrated strategy for electronic banking does not have a future in twenty-first–century banking.

CHAPTER

THIRTEEN

Brokerage Service:
Perspectives from a Decade in Online's Most Mature Segment

K. Blake Darcy, CEO, DLJdirect

Blake Darcy of DLJdirect has been in the online brokerage business since the beginning. In the following chapter, he provides a very personal view of trading securities on the Internet, which is arguably the most mature Internet industry. And he provides insights that are applicable to managers from any industry trying to do business over the Internet.

Orrin Beissinger of Prodigy called me at my desk at DLJ and asked, "Is this a bad day?" It was October 19, 1987, soon to be known as "Black Monday," as the stock market was in the midst of a precipitous fall. He went on to ask if we at DLJ still wanted to go on with the Prodigy-based online brokerage experiment our respective companies had been discussing for several months.

"Call back in a month," I replied, "and we'll see if we're still in business." Two weeks later the market had stabilized, and DLJ and Prodigy decided that there would still be a stock market, and that online trading was still a venture that was worth pursuing. Actually, the jammed telephone lines and the around-the-block lines at various Charles Schwab and Fidelity branches around the country served to convince many among the DLJ group studying this brokerage experiment that there really was a need to improve the communications and the trading mechanisms between investors and their brokers. Personal computers seemed like the best way forward.

Today, with at least 4 million investors trading over the Internet and every major financial-services firm either involved in or considering entry to the world of online brokerage, it is easy to imagine that the concept of offering consumers the ability to trade and control their own investments online was always widely supported. Such was not the case back in 1987. Then, the "state of the art" was clunky 286 chips inside of $3000 PCs, snail-slow 1200 baud modems that cost $350, and no Internet and no online trading. Covidea, a fledgling online service launched by AT&T, Bank of America, and Chemical Bank had just been a spectacular failure. PCs continued to appear on office desktops, but beyond simple word processing, calculating, and databases, practical uses for these expensive, bug-ridden early machines were quite limited. The boxes sat on the desktops and for the most part weren't connected to anything or anyone. Still, the concept was in the air that computers, if they could be separated from the huge old mainframes, made truly interactive, and made much more user-friendly, could create an information and communication revolution every bit as radical as the invention of the telegraph, the telephone, or the radio.

Even the most farsighted of us—the fortunate few who got into this new incarnation of an old industry at the beginning—had no idea that we would be creating something that could take off with such exponential growth. DLJdirect is now one of the most mature and experienced providers of online brokerage services in the world. In 1988, our first year, we began by doing eight trades per day, and signed up about three people each day. Ten years later, approximately ninety thousand people visit our sites each day, and we execute an average of twelve thousand trades per day.

In fact, online discount brokerage is the most mature segment of all e-commerce. As such, there are many lessons that can be learned from the evolution of online brokerage services that can be applied to other industries. Online channels have effectively altered the makeup of the brokerage industry, such that all brokerage services are now compelled to use online channels to reach their investors. This means that the category of "online discount brokerage" will disappear as online efforts become general to the brokerage industry. Raising the quality of the online experience, lowering prices while improving service, and building powerful brands worthy of investors' trust will be the key levers to the future of the online brokerage industry. The global market for online brokerage services is the new frontier.

A Few Lessons Learned

Having lived and worked through this "gold rush" period and seen the online brokerage industry begin to mature, I know that I may never experience this kind of ride again. That said, there are still frontiers to conquer. There is a global market in which the technology that serves our business will continue to evolve at a rapid pace, so that one day all types of online services may be taken as much for granted as tap water or electric power. The greatest lesson I have taken away from my pioneering experience online is that the sky is still the limit; none of us know how far or how fast we can go. We must continue to learn from our mistakes, keep innovating as we implement what we know, and stay flexible so that we don't miss the next big shift. Those basic ideas aren't original or new, but they still hold true.

To return to 1987, I was trying to make the most of the discount brokerage piece of DLJ's business. I was excited by computers and their promise. Prodigy, a true online pioneer, approached DLJ in May 1987 with the offer of creating an online brokerage system that would be far superior to the fledgling efforts of Charles Schwab and Fidelity. Those companies were offering software packages on dial-up services that added very little value to the transactions already offered over the phone.

I had always been interested in running my own business, but I didn't have a time frame or a plan for that goal. Brokerage seemed to me the way that I would get the business experience and the wealth to one day start my own shop—at what, I wasn't sure. I had been asked by some of the senior managers of DLJ and its Pershing division to develop a business plan for this online experiment, and when Dick Pechter (head of DLJ's Financial Services Group), along with Pershing's Gates Hawn and Rich Brueckner decided to pursue the experiment, I was offered the chance to run it. It was a wonderful opportunity: I felt that I was being given the chance to lead a start-up on the frontier of the brokerage business, and I could do it without risking capital of my own. When I look back at what that start-up venture has accomplished, what we've grown into, it's still that initial decision to make the venture happen that amazes me. That an institutionally focused brokerage firm was willing to take on a high-risk, retail-oriented project like this without having even seen the prototype service from Prodigy is a remarkable tribute to the foresight and courage of those senior managers.

Lesson One: *You need people of vision, who are willing to back a risky venture in the face of considerable barriers.*

In the case of DLJdirect, these managers believed in a fundamental idea—that PCs could bring customers closer to their brokerages, giving investors more control and greater value while giving brokerages a revolutionary tool to sell their products and services.

Looking back at those first few years, I would still say one of the biggest factors in our success was the fact that Dick Pechter said: Whatever you need, get; if you need support from any group, secure it, or let me know about it and I'll make sure that it happens. This form of leadership and support enabled us to succeed. Many of the other people in the firm thought that it was sort of a silly experiment and probably a waste of money. Dick had the vision that this concept was going to be big some day, as did Gates Hawn and Rich Brueckner. They continued to feed it and support the experiment, even before it was doing much business. There were many times over the ten years since the launch of what was then called PC Financial Network (or "PCFN" as we were known prior to September 1997) that we had to try to convince departments or areas within DLJ that this was going to be big, that we needed to give it ample support because eventually it was going to be a very large part of DLJ's future. It took some people longer than others to believe in this venture, but now everyone supports it. It may seem obvious, but it is a basic truth of any pioneering business: You need leaders of vision who will let you try, let you fail, and give you the backing you need to grow and succeed when it would be much easier, much more popular politically, for them just to keep doing things the old way.

Lesson Two: *You must design your business around what your customers value and what they are willing to pay for, and know that there may be a considerable difference between those two things.*

Early on in our development process, we started to do some focus-group work on what we thought were some interesting online applications, research products, and analytical tools. We heard our group members say: "Hey, I like this, and it should be free. And it has to be free, because I'm not going to pay for this."

We learned that our customers thought that certain features or products should just be part of what you get when you pay for our service. It is quite possible to test a product or feature and find that people really like it but aren't willing to pay for it. The assumption must then be that they're not finding a lot of real value in it. Some of the things we were testing were too expensive as products to build and offer on our platforms without additional charge, so we dropped those products. That decision has been proven correct by events: some of those very same applications—research products and analytical tools—are now available on the Web. They're either free, or if they are sold by subscription, they remain relatively unpopular. Our focus groups gave us this litmus test.

Lesson Three: *Design your organization around passionate people and their skills.*

Getting the most out of limited resources is the name of the game for all start-up business, and the most important assets a company has are its people. How does a company manage its human resources and create development processes to foster innovation?

If a company has someone who is really good, try to make sure that that person is properly deployed. From the very beginning, I've believed that innovation doesn't happen by design, but rather by a creative chaos, and the process shouldn't get in the way of that creativity. To be successful, it takes lots of people within an organization who are passionate about the industry they are in, passionate about their customers and their interests, and passionate about their industry's technological developments. It's not the job of the technology department, or the marketing department, or the CEO to come up with new ideas: it is everyone's responsibility. Innovation isn't a linear process where people sit around a room and say "Let's come up with a new product," after which a team is put together and put to work on a project. That's why we at DLJdirect don't have a "skunk works" or spend specifically on R&D. Part of everybody's job here is to absorb what is out there and make the best use of it. Innovation will come out of this free-form absorption of whatever is happening in the worlds of brokerage and technology and the realm of consumer behavior and preferences.

Even the most passionate, best motivated, most innovative people are, however, only human, and there is a limit to what they can do and how fast they can be redirected. In a start-up company, you expend your scarce resources on the most pressing tasks—in our case, after launching on Prodigy, our priority was launching on AOL. Then, in June 1995, with that site working well and providing us with the greatest flow of new accounts, we calculated that our priority was to enhance it and thus reinforce our success. Our people were, in effect, exhausted after their significant achievements, and as a company, we did not shift focus fast enough toward our next key development, the Internet. We continued to focus on our Prodigy and AOL sites, and judged that our Internet development could wait; we did not have the resources to pursue all three services at once. We needed to hire new people with new skill sets, to refocus our efforts in general toward the Internet. It took six months to make the transition, and we launched on the Internet in mid-1996.

Lesson Four: *Despite limited resources, an online start-up must execute today, but keep tomorrow always in its sights.*

It is a debatable point what, if any, impact that six-month delay may ultimately have upon our place in the industry. During this transition period, we had our first taste of the impact of "buzz factor" in the online world. The press had become enamored of this idea of doing business over the Internet, not over online systems— their story was the Internet. And it was very frustrating for us, because as far as we were concerned, our different platforms were all just different ways of doing brokerage online, and we had a strong history of doing it online through the two major existing retail gateways. But the press loved the idea of the Internet, so people who were on the Internet were considered pioneers and at the forefront, and they got the press.

Why did this idea of a division between the Internet and other online gateways gain such currency? Who decided that if a company was on AOL and Prodigy, it wasn't very "cool?" When one looked at the Internet, it was truly worldwide, it was somewhat chaotic, and above all, it was new. This was versus AOL and Prodigy, which were only national, were relatively ordered, and were rather "old news" at that point. AOL was still "cool" to some—they introduced the idea of chat, and started adding some pretty good content. But it was still a relatively controlled environment with a limited amount of information. Prodigy was no longer growing rapidly, and the same type of content found on the Internet couldn't be found on AOL or Prodigy. The Internet was a sort of wide-open wilderness that one could explore and in which one could find all sorts things. It was part of the excitement of the Internet that it was unregulated; anyone could go "up" on the Net—an individual could put up a Web page and be in business overnight. This as opposed to the other commercial systems, which were very closed, and which placed limitations on the content available.

It seems much longer ago than it really is, but we must remind ourselves that there was no Internet industry five years ago. It was really a grass-roots operation that took off. It started with word of mouth and then the press picked up on it. Their view was that this was something that was truly going to change the world. AOL and Prodigy, while interesting, were owned and controlled by companies with corporate agendas; they were nowhere near as exciting as this wide-open worldwide communication network that no one could control. The Internet seems to have a mind, and a life, of its own. It's very appealing, especially to Americans—it's the Wild West, the frontier. The Internet seemed to be changing every day, and that did not seem to be as true of the proprietary systems.

So PCFN, always proud of our reputation as pioneers, suddenly appeared a bit stodgy. I couldn't speak at conferences and talk about Internet brokerage trading, because we didn't have an Internet brokerage site. I remember instances in which people who had invited me to speak at a conference would actually withdraw the invitation upon learning that we didn't have an Internet site. They would say

"Sorry, this conference is only going to focus on companies that are on the Internet."

What's interesting about this is the "buzz factor" phenomenon of a concept catching on, which then directs the businessman to race to follow it, even though what he already has to offer may be superior to the hot concept. Our service on AOL and Prodigy was actually more effective than what it was then possible to do on the Internet. But the need to be "newer" and "cooler" drove us to play catch-up. Our site on AOL was superior to anything that we could then have done on the Internet from the standpoint of speed and reliability, yet it was viewed as "old" technology after having been up for all of a year.

The Maturing of the Online Market

Two years later, the online world had matured and segmented into separate markets. In particular, the online brokerage market, arguably the most mature of all e-commerce channels, is now big enough and sophisticated enough that it can be divided up into niches, and one can begin to think about applying business strategies toward separate pieces of the whole. A decade ago, we pursued all potential online investors because the target population was quite small. With online commerce now considered mainstream, and no longer the realm of "early adopters" of Internet technology, the decision becomes which segment of the online population to target.

The Three Levers of Online Brokerage Today

There are three basic levers that players in the online brokerage industry have to maximize their market share among existing and potential online investors: quality, price, and branding.

QUALITY

First, there is the overall quality of the experience. By this I mean the whole experience that our investors have each time they log onto our site, whether through the Internet or one of the proprietary online services. Each encounter with our site and our company must fulfill and hopefully exceed the customer's expectations. We can measure with accuracy certain parameters of the experience that our focus groups and other modes of feedback tell us are of the most concern to our investors: the reliability of each transaction, the speed of execution, the security of every account and all transactions. Every online brokerage firm is competing to execute trades more reliably, in less time, with more perfect security. But the other side of the quality question is what we can't easily gauge with objective measures. It is the more elusive parameters of customer service—the "feel" of the online world we create—all of the elements of the experience that derive from the much more subjective nexus where design, content, technology, and the company's organizational spirit come together. If there's a glitch and our site goes down for even a minute, that's bad. If some new piece of software is unstable and causes a PC to crash a lot, that's very bad. If a trade doesn't get executed correctly or takes a long time to be completed, that's extremely bad. But if an investor is having any of these problems and contacts us and doesn't get the problem speedily solved by a courteous, engaged, and efficient customer service team, well, that is a disaster. The customer may very well never give us a chance to serve him or her again. The online world is much more immediate, much more transparent to the customer, than the branch discount-brokerage environment, or the traditional full-service brokerage environment. If the phone lines into one of Schwab's branches are down one day, who knows about it the next day? If our service goes down for even a few minutes, word of that problem can and does go out over the Internet and around the world in minutes. We have to worry about our reliability and maintaining a high-quality experience overall for our customers, twenty-four hours a day, every day.

PRICE

The second lever is price. This is obvious but also has a number of more subtle facets. In one sense, all online brokerages are now discount operations. Our earliest market research confirmed a fundamental truth of online trading that continues to be ratified by today's customers: Online investors believe that if they are executing their own trades, they should pay less than they would for trading with a traditional full-service broker, and less even than what they might pay in a face-to-face transaction in a branch of a discount brokerage. Online brokerage firms must compete to keep prices low while providing ever greater levels of service and quality. That focus on quality and added-value—the reliable delivery of superior products and services—will be central to creating the third lever, branding.

BRANDING

Branding is perhaps the most crucial of the three levers to an online broker's continued growth and success. High-net-worth individuals, the most prized of customers for online brokerages, are unlikely to invest their wealth with a company that they do not know well and that has not earned their trust. Customers must know a company and like what they know of it. This is the heart of the definition of a brand, which I define simply as: an ownable, repeatable, relevant promise. This is true whether selling an online brokerage, soap, or corn flakes.

Branding is all the more crucial a lever in a field where traditional advantages like size and established infrastructure are less determinate. Just as the players within the maturing brokerage market know that most potential customers will soon be reachable via online technologies, they also know that their competitors, including the smaller and the newer players, will have access to the newest evolutions of the technologies and may profit by not having to replace old infrastructure; they will be in a position to benefit by learning from the mistakes of the pioneers. Computer and online technologies are arguably *the* technologies that have most greatly empowered the Davids to make successful attacks on the Goliaths. This is especially true of those giants who have grown complacent and fail to remain flexible and innovative.

A lesson concerning branding in the online world as a whole is well illustrated by Amazon.com's experience. This pioneer chose an excellent market for online sales, one that appealed to the well-educated, knowledge-hungry early users of the Internet: books. Amazon implemented and executed very well. They made good use of advanced search engines, which added value to their site and their service. In some cases, it has become a resource for people who might not actually be shopping for a book, but who, having visited the Web site to conduct a search or participate in the community of readers, might well end up buying a book. They used secure commerce technology, electronic order tracking, and express delivery, which made credit-card sales and speedy delivery a reality. They used discounts to compete well with superstore prices. But the real point is that they had this market to themselves for about a year and a half, and thus gained a strong foothold with their brand.

Now it appears that there will be two and possibly three big players in the online book market. Others may follow, and in a sense all booksellers may have to become online booksellers. Barnes and Noble and the other big companies in this market will profit by Amazon.com's example, and if they implement well, may each tear away a sizable hunk of the pioneer's market share. Then again, Amazon isn't standing still. Having expanded into music sales, they, and their competitors, are no doubt asking themselves: For what other products and services will our model work? As they extend the brand franchise, does the brand remain ownable, repeatable, and relevant to their target customers?

In the even more mature online brokerage world, the lesson can be even more starkly drawn.

Lesson Five: *Early movers have a chance to grab significant market share and customer bases, but big players can move in quickly after the pioneers and dominate a niche, or even the market as a whole, with stunning speed.*

For example, both Schwab and Fidelity were doing discount brokerage long before PCFN/DLJdirect, and both were even online before us, albeit with stand-alone technologies. They didn't move toward the proprietary online services quickly, and so the managers of DLJ saw their opening. Had either or both of these competitors been committed to Prodigy or AOL before us, we might never have come into existence. But then both of these firms recovered and got onto the Internet in good order; Schwab a bit before us, Fidelity at roughly the same time.

Hovering over all of us are the shadows of companies like Merrill Lynch, the traditional brokerage houses. Unlike DLJ's Financial Services Group under Dick Pechter, many of the traditional brokerage houses sat out the first decade of online brokerage. But then they didn't have the fortunate situation where the same manager who was responsible for traditional brokerage services also had the responsibility for online brokerage. Nor did they have a leader with the foresight to choose to cannibalize some small portion of his traditional business in order not to be left out of the online revolution. Had any of the traditional houses chosen to do so, they might easily have dominated the market. In the long term, perhaps very soon, they, too, will come to see that the anticipated pain of changing their culture and threatening parts of their traditional businesses is worth their potential gain, and they will participate in the online brokerage market.

The point we must return to is that selling a company's products and services in a rapidly evolving, segmenting industry will depend on establishing a brand that will set it apart from all its competitors in a crowded marketplace. There are now more than seventy brokerage firms online. The branded "buttons" or "tiles" that online brokers buy on various online sites help potential investors navigate to the brokerage site. They're fine for building awareness, particularly by having that button appear every time someone gets a quote on a particular Web site or search engine. But how does one name differ from another name on another button—how does a company make a brand statement? With so many choices everywhere online, there has to be a good reason why the customer is going to click on one company's button versus that of the competition.

As brokerage firms decide which segment of the market to target, they will be making marketing decisions that have long-term implications; longer-term, in all likelihood, than those involving systems or architecture, which have been moving so quickly that long-term plans are less applicable. In examining the demographics of the investor population, we see there are many lifestyle changes that customers go through. A twenty-five-year-old is typically saving up some money for the down payment on a house. After they buy that house, they're "poor" again. Then, they're spending on furniture, and getting the house ready. It isn't until they start to have kids that they start saving for college education and think about saving for other things. People who don't have kids probably start saving for retirement or for other major purchases. When people go through these different stages, they go from being cash rich, to cash poor, to cash rich again, and they make different decisions as they go along as to who they want their brokerage to be. There will be brokerage companies that will survive because they offer a quick, cheap trade. There is a segment of the online investing population that wants a quick, cheap, efficient trade. Such a person is a day trader who says: "I know what I want to do, just give me the screen and let me do it. And let me do it for the least amount of money, because I do this a lot."

Price, Profitability, and Channel Conflict: Issues for the Future

As discussed previously, price is one of the major levers that will continue to propel the growth of online discount brokerage. Every new entrant to the market comes under intense pressure to keep the prices of services low, and to go even lower through introductory or preferred customer pricing plans and promotions. The Internet is a world of very efficient shopping: It is easy for consumers to get information on price and features, to make their own comparisons, and indeed to switch their allegiances to a new service or product if an old one fails to deliver. This explains why, across the industry, we have seen the commission rates for online discount brokerage drop 50–60 percent over the last five years. At the same time, full-service and traditional discount-brokerage rates have remained unchanged. The prices of trades and other brokerage services online will stabilize in the current $5 to $30 range. A few players will try to use gimmicks to move their prices even lower, but these won't be sustainable. Any discount brokerage service that tries to price their trades much over $30, regardless of how stellar their service may be, will find themselves with the problem of how to do business with a very slim customer base.

Profitability will be threatened as the firms that have a large volume of trades from large customer bases, and that have been benefiting from the economies of scale these allow them, compete to improve service as they maintain low prices. Expensive branding campaigns and continual technical enhancements—both absolutely crucial to any online brokerage firm that wants to gain market share—are very hard to sustain when solid profits don't exist to support them. Firms without a large customer base will struggle to survive in this competitive market. A sustained bear market, which must come about eventually, will inevitably lead to consolidation in the online discount-brokerage industry.

Full-service brokers will see their traditional customer base erode as younger, computer-literate consumers who have grown up investing in the markets give more and more of their investment business to online discount brokers, and their older, noncomputer-literate customers are "actuarially" removed from the population. The full-service brokers will then have to decide whether to risk "cannibalizing" their own businesses by going online—or try to come up with a new pricing and service model that incorporates the power of online technology.

Currently, the established players in brokerage have no real incentive within their own organizations to be proactive in developing online services. A sustained bull market has allowed them to thrive in spite of the rise of online discount brokerage. They will continue to shy away from "channel conflict" as long as they are able to protect their profitable model of brokers generating commissions. They will resist the wholesale migration to online and will try to use online defensively instead. They will likely "bundle" services, providing online services to their customers based on account balances, providing a certain numbers of online features "free" if the customer keeps enough money on account with them and uses enough of their traditional services. The brokerage may collect a percentage of the assets held on account, versus commissions on trades performed.

Face-to-face brokerage services won't ever disappear entirely—though most of the faces may be appearing on your desktop PC screen—because many people still want the human interaction that helps them make their investment choices.

Even when they trust their own investment instincts more than their broker's, investors often want the customized feedback, the opinion, the ongoing dialogue their broker provides. For an investor inundated with huge quantities of raw, undigested market news from a multiplicity of sources, the continuing relationship with a broker can be a constant, guiding beacon. The broker still has value, but it is one that increasingly the online discount-brokerage firms will be providing. The investor-services representatives at the online firms will become the trusted faces and voices of the investment community. The traditional full-service brokerages will that find their customers will migrate to the online services, which give them the best commission rates, the fastest executions, the best information, and the most personalized relationship available.

But the end point for the industry remains the same: Online is the future, and all brokerage services will move online. Some firms will continue to court only the high-end customer and will charge higher commissions to support more human interaction, physical plant, and other select services. Other firms will continue the "race to the bottom" of the price war but will limit themselves to supplying only such limited services as rock-bottom discount pricing can support. The chief competition will be over the great middle market. The established discounters like Schwab and Fidelity will try to offer more traditional "full service" resources and services, and thus increase their revenue per investor to improve their profitability. Traditional brokers will need to incorporate the online technologies to satisfy the needs of the middle market.

Evolution of the Industry: Macro View

Regarding the continuing evolution of the entire financial-services industry as it affects the future of online brokerage, the recent merger mania in the financial-services industry does not yet seem to have played itself out. Further consolidation appears likely. In a market in which Davids often have a good shot at competing head-to-head with Goliaths, how important will mergers and partnerships, and the synergies they are intended to create, be to the future of our industry?

At present there is little evidence that the online financial-services world will be dominated by cross-selling (which has a dubious history in any case) or other supposed synergies. Cross-selling poses certain risks. It is easy for companies to get distracted from the core of their business in so fast-moving an industry. Companies that retain a focus on innovating within their own fields are likely to outperform companies that are spread too wide and too thin.

Further, while the idea of the online mall has gained some popularity, and there will be more online services that offer the multistore, multiproduct approach, ultimately, the products and services offered must be best-of-breed, or in the long run they won't succeed. DLJdirect may, for example, offer financial products from some of its business partners. We would then give our partners' products a favored place on our sites and in our service, and we might advertise and co-brand with our partners and their services. But if our partners' products and services don't measure up to market standards, in the long run they will fail, and no effort of ours will be able to save them.

The online world has brought everyone the ability to search out the best deals and compare them efficiently. Soon, there will likely be even more Web sites, services, or applications devoted to seeking out just what the user wants with even greater ease, speed, and accuracy. It is therefore hard to believe that with a better deal a click or two away, a bank, brokerage, insurance company, or any other financial-service firm is going to be able to hold onto market share just by offering a big umbrella of cross-branded, cross-sold products. Online customers will get more and more sophisticated, and their brand loyalty may well drop to even lower levels than we see at present.

The "Next Big Thing"

The "next big thing" we can be sure of in the immediate future is the growth of the global online brokerage markets. Without question, the United States will remain the best market online for brokers for several years to come. This is true because of this region's very high Internet penetration, the existence of a population that has the propensity to be self-directed, and the high degree of wealth overall. All of those things work in favor of online brokerage. All online brokerage firms are now trying to figure out how to take the U.S. model around the world. Most companies are looking at Western Europe, Hong Kong, Japan, Canada, and parts of Latin America. All want to know: Where are the next markets; how should they attack?

Several barriers to global trade must be surmounted by those online brokerage companies aiming for global customers. The first barrier, which affects all customer-service businesses seeking global expansion, is the issue of language. When you go global, your e-mail, customer service, and technical support must work in every language;

your whole presentation must work in each particular market. The second major barrier: Every country has different regulatory issues, which are time-consuming and costly to address. Then there are the issues of Internet penetration and education: All countries do not have large populations on the Internet. For example, in Japan many homes don't yet have a PC because there is physically less room for it—and that lack of computer availability and familiarity will hurt Japan as an online brokerage market to some degree. In some countries, the connection time to the Internet is slow and relatively expensive, and these factors reduce usage. In many countries, people are still very worried about security issues in regard to the Internet; only education about the online world will improve that.

Crucially, in most of these countries, there is as yet no well-developed, self-directed investing segment of the population. The United States started in this mode back in 1975, after deregulation, and it has taken until now to have 25 to 30 percent of our population doing self-directed trades. In Japan, there is no such population. The basic issue overseas is that people are just not used to trading and investing on their own.

It is therefore going to be a long process to get to the point where our global markets are as important to our base business as our U.S. market is. Long term, these foreign markets will evolve, and they will certainly incorporate online trading of equities and mutual funds. If a brokerage wants to be a major global player, it will have to establish a foundation in that part of the business now.

The "Next Little Thing"

On the "micro level" in the future, the "next big thing" might be hand-held devices. Everyone has misjudged them every time they've come around. Up until now, they've been a miserable failure from the standpoint of doing transactions, but it is likely they will work at some point. At least three of the standards many technology watchers have been waiting for—portability, battery life, and the wireless component—are now getting closer to being solved. If you look at the number of people walking around with Palm Pilots who love them, you have to believe that at some point, that type of device will also be a quote-retrieval and order-entry screen for brokerage. And when that starts to happen, the online brokerage industry will be there.

The End of the Online Category

Perhaps the overarching question about online brokerage is: Does this business fit within the traditional brokerage industry, take away from it, or subsume it all together?

Here is my vision of the future. I believe that the category today called "online brokerage" will go away. There is nothing now called "telephone brokerage." There is nothing now called "branch-office brokerage." Right now, companies are developing this thing currently known as "online brokerage," but I think that it will come to be called simply "brokerage." An investor will have a relationship with a firm or an individual. That investor will communicate within that relationship in a number of ways—by picking up the phone, seeing their broker face-to-face, using the Internet or WebTV,™ or whatever new technology comes down the road. That's going to be true if one has a Merrill Lynch relationship, a Charles Schwab relationship, a DLJdirect relationship, or a DLJ private-banking relationship—the investor will want all of those options. It will all fall within the investor's idea of "brokerage." Online brokers already have customer-service representatives available round-the-clock on their phones, and many will soon offer videophone cameras mounted on PCs so that if a customer wants contact that includes sound and vision, they can have that kind of interaction on a regular basis.

Brokers like Schwab and Fidelity now do over 50 percent of their trades online. Does that make them online brokers? They're simply brokers. They still have branch offices. And at these locations, they will still teach a customer how to use the Internet. That will help the process. Some brokers probably won't ever have that type of physical location. But soon, people will be more and more comfortable on the Internet, and they won't need to be taught as much about using it. They will also be more accustomed to doing business in general through their computers, and as you add audio and video capabilities, customers will feel like they are "there." This is already starting to happen.

I don't believe that there is ever going to be one "killer app" that dominates the technology sphere. We've almost grown beyond that. There are too many competing technologies and developers. One may win a temporary advantage, enough even to cause a shift in the marketplace, but in the end, the balance will be restored by the "next big thing," and the competition will continue.

In short, the successful online brokerage won't model itself as a high-tech firm. It will see itself as a brokerage firm that's trying to use technology as effectively as possible to deliver customer-oriented solutions. It is the opposite of what some companies are saying at this point—claiming to be technology companies, not brokerage firms. But the bottom line is: they are in the brokerage business. Their product is brokerage; technology is just the way they are delivering their product to investors. It is a very effective way of delivering that product to the market, but customers don't want to do their brokerage with a technology firm. They want to do it with a brokerage firm that is really good at incorporating the technology to serve its investors' needs. And when looking at who is dominating the market right now in online transactions, it is brokerage firms, not technology firms.

Delivering the basic services of brokerage—however the best-available technology delivers it, however people like it best—and being very flexible about moving forward with that changing technology: that is the future for online brokerage.

Publishing: Serving the New Consumers

Eric Hippeau, Chairman & Chief Executive Officer, Ziff-Davis, Inc.
You can't name a newspaper or magazine today that is not also publishing on the Internet. But many are doing so for purely defensive reasons. And none is doing it as well, or as profitably, as Ziff-Davis. Chairman and CEO Eric Hippeau is a technology visionary who has led his company to the Internet for all of the right reasons and has the track record to prove it. In this chapter, he dispels many of the myths about Internet publishing and shares some of the secrets of Z-D's success.

I believe in technology. I first realized this back in 1975, when I was twenty-four years old and the editor in chief of a daily English-language newspaper in Brazil. Deciding that the time had come to launch a computer publication, I started a section in the paper about computers and tried to convince my publisher that we should spin it out as a separate publication. Unfortunately, he did not believe that this was a very smart business decision.

Looking back, I shouldn't have blamed him for feeling this way about a publication focused solely on computers. It probably seemed like a tremendous risk. Computers and technology were still just a niche business that captivated mostly scientists, professors, and, of course, "geeks." There just wasn't an obvious market for these types of publications.

Now, fast forward about twenty years and look at the massive changes in society. Computers are everywhere, Bill Gates is more famous than our president and it is chic to be geek. Society has not only accepted computers, it has embraced technology as a critical part of everyday life.

The most popular and far-reaching application of technology today, which has truly become a critical part of everyday life, is the Internet. This medium has brought widespread changes to our society, especially in the way we communicate, conduct business, and even shop. And in spite of my Brazilian publisher's earlier renunciation, I have come to realize that the Internet actually complements and enhances print publishing by acting as a supplement and also by driving a large audience to this traditional medium.

The New Economy

Due to the impact of technology—especially the Internet—we are operating in a new economy that is firmly grounded in technology.

A decade ago, pundits were saying that manufacturing was dead in the United States, as productivity was slipping. Now, we are seeing a resurgence of the efficiency of manufacturing, significantly based on advances in technology. Technology is also having a big impact on a more individual front. Not since the Industrial Revolution have we witnessed the birth of so many billionaires. Gone are the days of the Rockefellers and Vanderbilts. Today's financial magnates are people such as Bill Gates and Larry Ellison. But what is startlingly different is the speed at which these entrepreneurs have made their billions and the profound influence they have had on Wall Street.

Technology is also changing the economic landscape of America. For years, Texas used to be known as the Oil State. Then it became known as the Energy State. Today, technology has surpassed energy as the number one industry in Texas. And take a look at what has happened to the farmland of South Dakota. Some of this state's most celebrated cow spots are now on Gateway computer boxes. You don't need to be obsessed with Silicon Valley to see the impact technology has had on the United States.

The New Consumers

In the 1980s, the new technology was the PC, and we can see in ret-
rospect the business opportunities it spawned. Today's new technology is the Internet, and it's becoming easier every day to imagine
the business opportunities that lie ahead. And, of course, the
Internet is really just another killer application of the PC.

Clearly, the Internet is changing the way we live our lives—
from the fourteen-year-old who is researching his science project; to
the forty-four-year-old who has refinanced his home, bought a car,
and shopped for Christmas presents; to the seventy-four-year-old
who is keeping an eye on investments while keeping in touch with
grandchildren. In fact, I frequently chat with my twelve-year-old
daughter on the Web when I am traveling.

These are the new consumers in this new economy. Making
smart business decisions on the Web requires understanding how
people's habits are changing because of the Internet. In this new
economy, consumers are not what they used to be. According to Ian
Morrison, the President of the Institute for the Future, new consumers are different from consumers of the past in five major ways:
They are better educated, more discriminating, better informed,
more individualistic, and what they value has changed. Consumers
today expect that they can have any product, anytime, any place,
and they expect to get it at a competitive price. And why not?

If we can shop for a new car on the Internet, what value does
the so-called bargaining of the local dealer add? Maybe that's
where we will go for a test drive and take our cars for service. But
the Internet is changing the role of the local car dealership. Web
sites like Auto-by-Tel and Carpoint are capitalizing on this trend.
And then there's the local grocery market. Who would have
guessed that you might buy your groceries over the Internet—then
have them delivered to your doorstep? And at a savings! New companies taking advantage of the new technology-driven economy
include NetGrocer and Safeway's Peapod system. Both are trying to
change the way Americans buy groceries. The number of new consumers is growing rapidly, and their presence is clearly trans-
forming the marketplace. Time to market is down, choice is up, and

consumer loyalty to brands is shifting based on their relevance in the new Web-centric economy.

Who would have forecast that Barnes and Noble would be fighting for market share against an upstart named Amazon.com? But, as Yogi Berra might have said, "Forecasting is hard—particularly the future." But it is not impossible if you realize that in order to understand the opportunities in media, you must first understand how people get their information.

Ziff-Davis and the Internet

We understand how people's habits reflect their interests, and we have always worked to serve the passions of avid readers. For example, before World War II, we believed that aviation would change the world and we focused on this niche. After the war, we believed Americans would want to spend their increasing disposable income in the pursuit of hobbies and special interests. So, we focused on that niche. Today, we deliver information on technology. Technology is neither a niche nor a special interest. It is the greatest factor influencing our society today.

Specifically, the Internet has dramatically transformed information, namely how we get it and where we get it. As a provider of information, Ziff-Davis has also felt the profound impact that the Internet is having on our business. It has shifted our business model, caused us to rethink our core business—publishing—and has encouraged us to expand into new areas, like television. From early on, our corporate strategy was to anticipate and serve the needs of the technology community through every possible medium. Our online history dates back to 1985, when *PC* magazine first launched a bulletin-board service. Out of that grew PC MagNet in 1988, which later became ZiffNet in 1991.

We launched our first "real Web site" in February of 1994. To put this in context, this was a full month before Marc Andressen and Jim Clark formed Mosaic Communications Corp., which was later renamed Netscape. Their work spawned the development of the World Wide Web, which arguably then spawned the Internet gold rush. At the end of the very first day that our Web site was up, its founders said "We got 200 users!" The rest, as they say, is history.

Today, our ZDNet Web site attracts approximately 6.8 million unique visitors a month. We went from zero to millions in four years. That's warp speed in media terms.

ZDNet is the Web's leading source for information about computing and the Internet. In fact, according to independent surveys, ZDNet is also the #1 Web site for news, information, and entertainment. To give you a relative sense of just how popular it is, www.zdnet.com reaches more people than www.usatoday.com and www.cnn.com combined. In addition to being pioneers in creating content on the Web, we were among the first in selling Web advertising. And advertising has become an important stream of revenue for our Internet business.

We jumped right into the online medium in 1985. When we decided to take the plunge early, we had one thought in mind. Starting a Web site didn't guarantee success, but not launching one guaranteed that we would never succeed. We decided to go out, do it, make mistakes, and then adapt and change to become successful. Our efforts paid off.

Clearly, ZDNet is a success stories for Ziff-Davis. But what has been the Web's impact on traditional publishing businesses? We believe it has been very positive. Take at look at print advertising. In 1994, we published eight leading computer magazines in the United States, with a combined circulation of 3.5 million. Today, we publish seventeen computer magazines in the United States, with a combined circulation of more than 6.5 million. Our growth in ad revenue and circulation has been dramatic. And contrary to popular belief, the Web has become a significant source of new subscribers to our print publications.

Survival of Print

When a new medium gains mass acceptance, there is often a question as to the survival of its predecessor. But television never replaced radio, radio never replaced newspapers, and the Internet won't be a substitute for reading newspapers or magazines. In fact, in 1997, over three hundred new magazines were launched industry-wide.

For some reason, people chose to ignore history and assumed that the Internet would wipe out print altogether. As the number of people utilizing the Internet began to increase exponentially, certain myths arose that heralded the demise of print. However, we believe that these myths have been proven to be false. In fact, research has shown that Internet users read 50 percent more magazines than the general public.

There are several specific reasons why print will continue as an essential source of information. First of all, magazines are easier to use than most online services. They are better suited for reading long documents. Magazines are more portable than the smallest and lightest laptop computer and they don't drain batteries on long flights. Roger Selbert, who edits and publishes the *FutureScan* newsletter, says, "If you look at the future, you have to look at historical patterns first to find the constants. The constants are the only thing that you can be sure about in the future. And the magazine format is one of those constants."

In our experience, the Internet actually drives people to magazines and newspapers, as some Web publishers are able to draw visitors by using samples of articles or pictures as a hook or a teaser for their print publication. This also allows consumers to view the material before they make a decision on whether they want to purchase a product.[1] Others use their online space as a supplementary medium to their print publication. These supplementary pages may offer additional in-depth coverage, extra editorial content, or additional pictures or artwork that is only available online. In fact, the Magazine Publishers of America states that over 1,750 magazines have established their own Web sites. All of these publications are likely trying to extend their audience by reaching out to a new audience over the Internet.[2] The reverse is also true. Online content can also drive people to read print publications because of a unique editorial style or type of content that may attract the reader. If someone reads articles online from the same Web site on a consistent basis and becomes familiar with a certain style, it is likely that they will seek out a print version, if one is available.

We divide the entire magazine industry into three categories: general interest publications such as *Business Week* or *Time*; special interest or category-specific publications such as our *PC Magazine* or *PC Week*; and publications that originated because of the

Internet, such as *Yahoo! Internet Life*. Since the Internet has become more popular, general interest publications have been the hardest hit, as people have been increasingly reading publications that are specifically suited to their interests. By contrast, it has been category-specific publications that have thrived in the Age of the Internet. For example, our research shows that during the first quarter of 1998, readership of computer publications increased 13 percent, while readership of general interest publications increased only 2 percent.

The new genre of publications are those that originated because of the Internet. In this group there are financial publications such as *Red Herring* and lifestyle magazines such as *Wired* and *Upside*. At the leading edge of the lifestyle group is *Yahoo! Internet Life*, a print guide to the Internet, providing information on select Web sites, as well as insight and commentary on the Internet.

A unique symbiotic relationship exists between this genre of magazines and the Internet. Neither the Internet nor these publications could exist without the other. In the same way that *TV Guide* could not exist without a television, *Yahoo! Internet Life* could not exist without the Internet. Martha Stewart's television program and magazine on cooking, decorating, and "home keeping" is another example of this type of cross marketing, as these two mediums supplement and feed off one another.

Previously, I discussed the Internet being a supplement to print, but in this case, *Yahoo! Internet Life* reaches an audience that looks at this magazine for a different set of reasons. These readers are interested in having a print companion to use when searching the Web or to read when their laptop batteries run out or where an extension cord does not reach the outlet! *Yahoo! Internet Life* has been extremely successful, and we expect its guaranteed circulation base to reach six hundred thousand by February 1999, which is double its initial base after its first year of operation in 1995. This is very strong growth for any magazine in any category and is yet another example of the complementary relationship of print and the Internet, where the Internet is complementing print, or vice versa.

The magazine industry as a whole has been quite prosperous. Over three hundred new titles were launched industry-wide in 1997, and magazines had their best year for ad growth since 1984, up 13 percent to $12.75 billion.[3] We have also felt the positive impact that the Internet has had on print publishing. In the thirteen years since we launched the online companion to *PC* magazine, the print version's paid circulation has grown from under three hundred thousand in 1985 to well over 1 million today. Interestingly, while the Internet audience is expanding, people who go online for news say that their news habits are unchanged, as they are still turning to traditional news sources such as magazines.

According to our research, people are spending less time watching network TV, making long-distance phone calls, and sleeping! Our research has also found that the time now spent on the Web has actually increased the time spent reading computer magazines and watching computer programs on cable television. According to InternetTrak, Web users are nearly three times as likely to read computer publications compared to the general public. During the first quarter of 1998, Ziff-Davis research shows that there was an 8 percent increase in people watching computer programs on network TV and a 3 percent increase in people watching computer programming on cable TV, while television viewership decreased by 22 percent during the same time period.

The New Audience

The Internet can also reach out to an entirely different audience that may not just go to a newsstand and look through various magazines before settling on one. We classify this audience as Internet-Only Driven. The Internet-Only Driven are the people whose only reason for walking into Circuit City is to buy a PC in order to e-mail grandchildren. Or they are the parents who would never buy a computer for themselves but know their kids need to be on the Internet. This is a rapidly growing group.

We reach this new audience by posting selected content online. Part of this audience is made up of people who utilized the Internet before becoming fully intrigued by technology. But after becoming hooked, many attempt to educate themselves further about technology by reading online publications. The Internet has the capability to bring information about technology to people who never thought that they were interested in the subject. I believe that if this new audience reads this content, it is likely that they will return to a given site on a consistent basis. After their attention is captured on the Internet, this audience will begin to look for specific brands elsewhere and might eventually seek out the print version of a publication for a long trip in a car or a long flight.

The Internet-Only Driven group is also extremely selective. This has become apparent by witnessing the success of specialty interest publications and Web sites. Nobody is interested in sifting through volumes of information to find a small article on their specific interest or favorite hobby. Search engines such as Yahoo! have made it possible to quickly find specific types of information on the Internet. By accepting key-word searches and aggregating information, Yahoo! provides exactly what the new audience wants.

We have also used the Internet to reach an audience with newer brands, such as ZDTV. ZDTV is a twenty-four-hour cable television channel that targets viewers interested in computers, technology, and the Internet. This network has an integrated Web site that provides the latest news, information on programming, and video and audio clips of select ZDTV shows. This Web site has been essential in launching our new cable channel, as it allows us to target an already interested audience. We also included a section on the Web site that allows visitors to proclaim "ZDTV Me." This function sends an e-mail stating that this visitor did not receive ZDTV through his or her local cable system and wants to voice his or her opinion that they do indeed want the channel. By mid-August 1998, nearly twenty-six thousand requests for ZDTV came through our petition form. In the case of ZDTV, the Internet has truly assisted us in extending our brand to a new, broader audience in the television arena.

ZDTV and the ZDTV Web site work in tandem to direct interested audiences to both mediums. These two mediums also provide separate, but integrated, forums for our editors and reporters to present information on computing and the Internet. By working together, these different mediums strengthen the corporate brand, the company's individual brands, and the entire category of technology-related information. We have proven that this model can also work across many different types of businesses, as we have six integrated media and marketing platforms, which are Publishing,

THE NEW SOCIETY AND THE INFLECTION POINT

This new audience is reflected in the ways that our society is rapidly changing, and technology is a major catalyst here as well. We see this in how people stay in touch, how people work, learn, spend money, and use their leisure time. When you think of major inventions that have changed the way people live, you might think of the telephone or the television. Well, add the Internet to that list. People are watching less television and in many households controlling the keyboard is a bigger victory than controlling the remote! E-mail has become an essential tool to keep in touch with family and friends scattered across the globe. In the past, the telephone was our best friend. These days, it's more and more likely to be the computer.

Success in this new Internet-driven economy is based on simple concepts. First, understand the inflection point. Opportunity in the new economy is not based on some whiz-bang business model. It is based on taking advantage of an emerging technology inflection point. This technology inflection point is the proverbial bend in the hockey stick where growth suddenly accelerates at a much higher rate.

This inflection point is so critical because it is about scoping the market and knowing where growth will come. If you can grasp the inflection point, then any business model can work. We break the adult population into four distinct groups. The first two

Events, the Internet, Education, Market Intelligence, and Television (ZDTV). Our six platforms provide us with an opportunity to cross market all of our products and provide unique solutions to our marketing partners.

Extension of the Brand

The Internet is a great tool to extend the reach of a company's brand. Some of the most recognizable brands today, such as Yahoo!, are solely driven by Internet exposure. Other companies, such as Gateway and Disney, have used the Internet to strengthen already powerful brands. Even older, more traditional companies, like General Electric and Ford, have realized the importance of extending their brands to an online audience by creating intricate and expensive Web sites. Ford even has online "showrooms" in which customers can view new Ford cars and trucks and educate themselves about Ford's different product lines. This Web site also includes historical information for enthusiasts on classic cars such as Thunderbirds or Mustangs!

The Internet is also utilized by publishing companies to extend their brand. *Modern Bride*, a magazine that provides information to are well established—the PC-Only Driven and the PC and Internet Centric.

The second two are still emerging and often neglected—the Internet-Only Driven and the Technology Hibernators. Our research indicates that approximately 26 percent of the adult population are PC-Only users, 29 percent are PC and Internet Centric, 3 percent are Internet-Only Driven, and 42 percent are Technology Hibernators.

Ziff-Davis has been focused on the first two groups—the PC-Only Driven and the PC and Internet Centric for many years. This has been a very robust market and we see continued growth in both groups. But what is becoming even more interesting is the growth we anticipate in the other two groups—the Internet-Only Driven and the Technology Hibernators.

The Technology Hibernators are those people who won't go near a computer until it is as straightforward as turning on their television. They want the Internet to come right into their living room. It is important to understand how the trend line bends here, because some really big growth comes from introducing these last two groups to technology and getting them hooked. As these new groups become technology users—specifically Internet users—lots of new business opportunities emerge. Part of anticipating technology inflection points is scoping the market and determining how consumers are using a new technology today and how they will use it tomorrow.

engaged couples to help them plan their wedding, honeymoon, and first home, features an interactive Web site. This site offers such things as sample wedding-planning calendars, checklists for the bride and groom, and tips on wedding insurance. It also provides a platform for the bride and groom to register online through the Wedding Network. Recently, *Modern Bride* and the Wedding Network joined together to offer a one-stop wedding-planning resource, registry retail, and online gift service for engaged couples and their friends and family. By providing a valuable service to all members of a wedding party, *Modern Bride* is able to reach an audience that may not have previously been aware of the magazine, Web site, or registry service they offer.

The magazine *Horticulture, The Art of American Gardening*, offers a Web site where visitors can plan out their garden online, down to every plant or flower. The site even includes a section where visitors can input the region of the country where they are planting their garden to find out which type of vegetation thrives there!

We utilize the Internet to extend our corporate brand as well as our individual brands, such as ZDNet, *PC Magazine*, and COMDEX. For example, COMDEX's Web site offers key information about upcoming events, such as preliminary event schedules, exhibitors, and potential attendees. This site also includes high-lights from previous shows, such as speeches, award lists, and photos. It is very important for us to put this type of information on the Web site, as it helps draw attention to our lesser-known or newer events. For example, our COMDEX/Fall event is extremely popular, draws a high level of traffic to our site, and therefore provides us with the ability to cross sell. When searching for information about an event in particular, visitors to our Web site will also learn about our other trade shows. Our Web site promotes and publicizes all COMDEX events, especially those that may be more segment-focused and not as well known as COMDEX/Fall, such as Seybold Seminars. Seybold events are a leading education and information provider for traditional and new media publishing industries. These shows focus on the latest technologies and products, design tools, and desktop applications. Being able to use the strength of the COMDEX brand has made it easier to draw visitors to our Web site and thus raise awareness about Seybold and other less-known events.

Online Revenue

There is one large hurdle facing all those who attempt to create a publishing business on the Internet, and that is the cost of creating, updating, and maintaining a site with new and interesting information. There are different ways to fund a Web site, which include selling advertising, sponsorships, classifieds, or directories. Another strategy, which has not yet proven to be completely viable, is to charge for content. Many Web sites have been successful charging for services, but few have found success charging for content. In fact, research has shown that two-thirds of Web users state that they will not pay for online content.

Not all Web sites that charge a fee to access content have been failures. In fact, the *Wall Street Journal* Interactive Edition has been extremely successful. It has over two hundred thousand paying subscribers to date, only one-third of which subscribe to the print edition. The median household income of subscribers to the online edition is $120,000, and the average age of subscribers for the online version is forty-two, while the average for the print edition is fifty-two.

Several Web sites that don't charge for content have also been extremely successful in terms of number of registered users. For example, the *New York Times* on the Web has approximately 4 million registered users but has never charged domestic subscribers to view its content. Originally, this Web site charged international viewers for reading content but has recently changed this policy. However, the *New York Times* lost between $12 million and $15 million from its Web projects in 1997, even though its online revenues (of an undisclosed amount) grew 66 percent. Instead of charging for content, the *New York Times* draws its revenue from other sources, such as advertising, sponsorships, archiving, and reselling articles to databases such as Lexis-Nexis and Dow Jones. This Web site has seen growth in revenues, registered users, and page views and has helped drive its viewers toward the print edition while strengthening the brand.

Although sites such as the *Wall Street Journal* Interactive Edition have been successful charging for content, I do not believe that this is a feasible model for the majority of other publications. The *Wall Street Journal* Interactive Edition provides uniquely targeted and high-level information about the financial community, that its subscribers may feel justified in spending money for content alone. Subscribers may believe that the information they find on the *Wall Street Journal* Interactive Edition is of such high editorial quality and is unique enough that they feel justified in paying a fee. Others may believe that the information obtained from this Web site is extremely valuable to their careers or financial well-being and therefore deem the subscription fee an investment in their financial security. While the *Wall Street Journal* Interactive Edition proves to be an interesting case study for the subscription model, we have chosen not to take the same route as they have.

We have been pleased with our online success to date and are not interested in charging for content alone. We have been successful in deriving revenue from advertising because of ZDNet's overall dominance and through fee-based services. Two of our most popular services are Computer Magazine Archives (CMA) and ZD University. CMA is a service that provides our Web site users with access to a collection of over 150-computer related magazines, journals, and newspapers, which include over one hundred thousand articles and abstracts on product reviews, company profiles, and high-tech industry trends, for only $4.95 per month. ZD University offers computer training via the Internet, forum-based virtual classrooms, interactive self-study tutorials, an online bookstore, and a reference library of tips and techniques. It features nearly one hundred courses that serve various levels of computer expertise and are led by a prestigious lineup of instructors, including book and software-program authors. Currently, we have more than sixty thousand students enrolled in ZD University who pay $7.95 a month to attend an unlimited number of Online classes. While that may not sound like much, ZDU is a successful subscription service on the Web.

The key to a successful Web subscription service is to provide users with the highest level of content that is integral to their everyday lives and is presented in a convenient manner. A Web site such as ZDU is a place where students can take as many classes as they want for one price and take these classes at any point during the month. Skills learned on ZDU, such as tips for Windows, Excel, PhotoShop, and select programming and operating systems, are applicable to the job requirements of many people and help develop the skill sets of those who take the time to sit in our "virtual classrooms." In fact, ZDU owns and operates a single-site training center that specializes in applications, programming, and certification training for Microsoft, Novell, and Lotus, and the Training Center Alliance, which provides qualifying training-center customers with enhanced marketing support and referral capabilities worldwide. In this day and age, when computers are increasingly penetrating all aspects of life, it is vital that all people know how to properly use a variety of programs, and ZDU presents a flexible format for people with varying types of work and social schedules to take advantage of this type of education.

In addition to services like CMA and ZDU, we also offer commerce over the Internet through Computer Shopper/NetBuyer. Computer Shopper is a print publication that provides buying advice, product evaluations, and technology coverage to readers who buy computer products directly from manufacturers. NetBuyer is its online companion and is one of the leading Web sites devoted to computer retailing. This site offers over 40,000 computer products from over 180 vendors. NetBuyer has been extremely successful, and we believe that e-commerce will continue to grow in the future and be an important and successful Internet business model.

Other companies have been very successful in offering a variety of consumer products over the Web. In fact, according to Internet Trak, over 7 million current Web users have purchased online in the past three months. Perhaps the most well known site is Amazon.com, an online seller of books and music that claims to have a catalog of over 3 million book, music, and other titles that can be purchased through its Web site. As previously mentioned, Amazon.com has posed a threat to the market share that established book retailers, such as Barnes and Noble, presently maintain. Companies such as Amazon.com have proven that some of the old rules of commerce do not apply to the Internet, as they do not rent or lease showroom property and have fewer employees than other bookstores. In turn, this lowers the company's overhead costs and makes their business more profitable.

Another Internet business model that has seen some success, as mentioned in previous chapters, is the community model. Companies such as GeoCities have attracted countless viewers to their specific chat rooms and Web pages on their main Web site. GeoCities comprises of a number of communities, each with a different theme such as sports or movies. The company has been able to take advantage of this type of community setting and generate revenue by selling sponsorships or advertisements to certain sections of the site. GeoCities can offer something that many other Web sites can't, and that is a targeted audience. For example, if an athletic-shoe company wants to advertise with GeoCities, they can advertise on the pages that are sports themed and ensure that they reach a targeted audience.

Challenges

One of the issues in building a Web site is creating original content. We do not believe in repurposing content, because the Web user has different tastes and a shorter attention span than the reader of print publications. If Web users cannot immediately find an article of interest, it is likely that they can and will immediately go to another

Web site for information. The vast majority of ZDNet's content is original to the Web, and while we do not repurpose content, we do reformat and reedit it for the Web. Actually, many of our editors and reporters will put a story on the Web first and then develop it further in one of our print publications. We believe it is important to present news in a timely manner and our Web sites are a way to disseminate information instantly. However, it is also important that news is developed in more detail after the initial report, and our print publications are a superb medium for doing so. Our Web sites and publications work in tandem to present the highest quality of information in the best possible format to our readers.

The widespread use of the Internet has brought about another series of issues such as copyright laws and privacy concerns, many recently involving the use of cookies. Cookies, as discussed throughout the book, are pieces of data written by a Web server that are stored on a user's PC. Cookies are used to track exactly what a user does on a Web site. Many Web sites assert that the use of cookies is a service to the user, as cookies record information that helps Webmasters better understand which sections of Web sites are more popular or heavily trafficked and helps Webmasters utilize targeted ad programs that may be of interest to the user.

Cookies are used to record frequency of visits, pages viewed, sections of the Web site visited, and any purchases that the visitor may have made on the Web site. Although cookies can be quickly removed by easily downloadable programs such as ZDNet's CookieMaster, they are reinserted into a PC whenever visiting a Web site that uses cookies. Although cookies were most likely created for harmless reasons, the information that they obtain can be used for purposes that the visitor may not want, such as certain types of market research and targeted mailings. Even thought there are limitations to the type of information that cookies can obtain, the unapproved use of information on personal Internet viewing habits is not right. We do use cookies on ZDNet but we notify our visitors that they are in use and give them the option of removing those cookies by offering CookieMaster.

We endorse privacy protection and take measures to ensure that any personal information that we collect from visitors to our Web sites is not distributed or used without their consent. If a visitor provides us with personal information, they are told exactly what this information will be used for and therefore have the choice of what information they want to disclose. Internet companies, not the government, should regulate privacy issues. It is up to every content provider and Web site to take this issue very seriously and not betray the trust that visitors place in their Web sites.

The use of cookies and programs such as CookieMaster have also brought up specific copyright issues on the Internet. Currently, a law is being proposed that will make it illegal to use tools to protect the privacy of Internet users, such as programs like CookieMaster. This law has been written to protect Web sites from copyright infringement by ensuring that Web sites can monitor the activities of visitors to their sites. While we are concerned about copyright issues, we are equally concerned about the privacy of our users. I do believe that a better system should be implemented to protect copyright issues, as eliminating privacy-ensuring tools will cause more problems and raise more issues in the long run.

Anticipating the Future

In the twenty-three years since I first decided to begin a publication focused solely on computing, our society has seen many changes. We have attempted to stay ahead of the rest of the industry by anticipating the future. Although this is not an exact science, we believe that our fine executive and editorial staff are dedicated to this endeavor and will always do what it takes to stay on the cutting edge. Over the years, we have been able to take advantage of new ways to educate and inform people about technology and have sought out business opportunities that may have seemed unconventional or unheard of at the time.

Spotting unique niches to develop has been one our strengths at Ziff-Davis, and we will keep searching for these areas. We are not waiting for the future to arrive to take advantage of the Internet, the Web, and other emerging technologies. As Robert Kriegel, the author of *If It Ain't Broke, Break It*, recently observed: "Successful leaders know that the future isn't found; it is invented. It is shaped by people with the vision, courage, and wisdom to think beyond the boundaries of the known." This is both a powerful and an empowering belief, and we at Ziff-Davis have the ability to continually present the future to our ever-growing audience.

■ ■ ■

1   Foote, Cone & Belding Report
2   FCB Report
3   Ibid

Health Care:
Operating in the
Third Dimension

Bob Pringle, President, InteliHealth, Inc.

Health care could be the next millennium's poster child for the Internet-ization of an industry. What other industry is a better candidate for the Internet's unique blend of information dissemination, user control, and system efficiency? Bob Pringle, President of Intelihealth, talks about the impact the Internet is already having on the industry that represents about 30 percent of the U.S. economy—and the even greater impact it will have in years to come.

Each month, I see hundreds of testimonials from people who have used the Internet for life-saving and life-changing health information. A woman in rural America recently wrote to say she would have never known that her asthma inhaler was recalled without an e-mail alert—and that as a serious asthmatic, this could have been a life-threatening situation. In Africa, a family was able to research and diagnose a rare condition in their young son; seeking treatment in a U.S. facility that will likely save the child's eyesight. A mother wrote to say that she finally understood her afflicted daughter's Attention Deficit Disorder and now has a posi-tive relationship with her child for the first time in almost five years.

Doctors in the United States and abroad have written to applaud the daily news updates they can now receive via e-mail of breaking news and commentaries in their specialties.

Each day, hundreds of thousands of people turn to the Internet to research serious health conditions. Hundreds of thousands more use the Internet to help them achieve a healthier lifestyle. Doctors tap the Internet to provide timely, accurate information to their patients. People research medications, diets, mental-health issues, allergies, cancer, neurological disorders, caregiving challenges, doctors, hospitals, studies, news, and more. Statistics show unprecedented consumer use of information to gain control of personal health and well-being.

At the same time, health-care institutions view the Internet as an unparalleled opportunity to improve communication, cost structure, and competitive advantage. Strategic opportunities abound for those companies positioned to meet the rapidly growing needs of consumers, physicians, hospitals, pharmacists, insurers, and others in the health-care industry. This chapter will address the emerging opportunities and predict many of the key factors for success.

Understanding the Third Dimension

I believe that success in the online world of health care will follow the three golden rules of real estate—"Location, Location, Location." Gold-miners called it a "land grab." Business scholars call it "disintermediation." Popular online pundits describe "community building." Conventional wisdom shouts "own the desktop" or "create a portal." Those who may reap the benefits will understand that it is all much simpler than that.

And also much harder. On the Web we have to deal with *virtual* locations. Historical marketplaces have been likened to traditional chess matches; the Internet adds a third dimension to that chess board—with an infinite number of levels. Those who benefit will use this third dimension to create unstoppable virtual distribution chains for their products—cementing efficient, valuable relationships with their new customers and adding almost unlimited worldwide potential for these new customers. Successful Internet

businesses know that eyeballs have to be converted to "RPEs"—
Revenue-Producing Events!

The Business Model Is Multidimensional

Who is going to make money and how? With over 1 trillion dollars
spent annually on health care, there will be no shortage of players
moving to leverage the Internet in the coming months and years.

Those who are successful in this category will create multidimensional business plans, improving access and efficiency to the
health care system. Major business plans will evolve for:

Content. Content may not be "King" anymore, but in health care
it is critically important. Access to quality, branded, trustworthy
information can save lives, reduce costs, and improve our overall
standard of living. Consumers and professionals alike are looking
for information on traditional medicine and on alternative therapies
and treatments.

Distribution. No matter what your health product, you need
people to see it. A Web offering is not a true offering until you can
drive traffic through the site. Successful undertakings will develop
affiliate programs to leverage their content and commerce opportunities across broad distribution networks.

Sponsorship. Leaders will emerge in obtaining sponsorship for
online content areas from pharmaceutical, managed care, provider,
nutrition, fitness, and major consumer-products companies.
Opportunities exist on international, national, and local levels.

E-commerce. With its early success selling books, CDs, and airline tickets, health-related products have a growing presence on the
Internet. As an example, we recently offered an online version of a
health newsletter, and converted as many as 7 percent of viewers
into paid print subscriptions.

Transactions. A significant percentage of the annual trillion-
dollar U.S. health tab is consumed by redundant and time-
consuming paperwork. Estimated cost savings for electronic medical records and associated improvements to medical quality are
staggering. For example, Aetna U.S. Healthcare just launched

"E-Pay," a new program that guarantees to pay physicians within fifteen days if both an electronic referral and claim are submitted—significantly reducing costly paperwork and manual transcription errors.

The Landscape

Health care may be the only industry changing as fast or faster than the Internet. The industry is extraordinarily fragmented—because health care today is regulated and delivered on a local basis. Consumers, health-care providers, insurance companies, and employers play ever-evolving roles amidst a sea of change.

While health-care spending accounts for more than 13 percent of the U.S. Gross Domestic Product, managed care has stabilized the overall rate of spending increases (figure 15.1).

Figure 15.1. Rate of Increase in Spending on Health Care

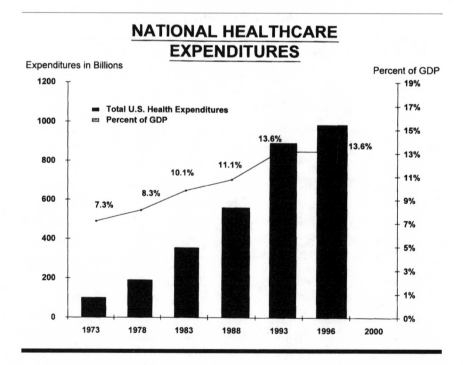

NATIONAL HEALTHCARE EXPENDITURES

CONSUMER SEARCHES

The top 20 pharmaceutical searches by consumers, based on more than five hundred thousand searches on InteliHealth consumer Web sites in July 1998.

1. Paxil (depression)
2. Zoloft (depression)
3. Viagra (sexual dysfunction)
4. Prozac (depression)
5. Lipitor (cholesterol)
6. Wellbutrin (depression)
7. Prednisone (inflammation/steroid)
8. Serzone (depression)
9. Ultram (pain)
10. Prilosec (digestive disorders)
11. Neurontin (seizures)
12. Meridia (weight loss)
13. Depakote (seizures)
14. Effexor (depression)
15. Xanax (anxiety)
16. Relafen (inflammation/nonsteroid)
17. Rezulin (diabetes)
18. Zyban (smoking)
19. Propulsid (digestive disorders)
20. Synthroid (thyroid)

Still, the roles of physicians, patients, insurance companies, hospital systems, pharmaceutical companies, and government are undergoing seismic shifts.

The Internet now plays a pivotal role in this shifting health-care industry. Forty-three percent of all adult users of the Internet have already accessed medical information online.[1] The same study estimates that 61 percent of all physicians will use the Internet for professional purposes by late 1998. And, a new industry is already mobilizing to meet the demand.

The Consumer

Consumers will be the driving force for change in the health-care industry. Remember just fifteen years ago, and think of the Financial Industry. As consumers, we had two choices for investment accounts—checking or savings. Consumers could not get real-time stock quotes or trade securities without calling a broker. Now, it's almost impossible to get through a day without knowing what the Dow Jones Industrial Average did. Over 30 percent of all individual stock trades are now executed on the Internet.

Likewise, families—especially sandwich-generation Baby Boomers—demand more and more control of personal and family health choices. They want information, choice, and access to quality care. As indicated by the previous chart, they are already turning to the Internet as a solution. Major medical information sites gather tens of millions of page views each month from both patients and providers. Healthy-living sites gather tens of millions more.

The quantity of information is not the problem. One can find two thousand Web sites indexed for cancer,[2] and over 2.5 million documents dealing with cancer.[3] Twenty *million* documents on the Web contain the word "health."[4]

The real concerns are:

Quality. Consumers need to find brands they can trust. Other industries have successfully done this on the Internet. Financial-information seekers trust the "Motley Fools," and book shoppers trust Amazon.com. But the issue is magnified with health information. In the early days of the "wild, wild, Web," credibility was hurt as fourteen-year-olds masqueraded as professionals giving advice on breast cancer. Unlike almost any other industry, poor health information can have a devastating impact. Likewise, timely, credible information can truly save lives.

Community. Particularly important for rare conditions, but of value to every patient and caregiver, online communities offer the ability to find other people "like me." Sharing experiences and learning can connect people across many miles. As extended families rarely live together any more, this virtual community results in tremendous support for individuals around the globe.

Personalization. The promise of personalizing information is tantalizing for the web of health-care issues faced by the average family today. "Let me know what I need to know when I need to know it." This can be particularly important for chronic conditions such as diabetes, high cholesterol, weight management, AIDS, cancer, and heart disease.

Confidentiality. Consumers and professionals alike are wary of providing detailed personal information when it is unclear how that information may be used. The anonymity of the Web allows people to get confidential information on sensitive topics such as AIDS and depression. Market leaders need to provide clear policies for how personal information will be used, which need to be backed by credible institutions with "staying power."

The Toughest Challenge

We are all consumers and we want it all. In the traditional world, people trade off authority for availability of information. The chart (figure 15.2) below shows how consumers traditionally viewed this trade-off. But with new information technologies, consumers expect increasing breadth and depth of quality, branded health information.

Traditionally, people have often asked an easily available family member or neighbor for health advice. The Internet now gives easy access to authoritative information from academic medical centers.

As an example, at InteliHealth.com we house over 2 million pages of information from distinguished sources such as Johns Hopkins, the National Institutes of Health, and the American Medical Association. InteliHealth also provides twenty-four-hour, search-engine-enabled, consumer-friendly access to highly authoritative information from Johns Hopkins—which has been rated the number-one hospital in the United States for the past eight years—

Figure 15.2: The information trade-off: Availability vs. Authority

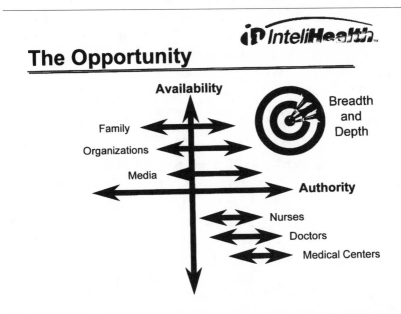

along with over one hundred other trusted sources of health-care information. Obviously, this is better than asking an uncle or aunt!

The American Medical Association: www.ama-assn.org provides online access to quality, peer-reviewed health information, as well as databases of physician credentials. Healthfinder: www.healthfinder.org, sponsored by the Department of Health and Human Services, is a Web site to help consumers find government-provided health information. Oncolink: www.oncolink.com, sponsored by the University of Pennsylvania, focuses on the information needs of cancer patients, caregivers, and health-care professionals.

The Health-Care Provider

With today's rapid change in medical knowledge, physicians are relying on the Internet for both medical and practice information. And as the industry consolidates and experiences a growth in the interrelated networks of doctors and hospitals, many of these providers are becoming increasingly efficient and technologically sophisticated.

A growing number of physicians access the Internet directly, and many more "delegate" the use of this technology to "proxies." Today, the online physician can readily access many of the latest peer-reviewed medical journals, tap into discussions with other physicians, and review the latest published medical protocols. Tens of thousands of doctors receive breaking e-mail updates of health news and information—an easy way to "push" personalized information directly to the professional desktop.

Because of the mature nature of the professional health-care industry, those interested in entering the online health-care market must create alliances with existing medical publishers and practice-management services. Information has always been an important aspect to these professionals. However, the issue is how to modify existing use of medical journals, medical textbooks, paper monographs, live medical-education seminars, and proprietary office-management software toward the use of Internet-based, open-standard products.

Several online communities for physicians have emerged with a critical mass of monthly users. Medscape: www.medscape.com provides aggregated information, along with the first online medical journals accepted for listing in the National Library of Medicine's Medline database. Physicians' Online: www.pol.net offers robust physician-only discussion groups. At InteliHealth, our Professional Network: ipn.intelihealth.com distributes a newswire and links to major medical databases and education resources.

But these businesses, along with publishers of journals and textbooks are still struggling to find an appropriate economic model. While advertisers covet this quality professional health-care demographic, the absolute numbers of users is still small. Physician offices have traditionally been slow adopters of new computer hardware and software platforms (many are still running DOS-based practice management systems). Adding to the complexity, traditional publishers are wary of providing "free" access to content that enjoys a strong base of subscription and traditional advertising revenue.

Still, entrepreneurial start-ups are rapidly entering the market with compelling offerings. One new venture will offer a solution set for physician offices that focuses on upgrading office answering-service technology and providing Internet-enabled transactions for managed-care claims, referrals, and encounters. Another venture will launch a "Bloomberg-like" terminal for physicians, with constantly updated news, information, and information links.

Most of these players recognize that the key to success does not center around providing quality clinical information. Instead, they are working to harness the unprecedented ability of the Internet to integrate the broad needs of health-care professionals. Successful visions will combine practice-management information and services; financial and leisure information; continuing medical education; connectivity with traditional hospital, laboratory, and managed-care systems; along with clinical news and databases. Tremendous opportunity exists for the companies that can determine how to use these technologies to improve the doctor-patient relationship and the quality of patient care.

Additionally, managed care and pharmaceutical companies are funding major initiatives to improve relationships with and access to physicians, consumers, and vendors. These initiatives focus around electronic transactions, disease-management programs, marketing programs, member retention, medication compliance, and clinical-trial recruitment.

Pitfalls

As more and more firms join the rush to fabled Internet gold mines, many will stumble. Even in this cyber-world where many of the old rules seem not to apply, we can predict some of the significant hurdles and failure points.

Government. Government regulators continue to watch the health-care industry with great interest. The rules can change at any time.

Going it alone. The Internet is a collaborative medium. Today's health-care giants, who have traditionally had very proprietary work practices, must learn to work with new strategic partners. Alliances with other key market leaders can accelerate successful product initiatives.

Legacy systems. Upstart companies with no historical baggage will enjoy a "start-from-a-blank-sheet-of-paper" advantage. However, most of the big players in today's health-care industry must deal with massive, fragmented, proprietary hardware and software systems. Huge portions of development and technology budgets are being allocated to Year 2000 software remediation.

Underfunding. In spite of the initial rush to have a presence on the Internet, it may be some time before emerging business models really strike gold. Successful businesses need committed, long-term funding partners.

The Fires of Change

The health-care industry changes more rapidly than any of its traditional brethren. However, the Internet is changing as fast, if not faster, than health care. Opportunities abound in this clashing world of moving trends and objectives.

Consumers will fuel this rapid rate of change, demanding more control and easier access to their personal medical data. They will demand the tools to make informed, joint decisions with doctors and managed-care organizations. Just imagine the impact of e-mail reminders in the following scenario. Diabetes is the leading cause of blindness in the United States, but only 32 percent of all diabetics get an annual eye exam.

Industry leaders will stoke the same fires of change as they seek competitive advantages in cost and communication. Double-digit annual health-care expenditure growth and merger mania in the provider, pharmaceutical, and managed-care industries will increase the synergies available from emerging technology.

Those who are successful in serving this dynamic marketplace will develop multipronged business models and will form broad alliances within the industry. They will focus on quality, community, personalization, efficiency, and confidentiality. Business models will include economic strategies for content, distribution, sponsorship, e-commerce, and transactions. Those who come out on top will leverage the brand recognition and staying power of major medical societies, major managed-care organizations, major academic medical centers, and major pharmaceutical manufacturers.

Covering All the Bases

If you are considering an Internet initiative in the health-care industry:

What are you doing differently? With hundreds of thousands of health-related sites on the Web today, along with major initiatives by industry titans, you must define your differentiating factors.

Who are you working with? Alliances with major health-care, media, and online companies are vital in this rapidly changing environment. Leverage existing distribution channels, brands, and technologies. Don't try to "go it alone."

How much will you need to spend? The cost of entry is rising. Look at competitive offerings and determine how much you will have to spend to reach parity, and then to move beyond. Be brutally honest.

Do you have access to the right expertise? Mistakes in medicine can cost lives. Regulations are complex. State-of-the-art changes regularly. Local health-care delivery networks and contractual intricacies are daunting. Lack of global standards in information and technology slow adoption rates.

Are you betting on the come? Do you expect early consensus of standards such as the electronic medical record? EDI transactions between doctors, hospitals, and managed care are still tedious and require heavy customization.

Are you passionate about your mission? Growing a new business initiative is a serious undertaking. Passion will help you overcome the inevitable setbacks and pitfalls.

■　■　■

1   FIND/SVP, 1997.
2   Yahoo search, 1998.
3   AltaVista search, 1998.
4   Ibid.

The Comeback of the Travel Agent

Andrew O. McKee, CEO, Vacation.com

The travel industry is among the most mature and active employers of Internet technology. But that doesn't mean that thinking "out of the box" and innovation are on the wane. Andrew McKee, an Internet travel entrepreneur, debunks many of the generally accepted "truths" of the Internet travel industry and provides some contrary thinking on the topic of disintermediation.

The Web was supposed to be the end of the travel agent. Yet, according to the US Travel Agency Survey conducted by *Travel Weekly*, the travel-agency business has never been stronger. Total travel-agency sales have risen to $126 billion in 1997, up from $101 billion in 1995. Profits are also up among agents, with 83 percent of all agencies expecting to post a profit in 1998. What happened to the Internet-as-executioner theory? The fact is that agents are beginning to *use* the Web to their advantage. While there are those consumers who will book everything online with a ubiquitous "booking engine," my point of view is that travel agents will become even *more* potent in the future, as baby boomers get connected to the Web and keep a bag packed, ready to go.

This contrarian view comes from the fact that I have been both a tour operator *and* a travel agent, in the brick-and-mortar world as well as the cyber-world. I am the founder of Vacation.com, a company that operates Web sites for tour operators and a network of retail travel agencies. My experience has lead me to conclude that Web-enabled travel agents will be a powerful, even dominant force in the future. I am so certain of this, I am willing to bet my company on it. Before we delve into the future, let's take a peek at the recent past by examining the existing travel industry—and where the bodies, and treasures, are buried.

Size Does Matter

The travel industry is large and growing, with travelers in the United States spending nearly $500 billion on travel and tourism in 1996, according to the Travel Industry Association of America. According to the U.S. Department of Labor, travel is expected to be one of the fastest-growing industries as the twenty-first century begins. The distribution channel for the sale of travel products—airline tickets, rental cars, hotel rooms, vacation packages—is highly diverse and fragmented, with travel agents historically handling a significant portion of all travel transactions, for both corporate and leisure travel. The country had 115,000 travel agents in 1996, and the number is expected to grow 62 percent by the year 2005, according to the Labor Department's *Occupational Outlook Handbook*, which contains overviews of occupations under sixteen classifications. Leisure-travel expenditures are expected to grow at an annual rate of 5 percent through the year 2006. Growth rates for cruise and tour sales are expected to approach 10 percent, with sales of cruises by travel agencies topping $22 billion in 1997.

As the population continues to age, and the baby boomers near retirement, discretionary leisure travel will expand, with growth outpacing the general economy. And the most affluent of these travelers are the ones most likely to already be online, using the Web. Given the confluence of these trends—an increase in high-value leisure travel in the economy and the utilization of technology by the most seasoned travelers—it becomes obvious that the Web will be a powerful tool for researching and planning all forms of travel, and that both consumers and suppliers will benefit from this powerful trend. Yet, what about the intermediaries—those packagers, resellers, wholesalers, consolidators, agents? What will happen to them in the new economy? Given the complex nature of most forms of leisure travel—travel that involves the packaging of tours, resort vacations, customized itineraries, and cruises—the likely effect will be a *share shift* from one type of intermediary (today's storefront agency, for example) to another form—a Web-enabled, independent travel agency, one that utilizes the technology to provide superior services to current and future customers.

Reintermediation

But if everything is so good today, why worry? Isn't there enough business to go around? In spite of the evident strength in the agency business, the current business model of the typical independent travel agent is under siege, with external forces—led by consolidation across agency groups, vertical integration, direct marketing by vendors, commission reductions, and the impact of the Web—all pointing to trouble ahead. The singular focus of each of these trends is to try and reduce distribution costs for the sale of travel products. Particularly damning is the effect of the internet on the travel agent: vendors are transacting directly with consumers over the Web, and "cyber-agents" will replace brick and mortar agencies. Although the outlook is not altogether rosy, the question is, can all agencies transform themselves into cyber-agencies? My belief is that those agents who transition to the new economy, *embrace* the internet as a *means* to improve and grow their businesses, will be successful; the others who cling to the old model will be left behind. The mission of Vacation.com is to help in that transition to the new economy, to *re*intermediate the travel agent.

Managing Complexity

In addition to forces trying to take business away from the traditional players, equally problematic for the traditional travel agent is the increasing proliferation of suppliers competing for the travel dollar. As product variety and complexity increases, the knowledge demands on the front-line agent have become daunting. In recent years, there has been significant growth in the number of "specialty travel" companies, those offering active and adventure vacations from western dude ranches in Wyoming to treks in Nepal, from cooking schools in France to weekend bike trips in New England. Yet with this increasing product complexity lies opportunity, which is the principal reason travel agents were created: to help consumers manage the vast array of available travel options. Given that necessity is the mother of invention, it's not surprising to discover the vast opportunities created by the Web in the travel arena. Dozens of companies have been formed to target opportunities in travel distribution created by the Internet, all geared toward simplifying the process of purchasing travel by consumers. The basic need for competent specialists—knowledgeable suppliers of service—will prove to be the salvation, indeed the fundamental reason, for the *expanded* role of the retail travel agent in the Internet era. This is admittedly a contrarian view, as there are forces at work focusing on using the Web as the intermediary *itself*, connecting suppliers to consumers, bypassing the middleman.

Disintermediation

Vendors are undermining the value of the agent, as many have elected to bypass the agency community and go directly to the end consumer by sending direct mail, setting up call centers for 800-number response, and, of course, setting up Web sites to market their products on the Internet. Furthermore, the historical core business proposition for most retail travel agencies has been in decline in recent years, as airlines have reduced commissions to the lesser of 8 percent or $50 for the sale of a round-trip ticket, reducing to crumbs what was once the staple of travel agents' diet: the sale of airplane tickets to their customers. The commission reduction has forced most travel agents to rethink their business models, inducing many to collect service fees for issuing now-unprofitable airplane tickets, and shifting their business mix to leisure/vacation travel. The Internet *phenomenon*, with its potential to radically change the economics and market-share characteristics of the travel distribution business, is at the center of every vendor marketing plan. What is it about travel that makes the Web such a potent force?

It's the Information

Given the sheer magnitude of the industry, it's no wonder that travel occupies the attention of so many Web strategists. The fit to the Web is so logical: the product is bought and sold on information, never touched or sampled. Information is central to the successful travel transaction, which is why people or entities who *control the information* have historically been the winners in the travel industry—note the success of the Computerized Reservation Systems (CRSs) like Sabre, Amadeus, and Apollo and publishers of information like the Official Airline Guide. What's happened to these players? The Web threatens their businesses by shifting power to new intermediaries and consumers. The last section of this chapter will present a business plan for the creation of a new, Internet-enabled digital trade network for the retail travel industry, the core mission of Vacation.com.

Keep It Simple, Stupid

If the Web was supposed to mean the death of the travel agent, what's taking its place? Certainly not vendor-direct bookings; suppliers have received a very small portion of online direct bookings. Most travel transactions are happening with agents—just a different *kind* of agent, one whose store is online, not at the local strip mall. Pundits predicted that consumers would abandon their travel agent and jump into cyber-bliss with their automated online travel agent as their guide. Wrong. Have you ever tried to book a complex airline itinerary on a Web-based booking engine like Preview Travel, Microsoft Expedia, or Travelocity (the "Big 3" of travel sites) and had a satisfying experience? Sure, for simple point-to-point airline itineraries, Preview and others do a decent job. But haven't you researched your flight options on the Web, and then called your trusted travel agent *just in case* there is a better deal out there that the automated systems won't tell you about? Of course you have. Travelocity won't tell you that you could fly direct into San Jose airport from Boston cheaper and more conveniently than connecting through Minneapolis to San Francisco, which is what you thought was the right airport for Palo Alto. Your travel agent would have told you that *in the first place*. Which is basically why one of the biggest stories behind the potential of the Web for the travel industry is the redefinition and empowerment of the traditional travel agent. Smart travel agents are using the Web to reinvent their business models, shifting business from the unsophisticated agents to the techno-savvy ones. Why haven't the automated agents gained greater share, particularly in the sale of complex travel products? For the same reason that people go out to restaurants instead of cooking at home: They want service.

It's All about Service

If you want evidence of this fact, consider that travel agents sell 95 percent of all leisure-travel products today. Why? Consumers want service. Translated: People want someone with prior experience, an expert who's been there, knows the product, makes it their *business* to sell travel; they want someone to yell at when things go wrong, who will fight for them when things go wrong or the product is different than advertised. How many times have brochures exaggerated the beauty of the beach or the quality of the food at that Caribbean resort? Suppliers will never criticize their own product; only independent agents can, and will, do that for consumers. My prediction is that will not change any time soon. If you want further convincing, look beyond travel to see where the Web is creating opportunities for intermediaries. Stock brokers are flourishing, despite the fact that enormous amounts of information is available online and being used by brokers' customers. You wouldn't buy a house on the Web without the advice of a real-estate professional, would you? Of course not . . . and many people feel the same way about their vacation investment—human interaction is critical to a successful travel experience. It's just the nature of the product; the Web will facilitate the transaction, provide information, even feedback from previous travelers, but my prediction is that the share of *complex* travel handled by travel agents will actually increase, and that the ones who are gaining the share will be *using* the Web to do so. No other industry (besides health-care delivery) requires such human interaction. It's human nature. Technology won't change that.

Figure 16.1: Complex Products Require Customer Support to Close the Sale

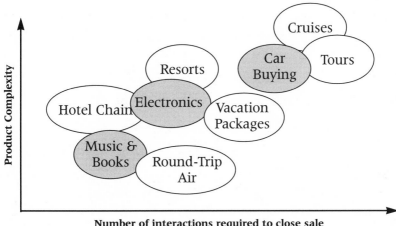

Product Complexity

Cruises

Car Buying

Tours

Resorts

Hotel Chain

Electronics

Vacation Packages

Music & Books

Round-Trip Air

Number of interactions required to close sale

As the chart above demonstrates, the higher the degree of complexity of a product, the less likely it will be purchased online—without the intervention of a human sales agent. Airline tickets, hotel rooms, and rental cars have demonstrated success in being sold online without human intervention, largely due to the fact that the product is simple and that it is sold based on information exchanged. This is why the Big 3 travel sites (Preview Travel, Travelocity, and Expedia) will generate over half a billion dollars in combined airline ticket sales in 1999. Where is all this business coming from?

Web-based travel agencies such as the aforementioned Big 3 have made it their mission to take market share from the traditional storefront travel agent. Like them, Vacation.com will fully participate and compete for customers in the online travel marketplace; however, unlike the Big 3, we believe that only a small percentage of vacation sales will be directly purchased by the consumer online without any human service component. The vacation travel transaction is simply too large in dollar amount, too risky in terms of the possibility of an unpleasant experience and too complex for the consumer to pursue without the free assistance of a travel professional. Which is why we expect that the use of our Internet-based technologies will only enhance the value and efficiency of agents.

So, it's pretty clear by now that I am bullish on the prospect of Web-enabling travel agents, but there have been other success stories in the online travel world. And some success stories come at the expense of others.

The Early Winners in the Online Travel World

INTERNET PORTALS

The early winners in the online travel business have been the Web portals that have exacted large fees in exclusive deals with search engines and other large aggregators of consumer traffic. Everybody knows that AOL and Yahoo! dominate the Internet audience business, with Excite and Infoseek in hot pursuit. Anyone who calls themselves a portal can expect a call from one of the Big 3 travel sites. Among all of them, Preview Travel has been the most aggressive spender: As of late 1997, Preview Travel had committed to spending over $60 million during five years in fees to distribution partners AOL and Excite. Since then they have locked up real estate on USAToday.com, and SNAP!, and they are rumored to have several other deals in the works. Travelocity has similar deals with Yahoo! and Netscape, and Expedia with Infoseek. Although these deals assure that these sites will have a strong branded presence, the economics of these arrangements is puzzling, given the slash-and-burn commission philosophy the airlines have imposed on "cyberagents." Airlines simply don't want the online travel agents to make any money selling tickets: they would rather drive customers to their own sites (and drive the general purpose travel sites out of business). Just for fun: figure out how many airline tickets the Big 3 will have to sell for them to break even on their estimated $100 million in portal investments? At $5 gross profit per ticket (after deducting fulfillment expenses), they need to sell around 20 million airplane tickets or about $6 billion in sales, or well over $1 billion per year, over the life of these agreements, just to pay for the portal cost. It doesn't begin to cover overhead and other costs (like their reservations centers) and technology. No matter how you slice it, that sales figure puts them squarely in the top 5 travel agencies in the United States. Will they be around long enough to realize these revenue goals? Not without finding higher-margin products to sell.

SUPPLIERS

Vendors have also been successful, but to a limited extent. Most tour operators have built "brochure" or "business-card" Web sites, which are designed to promote awareness of the suppliers' products to consumers who find them via search engines and other methods (site addresses printed on the vendors' collateral material, business cards, etc.). As most Web site managers have discovered, simply hanging a cyber-shingle out there is no longer enough; with over 200,000 travel Web sites out there, it's getting increasingly difficult to get noticed amidst all the noise. And very few of these vendors are truly Web enabled, where consumers are able to book their tour and packages online: The start-up costs are simply too high for all but the largest vendors, simply because there are too many legacy inventory-management systems out there that are based on proprietary designs that don't lend themselves to internet connectivity at a reasonable cost. And nobody knows if the investment will be worth the effort anyway, given the mediocre results of the "brochure sites" produced thus far.

AGGREGATORS

In the travel industry, what's happening today is a predictable awakening: Vendors (tour operators, cruise lines, hotels) have decided that they have to build a Web site to stay competitive. Now that they have done so, the inevitable question becomes: How do I generate more business from this? The next phase will benefit the aggregators, people with whom the vendors do business: Inns & Outs (bed and breakfasts), TravelWeb (hotel rooms from large hotel chains), Vacation.com (cruise, tour package). The aggregators will promise distribution with "portal deals." This will maximize reach for vendors who advertise with these services. Aggregators have built successful businesses around collecting content within different, specialized niches. Inns & Outs, Travelon, SkiNet, Adventure Quest, Golfweb—have all defined business models that serve specific markets. The aggregators then offer their content to portals and other hubs of commercial activity, who distribute the content to their audiences. Yet, the aggregators are starting to reach a plateau, as the number of new potential distribution partners is shrinking; all the deals include the usual suspects, and new frontiers are getting more difficult to conquer.

YOU AND ME

The biggest winners have been consumers, who have benefited significantly from the early initiatives in the online travel world, as new sets of tools have been made available to them to comparison shop and research different options, search for the best deals, receive e-mail notification of last-minute specials, and find that tour operator who excels in Tibetan kayaking adventures. As far as being an information resource, no greater tool has ever existed. The consumer will continue to win. Next to being a portal, I think that for a consumer looking to book travel, these are good times.

And the Losers

YESTERDAY'S TRAVEL AGENTS

One of the biggest beneficiaries of the explosive growth of the Web will be the travel agents—those who are Web-savvy marketers. There are countless success stories of travel agents, both cyberagents with reservation centers like Expedia and Travelocity, as well as traditional travel agencies that do a great job marketing on the Web, like 1Travel.com and others who have invested in building dynamic, consumer-friendly Web sites. These are companies who have adapted to the Web and are utilizing it to their advantage. They will only see their efficiency and market share grow. The losers will be "yesterday's" agents, those who shy away from the Web and make excuses for not developing a Web-based marketing and technology strategy. These agents will see their customer base erode as competitors emerge who can offer complete service and have access to a vast quantity of current information, including a state-of-the-art site of their own.

BROCHURE PRINTERS

There used to be a joke that the only people who consistently make money in the travel industry are the brochure printers. Think about it! When you enter into a travel agency, go to a consumer travel show, contact a tour operator—what do you see? Tons of brochures, most of which have a shelf life of less than one year! It goes without saying that the Web creates an opportunity for distribution of "better-than-brochure" information, complete with user feedback, instant pricing and availability, even direct booking capabilities. As the Web becomes even more ubiquitous, the need for excessive printing and distribution of brochures and catalogs will diminish, as consumers and agents rely more and more on electronic information.

COMPUTERIZED RESERVATIONS SYSTEMS (A.K.A. GLOBAL DISTRIBUTION SYSTEMS)

Built by the airline industry in the 1960s, the CRSs are a tool for travel agents to make air, car, and hotel reservations. Among their many strengths was the value of their distribution networks: Sabre, Apollo, Worldspan, Amadeus—all erected vast private networks that carry their information and capabilities into the office terminals of travel agencies worldwide. In order to cover the cost of the network, agents would enter into long-term agreements with guaranteed transaction levels to get these reservation terminals. With the advent of the Internet, the value of the CRS network diminishes, as the public network makes universal access readily attainable. No longer will travel agents be compelled by CRS into expensive, long-term, and restrictive contracts to gain access to the best of breed of the new reservations systems: They will be freely available over the Web. The Web provides a platform for new intermediaries to create booking engines—particularly for leisure products, which have traditionally been poorly represented on CRS systems—which threaten to undermine the hegemony of the incumbent distribution systems. If the internet threatens the power of the CRS, do they have a future? The real question is: Will they be a strong or a weak player? My view is that the smart ones will use the vast amount of information that they collect about consumer travel behavior to offer added-value services. It's not far-fetched to see Amadeus offering consumers a book to read on their flight to Seattle, or suggesting an umbrella because it's going to rain once they get there. As booking engines become ubiquitous and the

15 SECONDS OF FAME

So I was sitting at the head of an enormous conference table in the offices of *Rolling Stone* magazine, my back to the door, when the doors burst open and Jann Wenner, the magazine's owner and founder, walked in, with a CNN camera crew close behind, spotlights blaring. I was in the middle of defending to the Board of Directors my decision to go all out with our brochure last year, in the belief that a really great catalog would turn around the fate of Overseas Adventure Travel, the tour operator that I was attempting to rescue from the impact of the Persian Gulf War, the effect of which was to halt international leisure travel from the United States. Not a good thing for outbound tour operators. Wenner, one of OAT's shareholders, was being interviewed by CNN for a story on the twenty-fifth anniversary of the magazine, and the producers wanted some "live action" shots of Wenner at work. So they choose my meeting to film. The archives of this broadcast will show the furled brow, the beads of sweat, on the face of a man wondering "how did I get into this mess." Or, to paraphrase the words of many failed entrepreneurs, "what was I thinking, getting into the travel business?"

Weeks earlier, I was in the mailroom at Overseas Adventure Travel looking at the

internet becomes the true global distribution channel, transaction enablers will gain value from the ancillary products and services that enhance the selling experience.

The next generation of Web marketing services will focus on the 75 percent of consumers who do not shop online, or who have a relationship (or want one) with a travel agent. The Web will empower these cyber-agents, giving them access to a plethora of products *and* enabling them to continue to provide customer service.

The Revenge of the Travel Agent

CASE STUDY: BIRTH OF VACATION.COM

Back in 1994, the online services were just starting to penetrate double digits of consumer households. CompuServe, Prodigy, and AOL were battling each other for market share and travel was one of the differentiating categories, led by the presence of Easy Sabre in each of these online travel categories (they weren't called channels back then!). We approached Prodigy with an idea to create a vacation service that would offer its members access to hundreds of vacation products from dozens of leisure-travel vendors. Companies like Overseas Adventure Travel, Backroads, Mountain Travel, International Expeditions—all could reach a broad audience of number of brochures that were being returned by the Post Office as undeliverable. We had spent $175,000 on printing and mailing out twenty-five thousand copies of our glossy, four-color catalog. Approximately twenty-five hundred of them arrived back in our offices, plus probably another five thousand wound up in the trash along the way, discarded as junk mail. The catalog was the size of *Rolling Stone* magazine, a wonderful oversized glossy: *Rolling Stone* got us a good deal on printing. Looking at the sheer waste, in terms of dollars, effort, and *trees*—it occurred to me that there had to be a better way to get the word out about our product. OAT was one of the best companies in the popular category of adventure travel: Its products were unique, affordable, and eco-friendly; consumers were discovering "adventure" travel as a new, growing, and popular vacation category; and international travel was on the rebound, after several years of Persian Gulf–related aversion. *Why can't we make a profit?* I thought. The problem was marketing and distribution. We just couldn't get the word out about our company on an affordable basis—the answer, I believed, was in electronic distribution. Which led to the founding of Adventure Media, the company that became Vacation.com, Inc.

online consumers via a single easy-to-use interface. The idea resonated with Prodigy, and in the summer of 1996, Prodigy Vacations was launched, the first site in what has since become the Vacation.com network.

Vacation.com has developed into a comprehensive travel marketing database feeding a network of Web sites with the richest collection of leisure travel transactional content currently available on the Internet—and a very high rating for converting visitors to its sites into buyers. The Vacation.com Network consists of approximately twenty individual consumer-directed sites, selling the product of cruise, tour, packaged-vacation, and other leisure-travel vendors, including three hundred specialty travel tour operators. Vacation.com also has invaluable Internet portal relationships with Internet powers Yahoo!, AOL, AltaVista, and Excite.

The results have been outstanding, in large part due to the relationships we established with the online services and search engines who provide us traffic. As of late 1998, the Vacation.com network generates nearly 3 million page views per month, is visited by over four hundred thousand unique users and has a run rate of nearly $20 million in annual high-margin leisure bookings. Relative to other travel agencies, we barely break into the top five hundred; in the online world, we are in the top ten. Even though we have enjoyed some success offering our product to consumers directly, our view is that true economic leverage will come from the deployment of powerful Web marketing tools to empower the traditional travel-agency industry. Rather than trying to take share away from the agency community, we are building tools and a strategy to *partner* with the fifteen thousand independent travel agencies, who we believe will be the backbone of leisure-travel sales in the long run. How will we do this?

Consorting with the Consortia

Vacation.com plans to merge with several travel-agency consortia, membership organizations for the retail-agency industry. A travel consortium is an organization that gains independent travel agencies as members, offers them packaged training and marketing programs, and coordinates their vendor relationships and selling efforts to achieve enhanced commission rates on sales. Our plan is to "Web enable" the member agencies, as outlined below, creating a new technology-based membership association, where the revenues to the consortium are derived in large part by sharing performance-based revenue streams with the member agencies. This infrastructure will build upon the Vacation.com network's existing platform, as represented in the list that follows.

Delivering Value to Travel Agencies

Vacation.com delivers a menu of marketing and training programs to travel agencies. We use technology to do things for agents that no organization could ever do before, including:

- Preferred-vendor programs offering enhanced commission rates on a vast array of travel product from the company's cruise, package vacation, tour, and specialty-travel vendors;
- A world-class Web site under the agency's own brand with the *same* robust functionality as the Vacation.com flagship site. The company's Site Builder enables the agent to quickly and economically create a site of their own; easily maintain the content of the site (vendors, contact information, specials); and fulfill online orders via secure internet communication. Consequently, the retail agent becomes a

Figure 16.2: Vacation.com Distribution Model

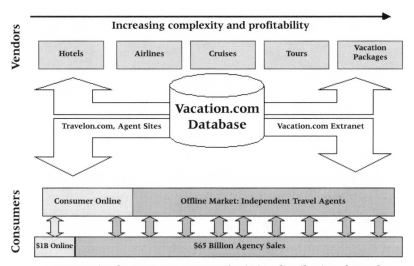

Aggregating buyers across new *and* existing distribution channels

world-class online marketer with a multimillion-dollar site of his or her own;

- Access to the agents-only Extranet providing travel product and destination research and transactions, agency forum for posting inquiries and chatting with other agents and consortium headquarters, and online transactions capability—empowering the agent to remain always authoritative and a step ahead of clients in sophistication in purchasing travel services;
- Ability to efficiently support the home-based travel agent: Our Web-based tools will empower any seller of leisure travel, no matter where they are;
- Access to last minute and special bargain-priced travel in a real-time environment;
- Access to controlled inventory of travel product with higher commissions and highly competitive pricing—giving agents the ability to compete on price with large agency franchises and megaretailers;

■ Ability to package travel product and expose it to a mass market as a specialty vendor customer of the company— economically reaching a mass market in a way that no small agency that also acts as a tour operator/cruise consolidator can do today.

REVENUE SOURCES

Vacation.com has a diversified revenue model. The sources of revenue fall into four categories: advertising sales, commissions on sales of travel, fees to travel agencies for membership services, and fees to vendors for marketing services.

■ *Advertising* sales for ads appearing online on the company's Travelon site, travel niche-oriented sites (allbiketrips.com, etc.), sites produced by the company for travel agencies, and sites on the company's agents-only Extranet. New ad revenue will be generated through the Extranet, agency sites, and increased niche-oriented sites as the product database grows deeper.

■ *Commissions/transaction fees* earned on sales of travel together with marketing fees paid by suppliers for measurable Web-based marketing.

■ *Fees for membership services* provided to travel agencies, such as annual membership dues, training programs, software sales and support, consulting services, trade shows, and conferences.

■ *Fees for marketing services* such as promotional-material design, database marketing-list services, agent direct mail, fax and e-mail promotions, trade shows, conferences, agent-training seminars, and consumer-oriented events.

The Future

The online travel industry has enormous potential, with many opportunities for existing companies who have a vested interest in the travel industry, or new companies with an entrepreneurial idea. Companies like Priceline.com have emerged, enabling consumers to set *their* optimal price for an airline ticket, rather than the vendor's. Once a sufficient number of suppliers are willing to participate, creating "liquidity" in the marketplace, such concepts will be successful. Tour operators will be able to gain access to new customers, especially if they participate in the services of the aggregators who perform marketing services for their clients. International opportunities also abound, as business models that are successful in the United States can be exported overseas to great success. I believe that inbound tour operators will be very successful on the Web, as consumers can shop for better deals by going directly to suppliers, bypassing the U.S.-based intermediaries. Similarly, I wouldn't be surprised if sometime soon we see overseas a Web-enabled network of travel agencies tied together with a leading consumer-branded travel site—unless, of course, we can get there first.

Author Profiles

How to Reach Us

We'd like to hear from you. For more information or to reach us, please visit us at our Website at: http://www.netsuccessbook.com

Christina Ford Haylock is President of Ford Communications, a management-consulting firm specializing in electronic commerce and the Internet. She is a true pioneer of interactive services. In 1987 at Bell Atlantic she was the founding product manager of its first online portal service, Gateway. From 1990 to 1996 she was Vice President Business Development and Marketing at Citibank where she played a pivotal role in the commercialization of online banking, including screen telephone based banking, where she forged and managed partnerships, led strategy development, formulated business plans, and launched several markets. Christina is a frequent speaker at conferences and a quoted expert on electronic commerce and management topics. She has been an active member of the Internet Alliance since 1988 and served three terms as an Officer of the Board of Directors.

E-mail: christinaf@aol.com

Len Muscarella is Managing Director of Interactive Media Associates, Inc. (IMA), a Parsippany, N.J., company specializing in the planning, development, and marketing of online and Internet services. Since Len founded the firm thirteen years ago, IMA has worked on the definition and design of new media businesses for companies including Citibank, HBO, *Newsday*, Time Warner, The New York City Ballet, The Topps Company, US West, and Ziff-Davis. He is a frequent speaker and often-quoted expert on new media topics. He served three terms on the Board of Directors of the Interactive Services Association, the trade association that is now known as the Internet Alliance.

A communications professional for almost twenty-five years, Len's corporate experience includes Dow Jones-Ottaway Newspapers, CBS Inc., and TRINTEX (the CBS-IBM-Sears venture that gave birth to Prodigy). He received his undergraduate degree from Boston College; has an MA in Communications from The Newhouse School, Syracuse University; and has an MBA from Rutgers University.

E-mail: len@imediainc.com

Ron Schultz is the Director of Publications and Publisher of Leadership Press for Senn-Delaney Leadership Consulting Group. Since 1982, he has authored or coauthored eleven books on business management, manufacturing excellence, and the future of American business. His most recent business book, *Open Boundaries—Creating Business Innovation through Complexity*, was published by Perseus Books in October 1998. He was also coeditor for the Smart Card Forum of the McGraw-Hill/Irwin publication *Smart Cards: Seizing Strategic Business Opportunities*. His book *Unconventional Wisdom—12 Remarkable Innovators Tell How Intuition Revolutionized their Decision Making* was published by HarperBusiness in March 1994. *Going Public*, written with Jim Arkebauer, was released in April 1991 by HarperBusiness and is currently in paperback with Dearborn Press.

E-mail: CreativeSG@aol.com

Richard P. Adler is a Principal of Digital Places, an Internet community consulting firm in California (www.digiplaces.com). From 1990 to 1996, Richard was Vice President for Development at SeniorNet, a national nonprofit organization that created the first electronic community for older adults. Richard was responsible for SeniorNet's business planning and launched its first Web site. Before joining SeniorNet, Richard was a director at the Institute for the Future, where he headed IFTF's research program in new information services. His clients included many high tech and Fortune 500 companies.

E-mail: radler@digiplaces.com

Regina (Reggie) Brady leads Internet direct-marketing initiatives for Acxiom/Direct Media. Brady announced the introduction of E-Mail Campaign Management, which is a total campaign-management solution for direct e-mail marketers that includes real-time analysis of results. She comes to Acxiom/Direct Media with more than eleven years at CompuServe, where she was responsible for the strategic development and management of e-commerce, interactive advertising, and direct-marketing activities. Ms. Brady established the direction for CompuServe's Electronic Mall, one of the first interactive venues to promote shopping and electronic commerce online. The Mall was home to more than 175 direct marketers and general advertisers that participated in global interactive marketing. Prior to CompuServe, Brady held senior positions at leading direct-marketing companies including Hearst, Columbia House, and Margrace.

Her book, *Cybermarketing: Your Interactive Marketing Consultant*, was recently published by NTC Publishing. She serves on the board of directors of the Interactive Alliance and is also a member of the New Media Committee of the Direct Marketing Association.

E-mail: rbrady@ix.directmedia.com

Bill Burrington is Vice President of Law and Global Public Policy and also serves as Associate General Counsel for America Online®, Inc., where he heads AOL's Washington, D.C., Law and Public Affairs Group. Mr. Burrington directs and manages AOL's international and domestic Internet and electronic commerce public policy advocacy and industry association activities. He currently serves as Chairman of the Internet Alliance, the Internet online industry's leading association in Washington, D.C.

Prior to joining AOL in early 1995, Mr. Burrington practiced new media and telecommunications law with firms in Milwaukee and Washington, D.C.; served as Chief of Staff and Counsel to a former member of the U.S. House of Representatives, and was Executive Director and General Counsel of the National Association for Interactive Services, which merged with the Internet Alliance in 1994. A recognized expert on Internet and e-commerce public-policy issues, Mr. Burrington has testified several times before the U.S. Congress, spoken widely and appeared frequently in national media about cyberspace policy issues, and was named one of Washington's "25 Most Wired People" by *Wired* magazine. Mr. Burrington is coauthor of *The Interactive Marketplace Regulatory Handbook*.

E-mail: billburr@aol.com

Anthony J. Christopher is a Principal of Digital Places, an Internet community consulting firm in California (www.digiplaces.com). From 1994 to 1998 he was Executive Director of Fujitsu's WorldsAway Product and Services Group where his team designed, developed, and operated online communities that generated $10 million in revenues in 1997. He was responsible for technology development, online service operations, marketing and sales; in this general management role he managed a team of forty-eight engineers, artists, marketers, Webmasters, sysads, and community managers.

At Apple Computer, he was the founding product manager for AppleLink in the early 1980s. AppleLink was an online network that connected Apple employees with its dealers, developers, and corporate accounts; it achieved phenomenal penetration of the company's distribution, developer, and partner communities and remained in service until the mid 1990s.

E-mail: AJC@digiplaces.com

K. Blake Darcy is Chief Executive Officer of DLJdirect Inc., a Donaldson, Lufkin & Jenrette company, located in Jersey City, New Jersey. In 1988, Mr. Darcy introduced DLJdirect (originally PC Financial Network), one of the first providers of online discount brokerage services. Since then, DLJdirect has become the leading provider of online brokerage services with over 450,000 customer accounts and over $30 billion in online transactions. DLJdirect is now available on the Internet at http://www.DLJdirect.com and through America Online®, Prodigy, CompuServe, and Microsoft Investor. In 1997, under Mr. Darcy's direction, DLJdirect created a separate technology company, iNautix Technologies, Inc., that develops online solutions for financial organizations. DLJdirect is the only online brokerage to be named the "#1 Internet Broker" four consecutive times by Gomez Advisors, Inc., and was named one of three "Web Sites to Watch in 1998" from *Business Week* magazine.

Earlier this year, Mr. Darcy was included on FutureBanker's list of the "10 Masters of Electronic Delivery." He was also on Institutional Investor's roster of "on-line elite," which featured the top twenty most important players on the financial Web.

E-mail: blakedarcy@dljdirect.com

Lauren Freedman founded the e-tailing group in 1994 to provide strategic and merchandising solutions to retailers, catalogers, and interactive developers. Client projects range from merchant strategy, added-value services development and competitive analysis with The Microsoft Network to state of the industry, electronic strategy development and user-interface design with Toys "R" Us, PBS, Oriental Trading, and The Vitamin Shoppe. Her electronic-shopping expertise has been applied to e-commerce solutions for Kodak, Encyclopedia Brittanica, and Bloomingdales online along with myriad assignments for US West, AT&T, iCat, and AETV, as well as virtual retailers like Buy Software, CyberShop, and Women.com. The company's mission is to further develop electronic commerce as a distribution channel for both entrepreneurs and large businesses through innovative commerce opportunities and customized marketing efforts. Their premier e-tailing report was released in June, 1998, analyzing e-commerce today, the online shopper, retail and catalog players, and the hows and whys of merchants moving online.

E-mail: lf@e-tailing.com

Eric Hippeau is the Chairman and CEO of Ziff-Davis, Inc. He is a member of the Board of Directors of Yahoo! and GeoCities. Marketing Computers has called him "The Man Who Would Be Content King" and the Software Publishers Association has called him one of the "leading industry visionaries." Hippeau joined Ziff-Davis in 1989 as publisher of *PC Magazine* and was promoted to several executive positions before being named Chairman and CEO of Ziff-Davis in October 1991. Prior to joining Ziff-Davis, Hippeau served as Vice President of IDG's computer publications in Latin America before moving to the United States in 1986 to become publisher of IDG's InfoWorld.

He started his publishing career at an English-language daily newspaper in Brazil, where he became Editor in Chief. Born in Paris, France, Hippeau became a U.S. citizen in 1992. He was educated in Switzerland and England and attended university at the Sorbonne in Paris.

E-mail: eric_hippeau@zd.com

Madelyn Hochstein is owner, President and cofounder with Daniel Yankelovich of DYG, Inc. Madelyn is well known in the business community for her speeches and presentations on social trends. Almost every week, she presents insights from DYG's social-values research to Fortune 500 companies and other major businesses nationwide.

E-mail: hochsteinm@dyg.com

C. Lincoln (Link) Hoewing worked for almost eight years on Capitol Hill, serving as a legislative aide and eventually Deputy Staff Director on the Senate Governmental Affairs Committee. In 1985, Mr. Hoewing left Capitol Hill to take a position at Bell Atlantic, one of the seven Regional Bell Operating Companies (RBOCs). He helped develop and manage the company's issues-management and strategic-issues-planning processes. In 1990, he became the director of a joint public affairs/public relations program funded by the seven RBOCs. In this role, he helped coordinate the government-relations program of the seven companies and assisted in message-development, advertising, and grassroots programs designed to influence policy makers to lift certain business restrictions that applied to the RBOCs.

In 1997, Bell Atlantic and NYNEX merged and Mr. Hoewing became Assistant Vice President, Issues Management and Corporate Relations. In that capacity, he is responsible for identifying and assessing emerging issues, developing corporate positions on Internet and technology-industry issues, and developing relationships with high-technology-industry members, interactive-technology associations, and research institutes and think tanks. He speaks frequently on high-technology issues and has written articles on using the Internet in the public-policy process.

E-mail: c.l.hoewing@bellatlantic.com

Jeffrey Kutler is Executive Editor of *American Banker*, the daily newspaper covering banking and financial services. He is responsible for much of the paper's coverage, including credit and debit cards, technology and operations, payment systems, and advances such as smart cards and digital cash. He also oversees coverage of major banking companies and the annual consumer survey project with the Gallup Organization. In 1996, he launched a monthly supplement, *FutureBanking*, covering these trends. He cowrote a chapter in the book *Smart Cards: Seizing Strategic Business Opportunities*.

E-mail: kutler@tfn.com

Leslie Laredo is the founder and President of The Laredo Group, the leading training, consulting, and research firm dedicated to online and interactive advertising; providing training, consulting, and research products and services to advertising and marketing executives, designed to increase their online advertising revenues and effectiveness.

Leslie is a true interactive pioneer and one of the first sales professionals to sell ads on the original interactive platform—public access videotex in 1983. Ms. Laredo helped forge the way for the online advertising industry to come of age by working with hundreds of companies to understand and successfully implement ad campaigns across several interactive platforms, including Prodigy, Interchange Online Network, and the Internet. During her six years at Prodigy, she was the first sales rep to achieve over $1,000,000 in ad sales in one year. From 1992 to 1996, Ms. Laredo headed up ad sales for Ziff-Davis Interactive, the Interchange Online Network, and AT&T Business Network. In her quest to grow the industry beyond its nascent stage, she was part of the group that launched the Internet Advertising Bureau and served as a founding board member. She is also active in the Interactive Services Association and was a member of the American Advertising Federation New Technology Committee.

E-mail: leslie@laredogroup.com

Edwin N. Lavergne is a partner at the law firm of Shook, Hardy & Bacon L.L.P. in Washington, D.C. Mr. Lavergne devotes much of his time to matters before the Federal Communications Commission, the Federal Trade Commission, and other regulatory officials regarding telecommunications policy and regulation, unfair trade practices, sweepstakes, advertising, and promotion law.

Mr. Lavergne's experience in the interactive-services field is nationally recognized. He has appeared on *Good Morning America* and has been quoted in numerous publications, including the *New York Times*, the *Wall Street Journal*, and the *Washington Post*. Mr. Lavergne has written over sixty articles on issues concerning telephone, online, and Internet services, which have appeared in the *Multimedia Law Report* and *InfoText* and *Voice Processing* magazines. Mr. Lavergne also coauthored *The Interactive Marketplace Regulatory Handbook* published by Thompson Publishing Group. The *Handbook* is a comprehensive guide to federal and state laws governing telemarketing, infomercials, home shopping, online services, and related interactive-media issues.

E-mail: Elavergne@shb.com

Paul D. Lewis is Vice President of Sales Operations at iVillage: The Women's Network. Prior to joining iVillage in 1998, Paul spent nine years at Prodigy, where he pioneered the development of interactive advertising sales, marketing, and operations. He is a past board member of the Internet Advertising Bureau. Paul holds a BS degree from MIT and an MBA from Wharton.

E-mail: paullewis@mail.ivillage.com

Harley Manning is a senior analyst for Forrester Research focusing on design, production, and content management strategies for new media. He came to Forrester after spending eighteen years designing and building interactive services for companies like Dow Jones, AT&T, MCI, Prodigy, and Sears. Most recently he was at Dow Jones Markets, where he was responsible for consolidating their regional Web sites into a single, international site targeted at brokers and traders. He was also responsible for the design, hosting, and operation of the Markets Intranet site, which was later expanded to become the Intranet site for all of Dow Jones.

Manning holds a master of science degree in advertising from the University of Illinois, Urbana.

E-mail: hmanning@forrester.com

Andrew O. McKee is the founder and CEO of Vacation.com. Prior to this, he was the President and CEO of Overseas Adventure Travel, a leading direct marketer of adventure and specialty travel programs. In September 1993, Mr. McKee sold the company to Grand Circle Travel, a leading database marketer of travel and related financial services. In 1990, Mr. McKee cofounded HEAR Music, a company that markets music to adults through the company's specialty retail stores. In 1992, CML Group, the parent of the Nature Company and Nordic Track, acquired the company. Mr. McKee has worked as an investment banker at Goldman, Sachs & Co. and as a marketing analyst in the magazine-circulation division at

Time Inc., where he specialized in direct-mail marketing. Mr. McKee was a White House Fellow Finalist in 1994 and is now CEO of Vacation.com, Inc. Mr. McKee holds a BA from Hamilton College and an MBA from Harvard Business School.

E-mail: drewmckee@aol.com

Jim Pisz is Director, Electronic Commerce, Intranet/Extranet Services for Toyota Motor Sales USA. For the past ten years, Jim has worked creating consumer and business online applications. Jim was responsible for the creation of Toyota.com in 1995; Toyota Vision, Toyota's corporate Intranet, in 1997; and Toyota's Dealer Daily, the corporate Extranet, in 1998. Toyota's Web sites have won numerous awards. Pisz has been a frequent guest speaker at conferences and has been quoted in the *Wall Street Journal*, *Adweek*, and other publications. Pisz was the recipient of The Cowles Award for Database Innovation in 1993, *Direct* magazine's market leader award in 1994, and the AMCI best automotive Web site in 1995.

E-mail: jim_pisz@toyota.com

Bob Pringle is President of InteliHealth, a joint venture of Aetna U.S. Healthcare and Johns Hopkins University and Heath System. InteliHealth is an industry leader in aggregating and distributing branded, trustworthy health information over the Internet (http://www.intelihealth.com). Bob brings a perspective from his background merging business and technology issues in a variety of industries, including finance (Reuters/Reality Online), consulting (Price Waterhouse), advertising (Competitive Media Reporting), and technology (IBM).

E-mail: bpringle@intelihealth.com

William M. Randle is Executive Vice President and Managing Director of Direct Access Financial Services of Huntington Bancshares Incorporated, a regional bank holding company headquartered in Columbus, Ohio, with assets of $28 billion. Huntington provides innovative products and services through more than six hundred offices in Ohio, Florida, Georgia, Indiana, Kentucky, Maryland, Michigan, New Jersey, North Carolina, South Carolina, and West Virginia.

Mr. Randle began his career in the Navy, where he achieved the rank of Lieutenant Commander. In 1969, he joined Atlantic Bancorporation of Florida, where he performed various assignments as Credit Card Manager, Director of Marketing, and, ultimately, as head of all Retail Bank Services until 1985, when the bank was acquired by First Union of Charlotte. Mr. Randle remained in Jacksonville as Senior Vice President of Retail Banking, which included Credit Card, Branching, Marketing, Public Relations, Electronic Banking, and Strategic Planning until 1987, when he moved to Charlotte to become Senior Vice President of Marketing with corporate-wide responsibilities.

E-mail: bill.randle@huntington.com

Elaine Rubin, an online retailer since 1992, has an electronic retail-consulting business to advise and support businesses interested in selling their products and services online. Elaine currently serves as Director of ibaby, a virtual retail store that specializes in essentials and gifts for babies and President of ekrubin inc. Prior to assisting her clients in building retail sites and strategies, Elaine served as Senior Vice President, Interactive Commerce for iVillage, where she created a commerce-within-community strategy for their targeted communities Parent Soup, About Work, and Better Health. Elaine joined iVillage from a position as Head of Interactive Services for 1-800-FLOWERS, where she was instrumental in generating more than $10 million of revenue in 1995 from a variety of interactive platforms.

Recognized by *Advertising Age* as one of the top twenty executives in interactive marketing, Elaine is a leader in her field and is responsible for the development and implementation of various interactive business models used today.

E-mail: ekrubin@aol.com

Samuel A. Simon is President, Issues Dynamics, Inc., and a nationally recognized authority on consumer and public affairs, with twenty-six years experience at the highest levels of his profession. Mr. Simon pioneered the practice of bridging gaps between industry and nontraditional consumer groups on public-policy, marketing, and consumer-affairs issues to achieve win-win solutions for clients. Most recently, Mr. Simon has adapted the Internet for use in public relations and public affairs, receiving national recognition for innovation in the media-relations and grassroots-mobilization arenas. He has also served as public relations and public affairs counsel to a variety of Fortune 500 companies.

Until 1986, Mr. Simon served as President of the Telecommunications Research and Action Center, the nation's oldest and largest consumer group concerned exclusively with telecommunications issues. He is a lawyer, graduating with honors from the University of Texas School of Law in 1970. He entered the public-interest movement immediately following law school, working as one of the first lawyers for Ralph Nader.

E-mail: sam@simon.net

Hilary Bryn Thomas is a pioneer of interactive services and has twenty years' experience as a consultant to firms on five continents. Today she heads Interactive Telecommunications Services, Inc. (ITS), which focuses on strategies for electronic business and electronic commerce. She is Director Emeritus of the Internet Alliance, President of the International Institute for Interactivity (III), and a self-styled "Interactivist."

E-mail: Hilary@interactivist.com

Brent Wilkey is a successful entrepreneur with a background in direct marketing, electrical engineering, computer technology, new media, and art. He has founded and served in leadership roles at several successful companies, including one of the ten largest independent direct-marketing agencies on the West Coast. He is active in various trade groups in North America and internationally, including board-member roles for the Interactive Services Association and the Internet Alliance.

E-mail: jbw@bixo.com

Index